# Microsoft® Excel 2000

## MICROSOFT® CERTIFIED EDITION

## Philip A. Koneman
Colorado Christian University

Prentice Hall

Prentice Hall
Upper Saddle River, New Jersey 07458

*VP Publishing:* Natalie Anderson
*Acquisitions Editor:* David Alexander
*Project Manager:* Monica Stipanov
*Assistant Editor:* Jennifer Cappello
*Senior Marketing Manager:* Sharon Turkovich
*Production Services:* Elm Street Publishing Services, Inc.
*Composition and Art:* Gillian Hall, The Aardvark Group
*Cover Images:* © 1999 PhotoDisc, Inc.
*Cover and Interior Designer:* Leslie Haimes
*Design Supervisor:* Pat Smythe
*Manufacturing Buyer:* Lynne Breitfeller

 © 2000 by Prentice-Hall, Inc.
Upper Saddle River, New Jersey 07458

Printed in the United States of America

10 9 8 7 6 5 4 3 2 1

ISBN 0-13-065110-9

Prentice-Hall International (UK) Limited, *London*
Prentice-Hall of Australia Pty. Limited, *Sydney*
Prentice-Hall Canada Inc., *Toronto*
Prentice-Hall Hispanoamericana, S.A., *Mexico*
Prentice-Hall of India Private Limited, *New Delhi*
Prentice-Hall of Japan, Inc., *Tokyo*
Prentice-Hall Asia Pte. Ltd., *Singapore*
Editora Prentice-Hall do Brasil, Ltda., *Rio de Janeiro*

# Dedication

To my wife, Tanya, and our children, Megan, Jonathan, and Andrew.
Thank you for supporting me during this project.

# Preface

The SELECT Lab Series uses a class-tested, highly visual, project-based approach that teaches students through tasks that use step-by-step instructions. You will find extensive 4-color figures that guide learners through the basic skills and procedures necessary to demonstrate proficiency using each software application.

*SELECT: Projects for Microsoft® Excel 2000* introduces an all-new design with ample space for note taking. The easy-to-follow, clean presentation uses bold color and a unique design program that helps reduce distraction and keeps students focused and interested as they work. We have developed additional instructional features to further enhance the students' learning experience as well as provide the opportunity for those who want to go beyond the scope of the book to explore the features of Excel 2000 on the Web. Each project concludes with a review section that includes a Summary, Key Terms and Operations, Study Questions (multiple choice, short answer, fill-in, and discussion), and two Hands-On Exercises. In addition, six On Your Own Exercises provide students the opportunity to practice and gain further experience with the material covered in the projects.

## Microsoft Certification

The content of this text is driven by the Microsoft Office User Specialist (MOUS) guidelines, and the author has developed the material from the ground up to reflect these objectives. Everyone who masters the projects in this text will be prepared to take the core level exam in Microsoft® Office 2000. It is becoming more and more important in today's competitive job market to have the skills necessary to be productive with today's most widely used applications software. *SELECT: Projects for Microsoft® Excel 2000* is designed with this purpose in mind.

## Organization

Before launching into the application, *SELECT: Projects for Microsoft® Excel 2000* familiarizes students with the operating system and some common elements of Microsoft® Office 2000 applications.

**Introduction to Windows** is a brief introduction to the operating system and can be used with Windows 98, Windows 95, and Windows NT, all three of which support Microsoft® Office 2000. Students become familiar with the Office interface, use a mouse, get Help, and work with multiple programs before launching the software applications.

The all new **Common Elements** section was created for *SELECT: Projects for Microsoft® Office 2000* to give students a basic overview of the elements common to the primary

Office 2000 software applications. This two-project section introduces students to basic features such as launching and exiting applications, basic file management tasks such as saving and opening files, printing techniques, and common methods for working with text and graphics. This section can be used as a reference throughout the text as students work through the individual applications or included as part of the course overview.

# Excel 2000

The new Microsoft® Excel 2000 spreadsheet tools can help you enter and manage your financial and numeric data more efficiently. New features include new date formatting options that address year 2000 concerns, see-through selection, list AutoFill, new cursors that provide visual cues, and improved chart formatting capabilities. Six new *SELECT: Projects for Microsoft® Excel 2000* teach students the certifiable skills and tasks that are important, both for business and for personal use. Students learn how to plan, design and format 3-dimensional workbook solutions.

# Features

## Running Case

The Selections, Inc. Department store is an all-new case for *SELECT: Projects for Microsoft® Excel 2000*. As a **Running Case**, Selections, Inc. puts students in an environment they can relate to, both as students and as future professionals. Each project begins with a scenario that puts students in the department store where they perform tasks that relate to a particular area or division of the store. Students relate what they're doing in Excel 2000 to a real-world situation that helps prepare them for what they may encounter in the business world as professionals.

## Challenge/Strategy/Setup

Once the student is familiar with the Running Case scenario for the project, the **Challenge** explains what they are actually going to do as they work through the tasks, and the **Strategy** summarizes a plan for achieving that goal. The **Setup** provides the settings necessary to ensure that the screen the student sees will match what is shown in the book.

##  Web Tip

This all-new feature for *SELECT: Projects for Microsoft® Excel 2000* provides the student with links to helpful Web sites and tips for locating additional information about specific topics on the World Wide Web. **Web Tips** often relate to Excel 2000, but include tips students can use in their everyday lives.

Each project contains at least three **Web Tips** that encourage students to explore Web sites that relate to the tasks they are performing in the application, highlight professional organizations that enhance the material, or direct them to topics of interest on their own. Because the Web is constantly changing, some links referenced in **Web Tips** may become inactive during the course. All **Web Tips** links will be updated through the SELECT Web Site at http://www.prenhall.com/select.

## Check Point

**Check Points** are placed at intervals throughout each project and provide review topics students can use to assess their skills or knowledge about related topics or about tasks previously covered.

## Break Point

Each project in *SELECT: Projects for Microsoft® Excel 2000* has been designed to take approximately one hour in the lab. Because students learn at different paces or may not have a full hour to complete a project, the **Break Point** feature appears at about the midpoint in each project and alerts students of a good stopping point if they need a break but want to continue the project later. **Break Points** take the guess work out of having to decide whether or not it's appropriate to stop and make it easier for students to start working on a project that they may not have time to complete.

## Tips and Troubleshooting Boxes

These feature boxes, popular with both instructors and students, appear throughout the text and have been revised and updated for *SELECT: Projects for Microsoft® Excel 2000.*

> TIP   *Tip boxes* include material that may be useful but that is not required in the step-by-step task instructions.

> **TROUBLESHOOTING**   *Troubleshooting boxes* alert students to problems they may encounter while using the applications and suggest possible causes for the problems along with potential solutions.

The **Introduction** sets the stage for the project and explains its purpose.

Clearly defined and measurable **Objectives** outline the skills covered.

The **Challenge** states the reasoning for the project.

The **Running Case** puts the student in the real-life environment of the Selections, Inc. department store.

The **Strategy** describes the plan for completing the project, which consists of tasks leading to the final product.

# Modifying Worksheets and Workbooks

Now that you have created the Selections, Inc. Sales Summary workbook, you can modify it so that it is easier to use and provides more information. In this project you will enhance the functionality of the workbook by adding worksheets for additional sales regions, deleting worksheets you no longer need, and repositioning the worksheets in the workbook. In addition, you will move, copy, and delete data, and create formulas that share information among worksheets in the Sales Summary workbook.

## Objectives

After completing this project, you will be able to:

➤ Open an Excel workbook
➤ Insert worksheets into a workbook
➤ Delete worksheets from a workbook
➤ Change the position of worksheets in a workbook
➤ Edit worksheets by copying and moving data
➤ Edit worksheets by revising data
➤ Enter additional text and number data into a workbook
➤ Create 3-D formulas that link information among worksheets

## Running Case

Mr. Traylor is pleased with the progress you have made so far. He enthusiastically accepted your initial design, and now wants you to finish defining the structure of your workbook to include quarterly sales for the remaining sales regions, and a summary of sales for all regions.

EX-44

---

**PROJECT** 2

## The Challenge

The regional worksheets need to be in order by region (North, South, East, West), with the summary worksheet appearing first in the workbook. The summary sales worksheet must contain formulas that dynamically list the regional sales data, so if the figures change for one or more regions, the changes are automatically reflected in the summary. When you are finished updating the workbook, Mr. Traylor will review your changes and approve the next phase of design.

## The Strategy

You can easily add worksheets to the workbook and then enter the appropriate data, create formulas, and modify the workbook structure by deleting any extra worksheets and ordering the remaining ones.

You can create 3-D linking formulas to dynamically include all regional sales data in the Sales Summary worksheet. Your workbook will look similar to the one shown in Figure 2.1 after you complete this project.

**FIGURE 2.1**

Project 2: Modifying Worksheets and Workbooks EX-45

An **illustration** shows the typical screen the student will see.

---

EX-46

## The Setup

Launch Microsoft Excel and make sure that you select the Excel settings listed in Table 2.1. This will ensure that your screen matches the illustrations and that the tasks in this project function as described.

**Table 2.1**

| Location | Make these settings: |
| --- | --- |
| Office Shortcut Bar | Right-click the Office icon on the shortcut bar and click Exit. |
| Office Assistant | Hide the Assistant. |
| Tools, Customize | Click the Options tab and deselect the option to show recently used menu commands first. Deselect the option to display the Standard and Formatting toolbars on one row. |
| Tools, Options | Click the Edit tab and select Move selection after Enter. |
| View, Formula Bar | Display the formula bar. |
| View, Status Bar | Display the status bar. |
| View, Normal | View the workbook in Normal view. |
| Maximize | Maximize the application and workbook windows. |

### Opening a Workbook

Before you can modify your workbook, you must open it. To open an existing workbook you must specify the file name and location.

**TASK 1:  To Open an Excel Workbook**

1. Select Open from the File menu.

2. In the File Open dialog box, select drive A.

> **TROUBLESHOOTING** If you saved your workbook to another location at the conclusion of Project 1, select the appropriate drive letter.

3. Open the Selections folder by double-clicking it, highlight the *Selections.xls* file, and click Open, as shown in Figure 2.2. Depending on your settings, your screen may differ slightly.

The **Setup** tells the students exactly which settings should be chosen so their computer screens match the illustrations in the book.

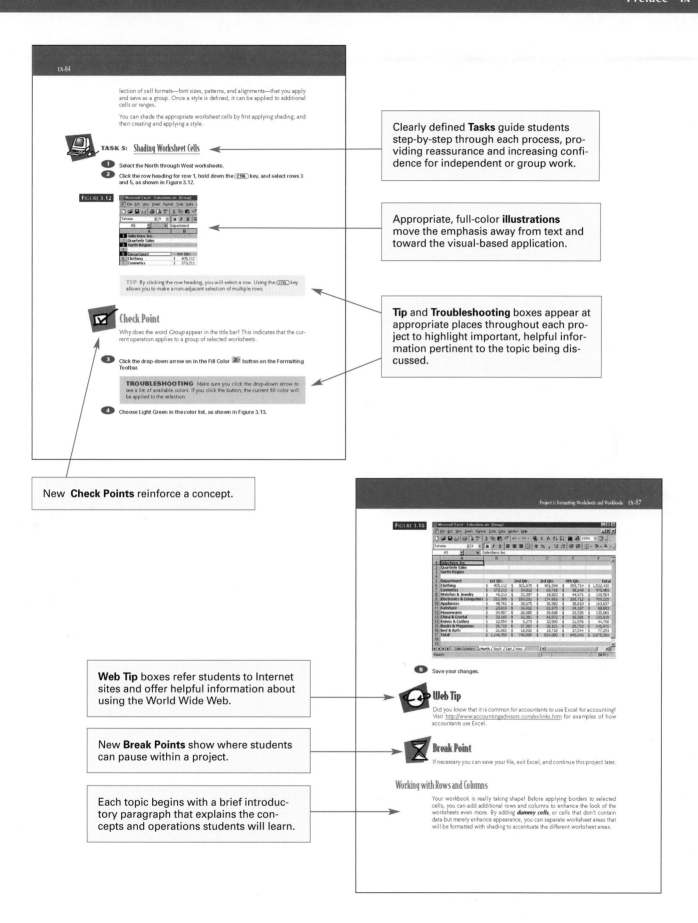

EX-84

lection of cell formats—font sizes, patterns, and alignments—that you apply and save as a group. Once a style is defined, it can be applied to additional cells or ranges.

You can shade the appropriate worksheet cells by first applying shading, and then creating and applying a style.

**TASK 5:  Shading Worksheet Cells**

1. Select the North through West worksheets.
2. Click the row heading for row 1, hold down the (CTRL) key, and select rows 3 and 5, as shown in Figure 3.12.

FIGURE 3.12

**TIP** By clicking the row heading, you will select a row. Using the (CTRL) key allows you to make a non-adjacent selection of multiple rows.

**Check Point**

Why does the word *Group* appear in the title bar? This indicates that the current operation applies to a group of selected worksheets.

3. Click the drop-down arrow on in the Fill Color button on the Formatting Toolbar.

**TROUBLESHOOTING** Make sure you click the drop-down arrow to see a list of available colors. If you click the button, the current fill color will be applied to the selection.

4. Choose Light Green in the color list, as shown in Figure 3.13.

Clearly defined **Tasks** guide students step-by-step through each process, providing reassurance and increasing confidence for independent or group work.

Appropriate, full-color **illustrations** move the emphasis away from text and toward the visual-based application.

**Tip** and **Troubleshooting** boxes appear at appropriate places throughout each project to highlight important, helpful information pertinent to the topic being discussed.

New **Check Points** reinforce a concept.

Project 3: Formatting Worksheets and Workbooks  EX-87

FIGURE 3.18

**Web Tip** boxes refer students to Internet sites and offer helpful information about using the World Wide Web.

New **Break Points** show where students can pause within a project.

Each topic begins with a brief introductory paragraph that explains the concepts and operations students will learn.

8. Save your changes.

**Web Tip**

Did you know that it is common for accountants to use Excel for accounting? Visit http://www.accountingadvisors.com/exlinks.htm for examples of how accountants use Excel.

**Break Point**

If necessary you can save your file, exit Excel, and continue this project later.

**Working with Rows and Columns**

Your workbook is really taking shape! Before applying borders to selected cells, you can add additional rows and columns to enhance the look of the worksheets even more. By adding **dummy cells**, or cells that don't contain data but merely enhance appearance, you can separate worksheet areas that will be formatted with shading to accentuate the different worksheet areas.

A **Summary** in bulleted-list format further reinforces the Objectives and the material presented in the project.

**Key terms** are boldface and italicized throughout each project, and then listed for handy review in the summary section at the end of the project.

**Study questions** bring the content of the project into focus again and allow for independent or group review of the material learned.

---

Project 3: Formatting Worksheets and Workbooks   EX-97

## Summary and Exercises

### Summary

- You can easily apply formats to numbers to make them easier to interpret.
- Font formats include size, style, and weight.
- You can easily change the alignment of data in one or more cells.
- A style is a set of formats that are stored with a name.
- Once you create a style, you can apply it to other selections.
- You can insert, delete, and resize the rows and columns in a worksheet.
- You can format cells by applying borders and shading.
- You can use the Web Page Preview to see how a worksheet will display if exported to the Web.

### Key Terms and Operations

#### Key Terms

| | |
|---|---|
| Borders button | Font Size box |
| cell alignment | Format Painter |
| cell border | number formats |
| cell shading | Select All button |
| currency style | style |
| Font box | Universal Document Viewing |

#### Operations

| | |
|---|---|
| add borders to cells | insert columns |
| apply font formats | modify number formats |
| apply number formats | resize columns |
| apply styles | save worksheets as HTML |
| change cell alignment | shade worksheet cells |
| copy number formats | use Web Page Preview |
| create styles | |

### Study Questions

#### Multiple Choice

1. Which of the following is not considered a number format?
   a. percent
   b. altitude
   c. scientific notation
   d. currency

---

EX-100

3. How does inserting columns into a worksheet differ from inserting worksheets into a workbook?

4. What is Web Page Preview? How does a Web Page Preview differ from a Print Preview?

5. List three common number formats.

### Hands-On Exercises

1. **Indenting and Rotating Text**

   Excel supports indenting and rotating text as a method for formatting worksheet data to make it more visually appealing. In this exercise you will indent and rotate text in the Java Sales workbook.

   1. Open the *Java Sales  4.xls* workbook.
   2. Click the First Qtr worksheet tab to make it the active sheet.
   3. Select cells B4:D4.
   4. Select Cells from the Format menu.
   5. Click the Alignment tab.
   6. Change the Horizontal alignment to Center, and click the polygon next to 90 Degrees, as shown in Figure 3.32.

   FIGURE 3.32

   7. Click OK. Change the font format to bold for the selection.
   8. Select cells A5:A8 and click the Increase Indent button on the Formatting toolbar, as shown in Figure 3.33.

In-depth **Hands-On Exercises** present tasks for building on the skills acquired in the project.

---

EX-102

FIGURE 3.35

5. Use the Format Painter to apply this format to the range A2:I2.
6. Apply formats to the Sales Summary worksheet so that your worksheet appears like the one shown in Figure 3.36.

FIGURE 3.36

Formatted Sales Summary worksheet for the Java Coffee Bar

8. Save your workbook as *Java Sales  6.xls*.
9. Close the workbook.

### On Your Own Exercises

### Web Tip

If you cannot obtain a copy of these files from your instructor, visit the SELECT Web site to download the necessary files: http://www.prenhall/select

1. **Formatting the Websites Workbook**

   Open the *Financial Sites 2.xls* workbook you modified in Project 1. Edit the workbook so it contains borders and shading to accentuate the sites. Save your workbook to the Investments folder with the name *Financial Sites 3.xls*.

2. **Formatting Your Class Schedule**

   Open the *Class Schedule  By Day.xls* workbook you modified in Project 2. Apply any formats you deem appropriate to each worksheet in the workbook. Save the workbook as *Class Schedule  By Day 2.xls*.

Six **On Your Own Exercises** are provided to invoke critical thinking and integration of project skills.

# Supplements

**Student Assessment Software**  *SkillCheck Professional Plus for Microsoft® Office 2000* features fully interactive test items that allow students to answer questions by performing complete tasks in virtually any correct way the software allows. All of the essential software features are all fully simulated, so no additional software is required. In addition to independently validated tests that cover beginning, intermediate, and advanced skills, each SkillCheck Professional Plus system includes a database of more than 100 interactive questions for each Office application. The instructor has complete control over every important aspect of testing and reporting, allowing users to customize or create tests with ease and speed.

**Companion Web Site**  *SELECT: Projects for Microsoft® Excel 2000*  is accompanied by a Companion Web site. Interactive online study guides offer interactive quizzes, chat rooms, and much more to help students with the material covered in the text.

## Instructor Supplements

**Instructor's Resource CD-ROM**   Instructors get extra support for this text from supplemental materials, including the Instructor's Resource CD-ROM with screen shots, diagrams, and tables from the text, and files that correspond to key figures in the book that can be used as electronic slides. Screen-by-screen steps in a project can be displayed in class or reviewed by students in the computer lab. The Instructor's Resource CD-ROM also includes the entire Instructor's Manual in Microsoft Word format, and Test Manager™, a computerized test bank designed to create printed tests, network tests, and self-assessment quizzes. Student data files and completed data files for Study Questions, Hands-On Exercises, and On Your Own Exercises are also on the Instructor's Resource CD-ROM.

**Test Manager**   Test Manager™ is a comprehensive suite of tools for testing and assessment. Test Manager™ allows educators to create and distribute tests for their courses, by printing and distributing through traditional methods or by on-line delivery via a Local Area Network (LAN) server.  Four question formats are available: multiple choice, true/false, matching, and completion exercises.  Answer keys and page references for test questions are provided.

**Printed Supplements**   The Instructor's Manual includes a test bank and transparency masters for each project in the student text, as well as Expanded Student Objectives, Answers to Study Questions, and Additional Assessment Techniques. The test bank contains two separate tests with answers and consists of multiple choice, true/false, and fill-in questions referenced to pages in the student text. Transparency masters illustrate key concepts and screen captures from the text.

# Acknowledgments from the Author

To Deanna Storey, Anita Devine, and Holly Rioux at Addison-Wesley: Thanks, Deanna, for going above and beyond the call of duty in making this work possible. You have truly been the best project manager any author could hope to work with. Thank you, Anita, for your insight, attention to detail, and great success in weaving our individual writing styles into a seamless whole. Thanks, Holly, for making sure our work meets each and every required certification objective. For getting this work into print, thanks to the Elm Street Publishing staff and especially to Michele Heinz; it has been a delight to work with you.

# Acknowledgments

Addison-Wesley Publishing Company would like to thank the following reviewers for their valuable contributions to the *SELECT Lab Series.*

James Agnew
Northern Virginia CC

Joseph Aieta
Babson College

Dr. Muzaffar Ali
Bellarmine College

John Anderson
Northeastern State University

Tom Ashby
Oklahoma CC

Bob Barber
Lane CC

Gina Bowers
Harrisburg Area CC

Robert Caruso
Santa Rosa Junior College

Robert Chi
California State
Long Beach

Pat Coulter
Pennsylvania Technical
College

Jill Davis
State University of New
York at Stony Brook

Fredia Dillard
Samford University

George Dollar
Clearwater Christian
College

Peter Drexel
Plymouth State College

David Egle
University of Texas, Pan
American

Linda Ericksen
Lane CC

Jonathan Frank
Suffolk University

Rebecca Gatlin
University of Central
Arkansas

Patrick Gilbert
University of Hawaii

Maureen Greenbaum
Union County College

Sally Ann Hanson
Mercer County CC

Sunil Hazari
East Carolina University

Ric Heismann
Northern Virginia CC

Gloria Henderson
Victor Valley College

Bruce Herniter
University of Hartford

Rick Homkes
Purdue University

Lisa Jackson
Henderson CC

Cyntia Kachik
Santa Fe CC

Vincent Kayes
Mount St. Mary College

Bennett Kramer
Massasoit CC

Charles Lake
Faulkner State Junior
College

Ron Leake
Johnson County CC

Randy Marak
Hill College

Charles Mattox, Jr.
St. Mary's University

Jim McCullough
Porter and Chester
Institute

Gail Miles
Lenoir-Rhyne College

Steve Moore
University of South
Florida

Karen Mounce
Somerset CC

Anthony Nowakowski
Buffalo State College

Gloria Oman
Portland State University

John Passafiume
Clemson University

Leonard Presby
William Paterson College

Louis Pryor
Garland County CC

Michael Reilly
University of Denver

Dick Ricketts
Lane CC

Dennis Santomauro
Kean College of New
Jersey

Pamela Schmidt
Oakton CC

Gary Schubert
Alderson-Broaddus College

Mike Scroggins
Southwest Missouri State
University

T. Michael Smith
Austin CC

Cynthia Thompson
Carl Sandburg College

Marion Tucker
Northern Oklahoma College

JoAnn Weatherwax
Saddleback College

David Whitney
San Francisco State
University

James Wood
Tri-County Technical
College

Judy Wynekoop
University of Texas

Minnie Yen
University of Alaska,
Anchorage

Allen Zilbert
Long Island University

# Contents

# Overview of Windows

# Overview of Windows

**W**indows is an *operating system*, a special kind of computer program that performs three major functions. First, an operating system controls the actual *hardware* of the computer (the screen, the keyboard, the disk drives, and so on). Second, an operating system enables other software programs such as word processing or spreadsheet applications to run. Finally, an operating system determines how the user operates the computer and its programs or applications.

As an operating system, Windows and all other programs written to run under it provide *graphics* (or pictures) called *icons* to carry out commands and run programs. For this reason, Windows is referred to as a *graphical user interface* or GUI (pronounced gooey). You can use the keyboard or a device called a *mouse* to activate the icons.

This overview explains the basics of Windows so that you can begin using your computer quickly and easily. In general, the information in this chapter is applicable to Windows 95, Windows 98, and Windows NT 4.0.

## Objectives

After completing this project, you will be able to:

➤ Identify the desktop elements

➤ Use a mouse

➤ Use the basic features of Windows

➤ Get help

➤ Work with multiple programs

➤ Exit Windows

### Identifying the Desktop Elements

Because Windows is an operating system, it launches immediately when you turn on the computer. Depending on the way your computer is set up, you may have to type your user name and password to log on (to gain access to the program). After Windows launches, the working environment, called the *desktop*, appears on the screen. Figure W.1 shows what a typical desktop might look like if you are using Windows 95, or the classic look of Windows 95 as the desktop style for Windows 98. If you are viewing the desktop as a Web page, the desktop may still look similar to Figure W.1, but the labels under the icons may be underlined. Table W.1 describes the icons that appear on the desktop.

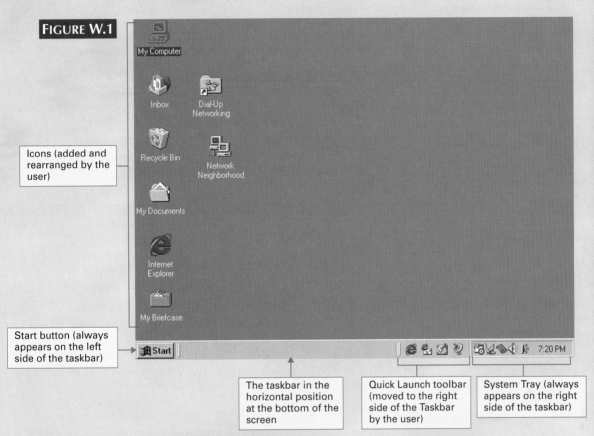

Icons (added and rearranged by the user)

Start button (always appears on the left side of the taskbar)

The taskbar in the horizontal position at the bottom of the screen

Quick Launch toolbar (moved to the right side of the Taskbar by the user)

System Tray (always appears on the right side of the taskbar)

**Table W.1**

| Icon | Description |
| --- | --- |
| **My Computer** | Enables you to organize your work and easily access your files and system folders. |
| **Recycle Bin** | Stores files that have been deleted from the hard disk. Files stored in the Recycle Bin can be restored to their original locations, if necessary. |
| **Internet Explorer** | Starts Internet Explorer, a program that browses the World Wide Web and provides access to other Internet services. |
| **My Briefcase** | Synchronizes files that are worked on using different computers. |
| **Network** | Accesses all the devices (drives, printers, and so on) on a network to **Neighborhood** which you've been granted access. |

At the bottom of the desktop is the *taskbar*, used for displaying the Start menu, starting programs, checking the status of various software and hardware components (such as the date and time or the volume control), and switching between programs. Table W.2 describes the elements of the taskbar.

**Table W.2**

| Taskbar Element | Description |
|---|---|
| Start button | Displays the Start menu, which has commands for launching programs, opening documents, finding documents, and so on. |
| Taskbar toolbars | Provide access to useful buttons. There are four taskbar toolbars available: the Quick Launch, Address, Links, and Desktop toolbars. Only the Quick Launch toolbar displays by default. It has buttons for launching Internet Explorer and other frequently used programs. It also has a Show Desktop button that you can use to quickly see the desktop without minimizing windows. You can display the other toolbars by right-clicking the taskbar and selecting a toolbar from the Toolbars menu. |
| System Tray | Contains icons for programs that are running in memory and displays the system time. |

# Using a Mouse

A pointing device such as a mouse is almost an indispensable tool for using Windows. Although you can use the keyboard to navigate and make selections, using a mouse is often more convenient and efficient. Table W.3 describes the actions that the mouse performs.

When you move the mouse on your desk, a pointer moves on the screen. When the pointer is on the object you want to use, you can take one of the actions described in Table W.3 to give Windows an instruction.

**Table W.3**

| Action | Description |
|---|---|
| Point | Slide the mouse across a smooth surface (preferably a mouse pad) until the pointer on the screen is on the object. |
| Click | Press and release the left mouse button once. |
| Drag | Press and hold down the left mouse button while you move the mouse and then release the mouse button to complete the action. |
| Right-click | Press and release the right mouse button once. Right-clicking usually displays a shortcut menu. |
| Double-click | Press and release the left mouse button twice in rapid succession. |

Windows interprets the instruction given by the mouse action based on the version of Windows or the desktop style that is used. For example, when you click the mouse once using Windows 95 or the classic Windows 95 style for Windows 98, Windows selects the item. If you double-click the mouse, Windows selects and executes. If you are viewing the desktop as a Web page, pointing is equivalent to clicking and clicking is equivalent to double-clicking.

> **TROUBLESHOOTING**  The steps in the Tasks in this chapter assume that Windows 95 or the classic Windows 95 desktop style is in use. If you are using the Web page style desktop, you might want to deactivate it by right-clicking the desktop and choosing Active Desktop, View As Web Page.

**TASK 1:**   To Use the Mouse

**1**   Point to the My Computer icon, press and hold down the left mouse button, and then drag the mouse across the desk. The icon moves.

> **TROUBLESHOOTING**  If the icon appears to snap back to its original location, turn off the Auto Arrange command by right-clicking the desktop and choosing Arrange Icons, Auto Arrange.

**2**   Drag the My Computer icon back to its original location.

**3**   Right-click the icon. A shortcut menu opens.

**FIGURE W.2**

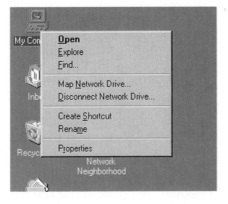

**4**   Click a blank space on the screen. The shortcut menu closes.

**5**   Double-click the My Computer icon. A window titled My Computer opens.

**FIGURE W.3**

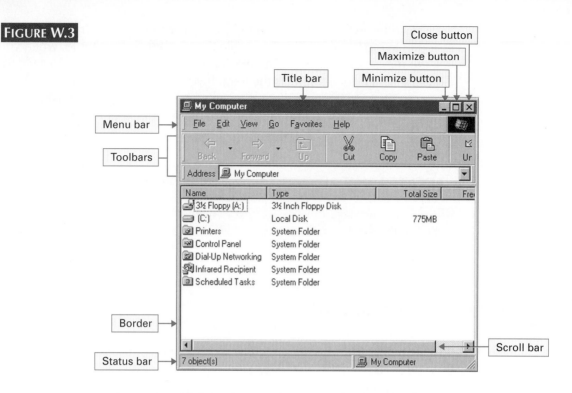

**TIP** Do not close this window, as you will manipulate it in the next task.

# Using the Basic Features of Windows

The basic features of Windows are windows, menus, dialog boxes, and toolbars. These features are used in all programs that are written to run under Windows.

## Using Windows

A **window** is one of the basic elements of the Windows operating system. All programs launched in Windows occupy a window. Figure W.3 shows the common elements of a window.

The **menu bar** displays options for performing **commands**. The **status bar** displays information such as menu descriptions and the size of files. The **borders** outline the boundaries of the window. The **scroll bars** let you see the entire contents. The **Close button**, the **maximize button** (which changes to a **Restore button**), and the **Minimize button** appear at the top right. Toolbars contain several specialized buttons. The **title bar** displays the application name.

## TASK 2:   To Work with a Window

**1** Click the Maximize ▢ button if it is displayed. If it is not displayed, click the Restore ⧉ button, and then click the Maximize button. The Maximize button changes to a Restore button and the window occupies the entire screen.

**2** Click the Minimize ▬ button. The My Computer window is no longer visible on the desktop. The taskbar now contains a My Computer button.

**FIGURE W.4**

**3** Click the My Computer button on the taskbar. The window becomes the current application.

**4** Click the Restore ⧉ button.

**5** Point to the right border of the My Computer window until the pointer changes to a double-headed black arrow, and then drag the border to make the window as narrow as shown in Figure W.5.

**6** Drag the bottom border up so the window matches the size shown in Figure W.5.

**7** Click ▢. The window occupies the entire screen.

**8** Click ⧉. The window returns to its former size.

**9** Click the Close ✕ button. The My Computer window closes.

**FIGURE W.5**

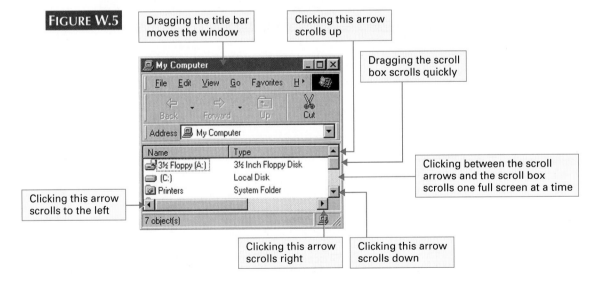

## Using Menus and Toolbars

Almost every program, including Windows itself, uses various types of **menus** and **toolbars** to make commands accessible to the user. In most cases, you can perform the same command either by using the menus or by using a button on a toolbar.

> **TIP** Toolbar buttons and keyboard shortcuts are considered faster methods than menus for accomplishing common tasks.

## Using Menus

Windows and Windows programs use several types of menus. One type of menu is the **drop-down menu**, appears when you make a selection from a menu bar. The menu bar in most programs appears at the top of the window under the title bar. Drop-down menus may also be referred to as **pop-up menus**. This term describes the way the menu displays when the menu bar is moved to the bottom of the screen. The Start menu in Windows is an example of a pop-up menu.

Figure W.6 shows a Word menu with many elements common to the menus used in other Windows programs. An option with an ellipsis displays a dialog box. Dimmed options are not available in the current circumstance.

**FIGURE W.6**

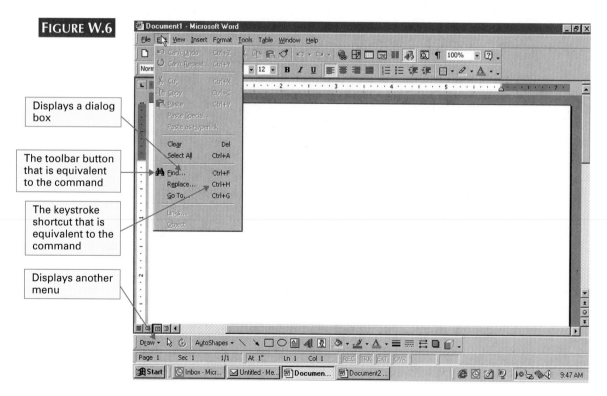

Displays a dialog box

The toolbar button that is equivalent to the command

The keystroke shortcut that is equivalent to the command

Displays another menu

The shortcut menu that you saw in Task 1 is a **context-sensitive menu**. This means that the menu displays only those options that are appropriate to the context, or current task. For example, in Task 1, when you right-clicked the My Computer icon, a shortcut menu opened with options that pertain only to My Computer. If you had right-clicked the Recycle Bin, a different shortcut menu would have opened. Shortcut menus are always displayed by right-clicking an object or an area of the screen.

You can select menu options, whether in a menu bar, a drop-down menu, or a shortcut menu, by clicking the option. If you prefer to use keystrokes, you can type the underlined letter for the option. To select an option from the menu bar, first press (ALT) to activate the menu bar and then type the underlined letter of the option.

> TIP  Because you can select menu commands in two ways, the steps with instructions to select a menu command will use the word choose instead of dictating the method of selection.

## Using Toolbars

Many programs have multiple toolbars. The buttons on a toolbar are usually related in some way, or the toolbar is a multipurpose toolbar, and the buttons are grouped by related functions.

To use a toolbar button, click the button; Windows takes an immediate action, depending on the button's function. Some toolbar buttons perform commands; others display drop-down lists or dialog boxes.

> TIP  If you don't know what a button on the toolbar does, point to the button; a **ToolTip**, a brief description of the button, appears near the button.

**TASK 3:   To Use Menus and Toolbars**

1  Click the Start button, point to Programs, and click Windows Explorer. The Exploring window opens.

2  Choose View from the menu bar. The View drop-down menu appears.

3  Choose Large Icons if it is not already selected.

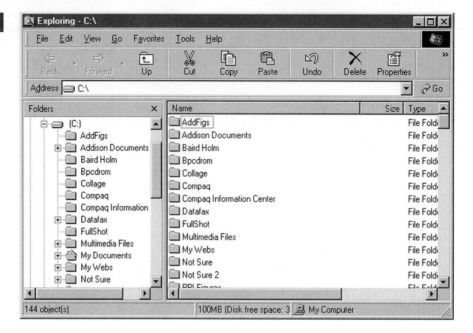

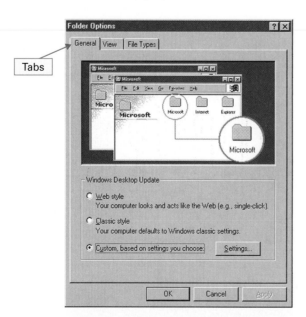

**4** If the toolbar is not displayed, choose View Toolbars (in Windows 95) or View, Toolbars, Standard Buttons (in Windows 98).

**5** Click the down arrow on the Views button and choose Details. The Details view appears. This can be the most helpful view when you are performing file maintenance because it displays the most information about a file.

**6** Click ⊠.

## Using Dialog Boxes

When many options are available for a single task, Windows conveniently groups the options in one place, called a **dialog box**. Some functions have so many options that Windows divides them further into groups and places them on separate pages in the dialog box. Figure W.8 shows an example of a dialog box with three pages.

## Working with Multiple Programs

The Windows **multitasking** feature allows you to launch multiple programs and switch back and forth between them. A button on the taskbar represents each open program, as each program is a specific task the user is accomplishing.

 **Check Point**

When you run multiple applications, more than one program is running, but only one program is active at any given time.

 **TASK 4:  To Switch between Windows**

**1** Click Start and point to Programs. The Programs menu appears.

**2** Point to Accessories and click Paint. Maximize the window if necessary.

**FIGURE W.9**

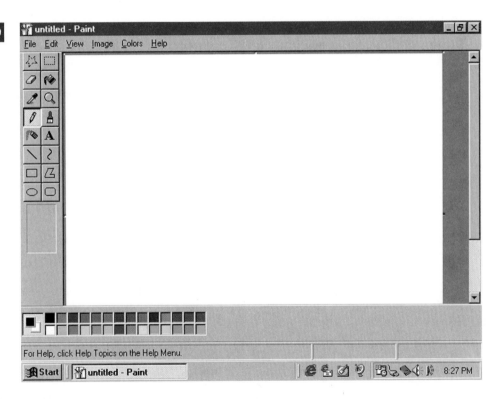

**3** Choose File, Open, and select the Windows folder for Look in. Then double-click on any file name that has a *.bmp* extension. The file opens.

**4** Click Start, point to Programs, point to Accessories, and click WordPad. The WordPad window opens.

**5** Type **What do you think of this graphic?** and press (ENTER) twice.

**6** Click on the Paint button on the taskbar. Windows switches to the Paint program.

**7** Choose Edit, Select all. The graphic is selected.

**8** Choose Edit, Copy. Windows copies the image to the Windows Clipboard.

**9** Click the WordPad button on the taskbar. Windows switches to the WordPad program.

**10** Choose Edit, Paste. The graphic file appears at the insertion point in the WordPad file.

**11** Choose File, Save. The Save As dialog box opens.

**12** Specify the drive and folder where you save your files in the Look in text box.

**13** Type **My File** for File name and choose Save. The file is saved and the dialog box closes.

> **TIP** You also can use the keyboard shortcut (**ALT**) + (**TAB**) to switch between programs.

## Getting Help

Instead of opening a Windows reference book, you can get help right at your computer using the Windows **Help** feature. Windows provides you with three methods of accessing help information: You can look up information in a table of contents; you can search for information in an index; or you can find a specific word or phrase in a database maintained by the Find feature.

Additionally, Windows provides context-sensitive help, called **What's This?** for the topic you are working on. This type of help is generally found in dialog boxes.

After you learn to use Help in Windows, you can use help in any Office 2000 application. The Help feature in Windows 98 is a little different from the Help feature in Windows 95. Perform Task 5 if you are using Windows 95 as your operating system; perform Task 6 if you are using Windows 98.

 **TASK 5:** To Use Help in Windows 95

**1** Click the Start button on the taskbar and click Help. The Help window opens.

**2** Click the Contents tab if a different page is displayed. The Contents page appears.

**3** Double-click Tips and Tricks, and then double-click For setting up the desktop efficiently. The topics on this subject appear.

**4** Double-click Putting shortcuts on the desktop. The Help topic opens.

**5** Choose Help Topics and then click the Index tab. The Index page of the Help feature appears.

**6** Type **calculator**. The list scrolls to the first occurrence of the word calculator.

**7** Double-click *starting*. The Help topic appears.

**8** Choose Help Topics and then click the Find tab. The Find page of the Help feature appears.

**9** Type **print** and click Find Now if necessary. A list of topics that contain the word *print* appears.

**10** Double-click Changing printer settings. The Help topic appears.

**11** Click the button in the first step. The Printers folder opens.

**12** Select any printer that is listed (as instructed in the second step in the Help topic) and choose File, Properties (as instructed in the third step in the Help topic). The Properties dialog box opens.

**13** Click the What's This button ? as instructed in the Help Tips, and then click any option in the dialog box. A pop-up box with an explanation of the option appears.

**14** Click the pop-up box to hide it and then close the Properties dialog box as well as the Help topic.

TASK 6:   To Use Help in Windows 98

**1** Click the Start button on the taskbar and click Help. The Help window opens.

**2** Click the Contents tab if a different page is displayed. The Contents page appears.

**3** Click Using Windows Accessories. The topic expands.

**4** Click Calculator.

FIGURE W.10

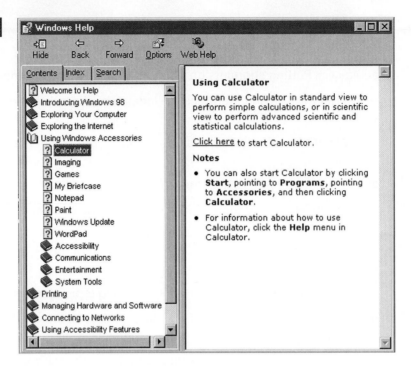

5 Click the Index tab, scroll the list, and double-click Active Desktop. The topic displays in the right pane.

6 Click the Search tab, type **print** in the text box and select List Topics. The topics display in the Topics list at the bottom of the dialog box.

7 Double-click To change printer settings. The topic appears in the right pane.

8 Click the Hide button on the toolbar. The left pane closes.

FIGURE W.11

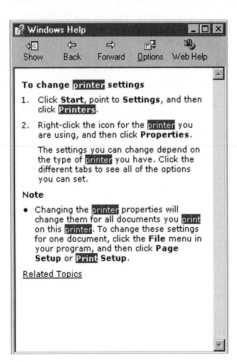

9 Click the Show button. The left pane appears again.

**10** Click the Options 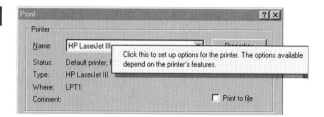 button. A drop-down menu appears.

**11** Choose Print. The Print dialog box opens.

**12** Click the What's This ? button. A question mark is attached to the mouse pointer.

**13** Click the Properties button. An explanation appears.

**FIGURE W.12**

Print

Printer

Name:   HP LaserJet III

Click this to set up options for the printer. The options available depend on the printer's features.

Status:   Default printer;

Type:   HP LaserJet III

Where:   LPT1:

Comment:                                    Print to file

**14** Read the message and then click it. The message closes.

**15** Click X in the Print dialog box.

**16** Click X. The Help dialog box closes.

> **TIP** You can print any help article by right-clicking anywhere in the article and choosing Print Topic.

# Exiting Windows

When you are ready to turn off the computer, you must exit Windows first. You should never turn off the computer without following the proper exit procedure because Windows has to do some utility tasks before it shuts down. Unlike most of us, Windows likes to put everything away when it's finished. When you shut down improperly, you can cause serious problems in Windows.

**TASK 7:** To Exit Windows

**1** Click the Start button and then click Shut Down.

**2** In Windows 95, choose Shut down the computer?, and then choose Yes. In Windows 98, choose Shut down, and then choose OK.

**3** When the message "It's now safe to turn off your computer" appears, turn off the computer.

> **TROUBLESHOOTING** You may not see a message that says "It's now safe to turn off your computer." If you are using a computer in a lab, follow the shutdown procedures used by the lab. Instead of choosing Shut down (the computer) and turning off the computer, you may be instructed to choose Close all programs and log on as a different user and leave the computer on.

# Summary

- Windows is an operating system with a graphical interface.
- The working environment is called the desktop.
- The Start menu has commands for launching programs and opening documents.
- The mouse gives instructions to Windows, which Windows interprets based on the interface that is in use.
- A window has a border, sizing buttons, a Close button, and other elements that are unique to a window.
- Menus and toolbars contain commands for performing procedures.
- Dialog boxes display options for commands.
- You can get help right at your computer using the Windows Help feature.
- You can copy, rename, move, delete, and restore files.
- The multitasking feature of Windows allows you to launch multiple programs and switch between them as you are working.
- You must exit Windows properly to allow Windows to perform its necessary functions.

## Key Terms and Operations

### Key Terms

| | |
|---|---|
| command | My Briefcase |
| Close button | My Computer |
| context-sensitive menu | Network Neighborhood |
| desktop | operating system |
| dialog box | pop-up menu |
| drop-down menu | Recycle Bin |
| Graphical User Interface | Restore button |
| graphics | scroll bar |
| hardware | shortcut menu |
| Help | Start button |
| icons | status bar |
| Internet Explorer | taskbar |
| Maximize button | title bar |
| menu | toolbar |
| menu bar | ToolTip |
| Minimize button | What's This? |
| mouse | window |
| multitasking | window border |

### Operations

| | |
|---|---|
| click | open a window |
| double-click | point |
| drag | right-click |
| exit Windows | switch between windows |
| launch a program | |

# Common Elements In Office 2000

# Basic Common Elements

One of the greatest advantages of using the ever-popular Microsoft Office suites is the number of features common to all programs that make up the office suite. Microsoft Office 2000 takes full advantage of many common elements. The increased number of common elements means that techniques you learn in one Office 2000 application can be used to accomplish the same task in other Office 2000 applications. This section introduces you to many of the features common to Office 2000 applications and describes some of the unique twists you'll find with these common features as you move from application to application in Microsoft Office 2000.

## Objectives

After completing this project, you will be able to:

➤ Launch applications

➤ Perform basic file management tasks

➤ Use Help

➤ Select printers and print

➤ Exit applications

## Launching Applications

Office 2000 offers a variety of techniques for launching applications. The procedure you use will depend on how Office 2000 is installed on your computer and your personal preference.

To launch Office 2000 applications, use one of the following procedures:

• Click Start, Programs, and then click the Office 2000 application you want to launch.

**FIGURE 1.1**

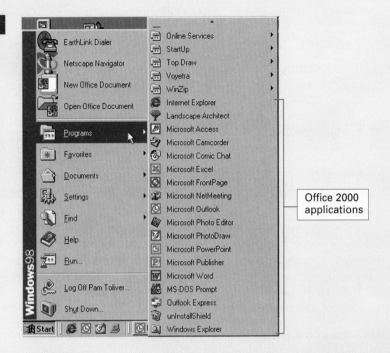

Office 2000 applications

**TROUBLESHOOTING** If shortcuts to the Office 2000 applications do not appear on your Programs list, click the arrow button at the bottom of the Programs list to scroll until the applications appear.

- Click Start, New Office Document, and then double-click the Blank file type that represents the application you want to launch. The application required to create the file launches. Blank files are identified by type on the General page of the dialog box. Design templates are grouped by type on additional pages of the dialog box.

**FIGURE 1.2**

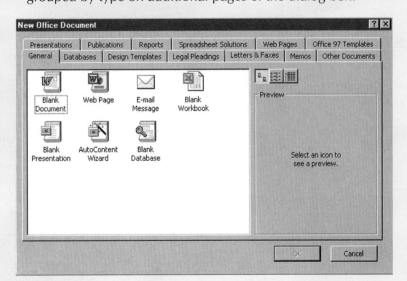

**TIP** Office 2000 also offers a series of professionally designed file formats called *templates* that you can choose to create your file. Simply click the tab for the type of file you want to create, click a template name, and review the template preview.

- Double-click an application shortcut icon on the desktop.
- Click the application icon on the Microsoft Office Bar, if it is installed on your computer. The Microsoft Office Bar usually appears at the top of the computer screen when it is installed.

**FIGURE 1.3**

This Microsoft Office Bar has been customized to display application icons. Your bar may differ from the one shown here

**TIP** You can also launch an Office 2000 application by selecting an Office file on the Start menu Documents list or by selecting the file in the Exploring or My Computer window. When you click a file shown on the Documents list, or double-click a filename in the Exploring or My Computer window, the application used to create the file launches and the file opens.

Depending on the application you launch, the item that appears on-screen will differ:

- Word and Excel display new files: Word displays a new blank document. Excel displays a new blank workbook template.
- Access and PowerPoint display dialog boxes that contains options for creating a new file or opening an existing file.

Because Word makes accessing and using all the common elements covered in this section easy, it was chosen as the application to introduce many of these features. The procedures for launching Word 2000 described here should be accessible from all computers on which Office 2000 is installed.

**TASK 1: Launching Microsoft Word 2000**

**1** Choose Start, Programs.

**2** Scroll to the bottom of the Programs list, if necessary.

**3** Click Microsoft Word. Screen elements common to all Microsoft Office 2000 applications are identified in Figure 1.4.

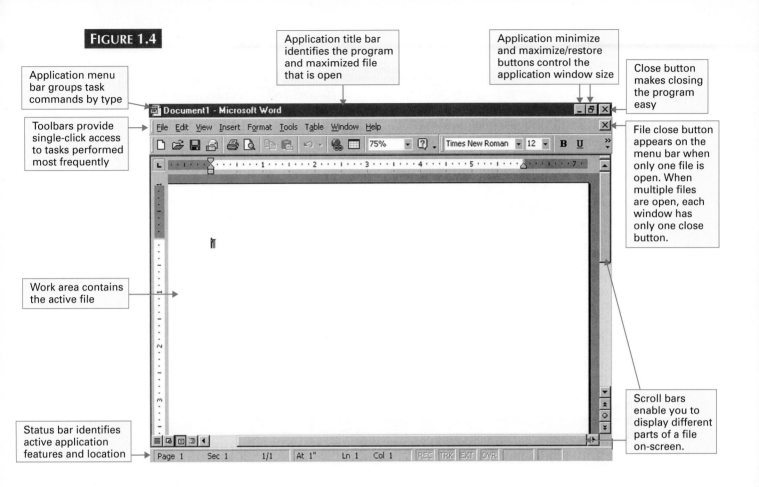

FIGURE 1.4

Application menu bar groups task commands by type

Application title bar identifies the program and maximized file that is open

Application minimize and maximize/restore buttons control the application window size

Close button makes closing the program easy

Toolbars provide single-click access to tasks performed most frequently

File close button appears on the menu bar when only one file is open. When multiple files are open, each window has only one close button.

Work area contains the active file

Scroll bars enable you to display different parts of a file on-screen.

Status bar identifies active application features and location

# Performing Basic File Management Tasks

Basic file management tasks include opening files, creating new files, saving files, and editing file properties. The procedures for accomplishing these tasks are similar in all Office 2000 applications.

## Opening Files

Office 2000 provides a number of different procedures that you can use to open an existing document, workbook, presentation, or database. The Open dialog box has been redesigned in Office 2000 and presents a Web-like look. To open a file:

- Choose File, Open.
- Click the Open button on the Standard toolbar.
- Press (CTRL) + O.
- Choose Start, Open Office Document.

Regardless of which of these four procedures you use, an Open dialog box similar to the one shown in Figure 1.5 appears. Features of the Open dialog box are described in Table 1.1.

FIGURE 1.5

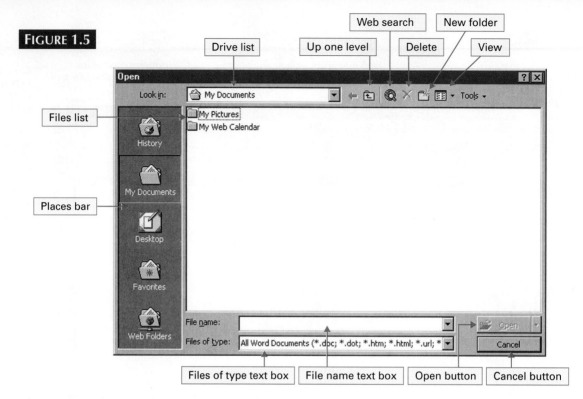

Table 1.1

| Feature | Description |
|---|---|
| Drive list | identifies the current drive and/or folder |
| Up One Level button | accesses the "parent" folder when a folder is active or My Computer when a drive is active |
| Search theWeb button | launches Internet Explorer 5 or your default Web browser to the Microsoft Home, all in one page so that you can perform a search for the document to open |
| Delete button | removes the active document from the folder or drive |
| Create New Folder button | creates a new folder within the active drive or folder |
| View drop-down list | enables you to change the way files and folders are displayed in the dialog box and rearrange files |
| Tools drop-down list | contains commands often found on Open dialog box menus in other applications |
| Places Bar | contains folders and file storage locations so that you can open them quickly |
| File name text box text box | enables you to type the name of the document to locate or open |
| Files of type text box | identifies the types of files displayed |
| Files list | shows all folders and files in the active folder or on the active drive. |
| Open button | opens the selected (highlighted) file and contains a drop-down list that enables you to open a copy of the file, open the file in Read-Only mode, or open a Web document in a browser |
| Cancel button | closes the dialog box without opening a document |

**TIP** A folder in Windows can contain files or additional folders.

**TIP** By default, if the file you want to open is one of the last four files opened on the computer you are using, the file name may appear at the bottom of the File menu. Click the file name to open the file. You can change the number of files that appear at the bottom of the File menu for any application using the Tools, Options command and then setting the number of files on the General page of the Options dialog box.

**TIP** You can also open one of the last fifteen files saved on the computer you're using by selecting the file name from the Start menu Documents list. In addition, you can open a file by double-clicking the file name in the Exploring or My Computer window. If the application used to create the file is not running, it launches when you open the file.

# Web Tip

If you do not have a copy of the *Selections.doc* file on your student disk, you can download it from the SELECT Web site at
http://www.prenhall.com/select

## TASK 2:   Opening a Copy of a Document

**1** Choose File, Open.

**2** Open the folder or disk drive containing the *Selections.doc* file that you downloaded from the SELECT Web site, or follow the directions from your instructor to locate the file. The folder or disk drive name appears in the Look in text box.

**3** Click the *Selections.doc* file. The file name appears highlighted.

**4** Click the drop-down list arrow on the Open button.

**FIGURE 1.6**

**5** Choose Open as Copy. Opening a copy of an existing document leaves the original intact so that you can use it later, if necessary.

**FIGURE 1.7**

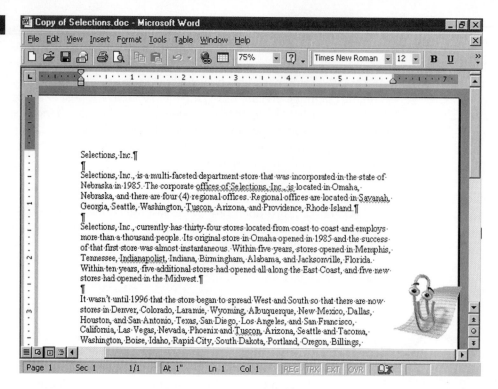

---

**TIP** Word underlines suspected spelling and grammar errors; Excel and Access do not.

---

**TIP** The settings active on your computer control the appearance of the document on your screen.

---

## Creating New Files

As you discovered with opening files, Microsoft Office 2000 offers a variety of different techniques for performing tasks. A new document automatically appears when you launch Word, and a new blank workbook is created each time you launch Excel. As you explore all Office 2000 applications, you'll find that options for creating and opening files are presented when you launch PowerPoint and Access. To create a new file in any Office 2000 application after it is launched:

- Click the New ☐ button on the Standard toolbar of any Office 2000 application. A new blank file automatically appears in Word and Excel. In Access, clicking the New button displays the New dialog box so that you can create a blank database, or a database using a template. In Power-Point, the New Slide dialog box opens so you can select a slide format for the first slide in the new presentation.

- Press (**CTRL**) + N. A new blank file automatically appears in Word, Excel, and PowerPoint. In Access, the New dialog box opens so that you can select the type of database you want to create. In PowerPoint, the New Slide dialog box opens so you can select a slide format for the first slide of the new presentation.

- Choose File, New. The New dialog box opens and displays a list of templates—professionally designed, preformatted file formats specific to the application you're using—that you can use to format your file.

The number of the new file on the title bar is incremented by 1. Another document button appears on the Windows taskbar.

> **TIP** You can also create a new Office 2000 document by choosing Start, New Office Document. A dialog box that contains a comprehensive listing of all Office 2000 templates grouped by type opens so that you can choose the type of document you want to create. After you choose the document type, the application required to create the file launches automatically, if it isn't already running.

## Check Point

Create a new blank document in Word by clicking the New Blank Document button on the toolbar.

FIGURE 1.8

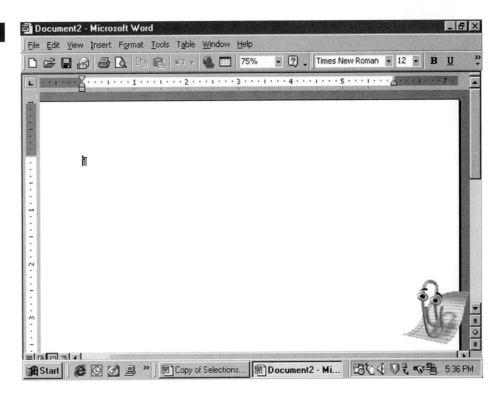

## Switching among Open Files

Word, Excel, and PowerPoint enable you to open or create multiple files without closing files that are already open. These three applications place a file button on the Windows taskbar for each file you have open. To switch from one open file to another, you can:

- Click the Windows taskbar button for the open file you want to access.
- Press (CTRL) + (F6) to browse open files for the active application. Press (CTRL) + (SHIFT) + (F6) to move backward among open files.

> **TROUBLESHOOTING** This technique accesses open files for the active application only. Because each application and file you have open appears as a button on the taskbar, you can press (ALT) + (TAB) to move from one open application to another as well as from one open file to another.

- Choose the Window menu and then select the file you want to access from the bottom of the menu.

 **Check Point**

When you use multiple applications in Office, more than one program may be open, but only one is active. Similarly, when you open multiple documents, workbooks, or presentations, more than one can be open, but only one is active at any given time.

## Closing Files

Office 2000 applications provide a variety of techniques for closing files. To close the active file:

- Click the file Close ☒ button at the right end of the menu bar.

> **TROUBLESHOOTING** In Word, the Close button appears on the menu bar only when one document is open. When multiple documents are open, click the Close button at the end of the title bar—Word stays open until all documents are closed.

- Right-click the Windows taskbar button for the file you want to close and choose Close.
- Choose File, Close.
- Press (CTRL) + (F4).
- Click the file control icon at the left end of the menu bar and choose Close.

TIP Regardless of which procedure you use to close a file, if you have edited the file, the Office 2000 application will prompt you to save the file. Be sure to read the message carefully to determine your response and prevent unwanted loss of data.

## Check Point

Before continuing with the rest of the features, use one of the close procedures identified to close the blank document you created earlier. After you close the file, the *Copy of Selections.doc* should appear.

## Saving Files

Each new document you create, each copy of an existing document you open, and each document you edit all need to be saved. You'll find a number of different Save commands listed on the File menu of Office 2000 applications. Knowing the difference between the Save commands is important. Here's how they work:

**Table 1.2**

| Command | Description |
| --- | --- |
| Save | Opens the Save As dialog box so that you can select a storage location for *new* files you create. The dialog box contains text boxes where you can type a file name and select a save format.<br><br>Automatically overwrites previously saved files that you open and edit and saves existing files for which you opened a copy in the same folder of the same disk using the file name *Copy of xx*. |
| Save As | In Word, Excel, and PowerPoint, opens the Save As dialog box so that you can save changes to an already saved file and/or copies of existing files in a different storage location or using a different file name or file type.<br><br>In Access, Save As allows you to export a specific database object only. |
| Save as Web Page | Opens the Save As dialog box, automatically activates Web Page (*.htm; *.html) as the Save as type, and adds a page title. |

To initiate the Save command, you can use one of the following techniques:

- Click the Save ▣ button on the Standard toolbar.
- Press (CTRL) + S.
- Choose File, Save.

When you save a file, you may also want to create a new folder in which to store the file. You can create the folder "on the fly" using the Save As dialog box and prevent having to move the file later.

## TASK 3:  To Save a Copy of a File in a New Folder

**1**  Click the title bar of the *Copy of Selections.doc* file to make it active, if necessary. Active windows usually have a darker title bar than inactive windows.

**2**  Choose File, Save As. The Save As dialog box opens.

**3**  Open the disk drive on which you want to create a new folder and click the Create New Folder ▣ button. The New Folder dialog box opens.

**4**  Type your name in the Name text box and choose OK. The new folder appears in the Save in text box at the top of the Save As dialog box.

**5**  Choose Save. The new file named *Copy of Selections.doc* appears in the new folder, and the file name also appears in the title bar of the document.

## Web Tip

You can save a Web page using the same basic save techniques used to save files in Office 2000 applications. Simply display the page or open the file you want to save and choose File, Save, select a folder to contain the file, type a file name for the file, and choose OK.

# Changing File Properties

***Properties***, information about files, are automatically stored with each Office 2000 file you save. Properties are grouped into different categories and provide information such as the date on which the file was created, the date on which it was last edited, the author's name, the author's company, file size, and other application-specific information (such as number of words in a Word document). In addition, the Office 2000 application used to create the file automatically assigns a title for the file based on the file name assigned to the file. You can edit or add additional bits of information about the file and check existing information.

**TASK 4:  Editing File Properties**

**1**  Click the File menu. The File menu appears. Pause until additional commands appear.

> **TIP** Only menu commands used most frequently appear when a menu is initially displayed. After the menu is displayed for a few seconds, additional commands appear on the menu.

**2**  Choose Properties.

> **TIP** In Access, the command on the File menu is Database Properties.

**FIGURE 1.9**

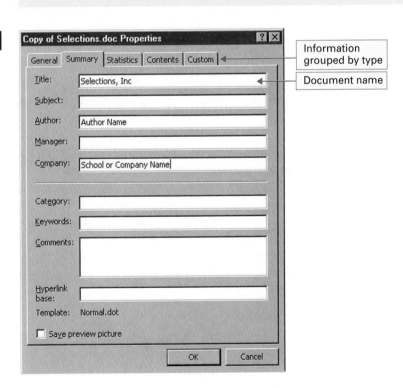

**3** Position the mouse pointer before the *S* in *Selections* in the Title: text box and click.

**4** Type (**Your Name**)**'s Edits to**. The title now appears as (Your Name)'s Edits to Selections, Inc.

**5** Choose OK.

 ## Check Point

Launch Microsoft Excel 2000 using the same launch procedures you used to launch Microsoft Word 2000.

 ## Break Point

If time is running short, save changes to the file. Then close Word. You can now power down your computer, if necessary, and continue this project later.

# Using Help

In the Windows section, you learned how to use Windows Help and how to locate information about specific topics. Each Office 2000 application comes equipped with quite a variety of help features that will have you getting help from all over the world—right on your computer as you work!

## Using the Office Assistant

The Office Assistant is a help feature that is growing in popularity. The Office Assistant is easy to use, is personably animated, and provides a focused list of help topics related to questions you "ask" the assistant. Depending on how the person using your computer left the Assistant, it may appear on-screen when you launch applications. When closed, the Assistant waits on the Standard toolbar and appears when you call it to look up information about topics for which you need help. After you start the Office Assistant in one application it remains on screen until you close it—even when you open another Office application. The information it provides when you ask it a question relates to the application that is active at the time you ask a question—regardless of what application was active when you started the Office Assistant.

## TASK 5:   To Use the Office Assistant

**1** Click the Microsoft Help [?] button on the Standard toolbar. Clippit, the default Office Assistant, appears; it appears the same in all Office Applications. You can type questions or words related to the application, and Clippit will fetch a list of related topics. Light bulbs indicate hints and ideas that Clippit has. Notice that Excel is the active application in Figure 1.10.

**FIGURE 1.10**

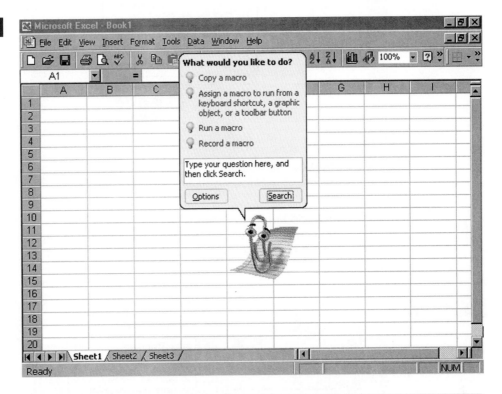

**TIP** The Office Assistant dialog box appears in different shapes and sizes, depending on how it was last used.

**2** Type **How do I print a worksheet?** The Office Assistant takes notes as you type.

**3** Click Search. Acting pleased with itself, Clippit displays topics related to printing worksheets.

**FIGURE 1.11**

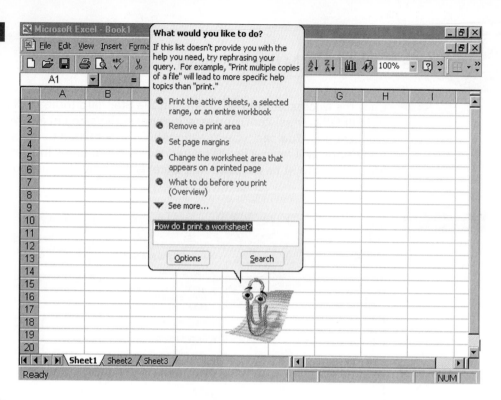

**4** Click What to do before you print (Overview). The Excel window resizes to accommodate the Help window. The Microsoft Excel Help window displays a graphic button to access additional help. Clippit is watching what you are doing.

**FIGURE 1.12**

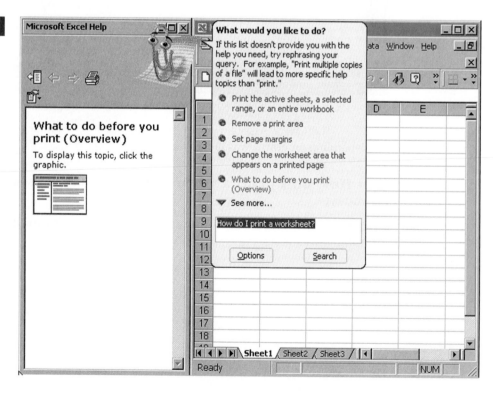

**5** Click the graphic. The Microsoft Excel Help window enlarges and provides additional information.

> **TIP** As you work with Help, you'll discover that the format of information displayed after you select a topic varies. In some cases a list of step-by-step instructions appears in the Help window, while at other times another list of topics related to the topic you select will appear.

**6** Close the Help window and then close the Help palette. The Excel window resizes to its original size.

**7** Right-click Clippit. A shortcut menu opens.

**FIGURE 1.13**

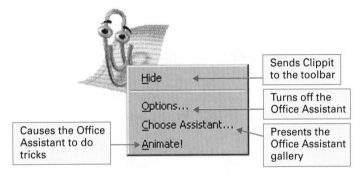

**8** Choose Choose Assistant.

**FIGURE 1.14**

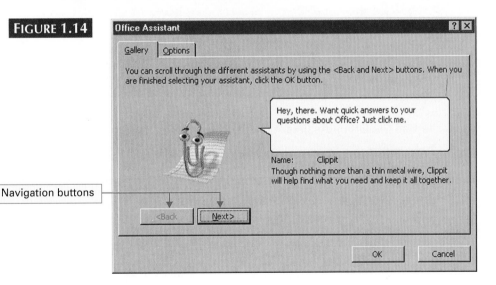

**9** Click the navigation buttons to review additional assistants until you find one you like.

**10** Choose OK.

## Turning Off and On the Office Assistant

When the Office Assistant feature is active, it often offers unsolicited help that can become quite annoying. You can disable the feature in Office 2000 applications. After you turn off the Office Assistant, a Help window automatically opens when you click the Microsoft Help button.

### TASK 6: To Turn the Office Assistant Off and On

**1** Display the Office Assistant and right-click to display the shortcut menu.

**2** Choose Options.

FIGURE 1.15

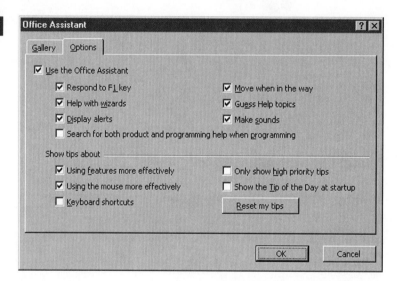

**3** Clear the Use the Office Assistant checkbox. All other options are dimmed.

**4** Choose OK. The Office Assistant closes.

**5** Choose Help, Microsoft Excel Help, and then click the Answer Wizard tab, if necessary.

**FIGURE 1.16**

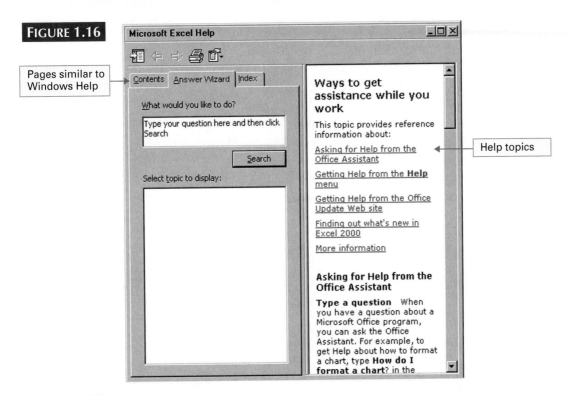

Pages similar to Windows Help

Help topics

6 Close the Help window.

7 Choose Help, Show the Office Assistant. The Office Assistant feature is reactivated so that clicking the Microsoft Help button will now call the Assistant.

8 Right-click the Office Assistant and choose Hide. The Office Assistant disappears and waits to be called again.

**TROUBLESHOOTING** After you choose Hide several times, a dialog box will appear asking if you want to deactivate the Office Assistant. Read the options carefully and choose the option that best represents how you want to use the Office Assistant.

## Web Tip

If you're connected to the Internet, you can access one of several Web sites maintained by Microsoft to provide up-to-the-minute help online. The Web provides information directly from Microsoft support team members as well as information and helpful hints from other Office users. To access the Microsoft Web site directly from an Office 2000 application, choose Help, Office on the Web. Your default Web browser launches and displays the Office 2000 Update page.

# Selecting Printers and Printing

While each Office 2000 application has printing features that are specific to the application, printing basics are the same for all applications. There are three basic methods for printing documents:

- Choose File, Print to display the Print dialog box and set print options.
- Click the Print 🖨 button on the Standard toolbar to print the active file using default settings.
- Press (CTRL) + P to display the Print dialog box and set print options.

Before printing files, you must first select a printer.

## Selecting Printers

By default, Office 2000 uses the default printer set up in Windows. You can change the printer selection to any printer that is installed on the computer. You can select the printer from the Print dialog box.

**TROUBLESHOOTING** If the printer you want to use is not installed on your computer, check with your instructor or the lab assistant to obtain the necessary installation disks and information for the printer.

**TASK 7:** **To Select a Printer**

**1** Switch to Word and choose File, Print.

**FIGURE 1.17**

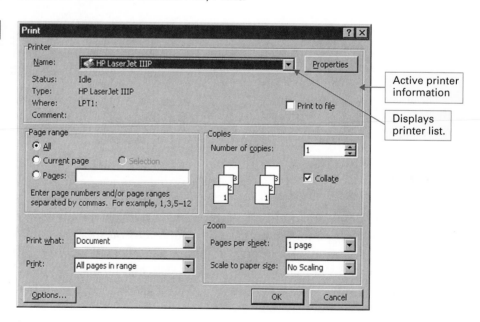

Active printer information

Displays printer list.

**2** Click the Name drop-down list arrow. Note that fax setups are listed as printers.

**FIGURE 1.18**

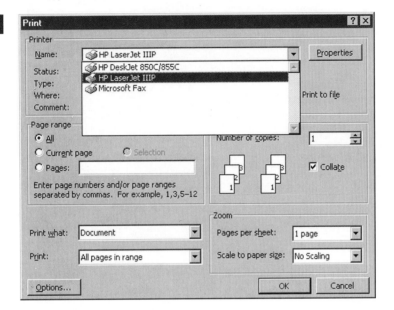

**3** Select the desired printer.

**4** Choose OK.

> **TIP** The selected printer appears in a Screen Tip when you point to the Print button on the Standard toolbar when the feature is activated.

## Setting Print Options

Options displayed in the Print dialog box vary among Office applications. There are a number of options, however, that are similar in the Print dialog box of all applications. These are identified in Figure 1.19.

FIGURE 1.19

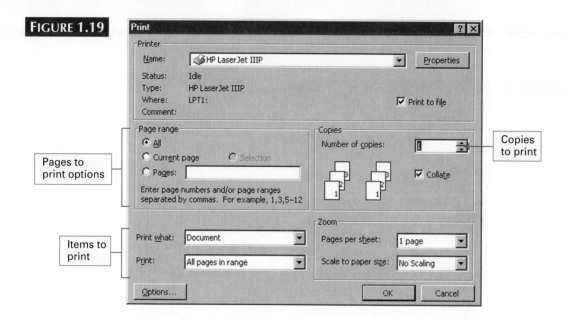

Figure 1.19

After you set the desired print options, all you have to do is choose OK to print the active file or other object you selected.

## Web Tip

You can print information from a Web site using the same basic procedures used to print an Office 2000 file. Display the page you want to print and choose File, Print from the Web browser menu.

## Previewing Pages

Even though most applications display files in **WYSIWYG** (what you see is what you get) format, sometimes what you see on paper is not what you expected. It is always a good idea to preview pages of the file before sending the page to the printer to help prevent some of these surprises. Each Office 2000 application has some type of Print Preview feature that enables you to see what the file will look like when it's printed.

- For Word, Excel, and Access, display the preview by choosing File, Print Preview, or click the Print Preview ⧉ button on the Standard toolbar.

- In PowerPoint, display each slide on-screen by choosing View, Slide Show, by pressing (F5), or by clicking the Slide Show 💻 button at the bottom of the presentation window.

## Check Point

Print Preview toolbar buttons vary by application. Display the *Copy of Selections.doc* in Print Preview and use the Context Sensitive Help ▶? button to find out what each tool does.

When you're finished, close Print Preview, save, and close the document.

# Exiting Applications

Before you exit Office 2000 applications, it's a good idea to save work that you want to keep and close files you have open. If you exit an application without saving changes to open files, the Office 2000 application prompts you to save changes to the file. Be sure to read these prompts carefully to ensure that you take the action you want to take and avoid unnecessary loss of data.

To exit Office 2000 applications, use one of the following procedures:

- Click the application Close ✖ button on the last open file in the application.
- Choose File, Exit. If multiple files are open in the application, all files close as you exit the application.
- Click the application control icon (for example 📝) at the left end of the title bar, and choose Close.
- Press (ALT) + (F4).
- Right-click the application button on the Windows taskbar and choose Close.

## Summary and Exercises

### Summary

- The many common elements of Office 2000 allow you to use techniques learned in one application to accomplish the same task in other applications.
- Applications can be launched in a variety of common ways, based on your preference and how Office 2000 is installed on your computer.
- File management tasks include opening files, creating new files, saving files, and editing file properties.
- Documents can be opened as a copy or as read-only to ensure that your original remains intact.
- New documents can be created as blank files or by using a pre-designed template.
- Word, Excel, and PowerPoint enable you to open or create multiple files without closing files that are already open.
- When you elect to close a file that has been edited, regardless of which procedure you use, the application will prompt you to save the file.
- File properties are automatically stored with each file you save.
- Help is available by using the Office Assistant.
- Printing basics such as selecting a printer and setting print options are basically the same for all Office 2000 applications.

### Key Terms

collate                                     save
Office Assistant                            templates
properties                                  WYSIWYG

### Study Questions

#### Multiple Choice

1. Which procedures for accomplishing tasks are basically same in all Office 2000 applications?
   a. presentation design
   b. file management
   c. data management
   d. toolbar options

2. Which of the following procedures is not an option to open an existing document, workbook, presentation, or database?
   a. choose Start, Open Office Document
   b. choose File, Open
   c. press (CTRL) + P
   d. click the Open button

3. To create a new file after an application is launched,
   a. press (CTRL) + N.
   b. click the New button on the Standard toolbar.
   c. choose File, New.
   d. all of the above.

4. Which are the three options for initiating commands in Office 2000?
   a. design buttons, keystrokes, and mouse options
   b. taskbar buttons, menu commands, and keystrokes
   c. menu commands, keystrokes, and design buttons
   d. both b and c

5. The programs that display new files automatically when you launch them are
   a. Access and Word.
   b. Excel and PowerPoint.
   c. Access and Excel.
   d. Word and Excel.

6. The Print Preview feature is the same in all Office 2000 applications except
   a. Word.
   b. Excel.
   c. Access.
   d. PowerPoint.

## Fill in the Blank

1. _____ enables you to see what your printout will look like before you print it.

2. Click the _____ button to switch to a different open file.

3. _____ in the default Office Assistant.

4. The _____ appears down the left side of the Open and Save As dialog boxes.

5. When you want to leave the original file intact but want to use the file as a basis for a new file, you can open a(n) _____ of the original file and save it as a new file.

## Short Answer

1. List three different ways you can launch an application.

2. Identify several different ways to exit an application.

3. The Word screen on one computer in the lab looks different from the Word screen on another computer in the lab. Explain the possible reasons why.

4. Regardless of the procedure you are using, what feature will help prevent unwanted loss of data, and when will this option be presented to you?

5. How can you turn off the Office Assistant?

## For Discussion

1. Discuss the different ways to save a document, and explain when and why you might choose each particular option.

2. Briefly discuss when, how, and why you would use the Office Assistant.

# Common Text and Art Elements

In the previous project, you learned some of the basic elements and features that all Office 2000 applications have in common. In this project, you learn some techniques for working with text in all applications, how to proof files, and how to insert pictures and change words into art work.

## Objectives

After completing this project, you will be able to:

➤ Work with text

➤ Use proofing tools

➤ Add graphics to Office 2000 files

➤ Edit and format graphic objects

## Setup

To ensure that your screen looks like those pictured in this project, you need to check some of the settings, as described in Table 2.1.

**Table 2.1**

| Item | Action |
|---|---|
| **Office Assistant** | Hide the Assistant. |
| **Toolbars** | Reset default toolbars by choosing Tools, Customize, and then display the Toolbars page of the dialog box. Check the Standard and Formatting toolbars and the menu bar. Select each of these items individually and choose Reset. Choose OK to confirm each change.<br><br>Click the Options tab and ensure that all Personalized Menus and Toolbars options are deselected. Then click the Reset my usage data button and choose Yes to restore menus.<br><br>When all toolbars and the menu bar have been reset, choose Close. |
| **View** | Click the Print Layout View button at the bottom of the Word window. |

# Working with Text

Whether you're typing a letter in Word, entering values in an Excel worksheet, adding data to an Access table, or creating slides in Power-Point, you'll type and edit text using Office applications. Learning how to navigate, edit, enhance, format, align, and move and copy text now will make working with text in each module easier.

 Check Point

Open the *Copy of Selections.doc* you saved in the Basic Common Elements project and use it to practice the following techniques.

## Navigating Text

Navigating text simply means moving from character to character, paragraph to paragraph, screen to screen, or page to page in text. You can use both the keyboard and the mouse to move the insertion point within a file. Mouse techniques common to all Office applications include using scroll bars to display different parts of a file or view and clicking to position the insertion point in the paragraph, cell, or field you want to edit.

Table 2.2 identifies keystrokes common to all Office 2000 applications for moving from place to place.

**Table 2.2**

| Key | Action |
| --- | --- |
| ← | Move left one character or column |
| → | Move right one character or column |
| ↓ | Move down one line or row |
| ↑ | Move up one line or row |
| PGUP | Move up one screen |
| PGDN | Move down one screen |
| HOME | Beginning of a line or row |
| END | End of a line or row |
| CTRL + END | End of a file |
| CTRL + HOME | Beginning of a file |

TIP These keystrokes apply only to datasheets in Access.

TIP As you work with each application you'll discover additional keystrokes specific to that application. For example, in Excel, you'll learn to move from worksheet to worksheet in a workbook, in PowerPoint you'll learn to display presentation slides, and in Access, you learn to move among records in forms using the navigation controls.

## Inserting, Deleting, and Typing Over Text

All Office 2000 applications are set with **Insert mode** active so that to insert text, you simply position the insertion point and start typing. Existing text moves over to make room for the new text. To replace existing text with new text, you can select text that you want to replace and type the new text.

TIP In Word, you can also switch to **Overtype mode** by pressing (INS) on the keyboard or by double-clicking the OVR area of the status bar to replace existing text as you type new text.

The position of the insertion point controls the technique to use to delete text:

- Position the insertion point immediately before the text you want to delete and press (DELETE) once for each character and space you want to delete.
- Position the insertion point immediately after the text you want to delete and press (BACKSPACE) once for each character and space you want to delete.

The easiest way to learn how to insert, type over, or delete text is by practicing navigation and selection techniques and seeing how they work.

## Enhancing and Formatting Text

Word, Excel, and PowerPoint share common methods for changing the appearance of text. Special features enable you to enhance and format text by changing the text **font**—the way text characters are shaped and the text size—as well as text **attributes**—how text characters appear. Changes you make to text that has already been typed affect selected text only. However, you can "turn on" an enhancement or change font characteristics before typing text and then turn the enhancement off or change the font again when you are finished.

TIP In Access, these formatting methods apply only to datasheets.

## TASK 1:   To Enhance and Format Text

**1** Open the *Copy of Selections.doc* file and select the title **Selections, Inc.** The text appears highlighted.

**2** Click the Bold **B** button on the Formatting toolbar. In Figure 2.1, the Bold button is lighter and depressed. The title appears darker and remains selected.

**FIGURE 2.1**

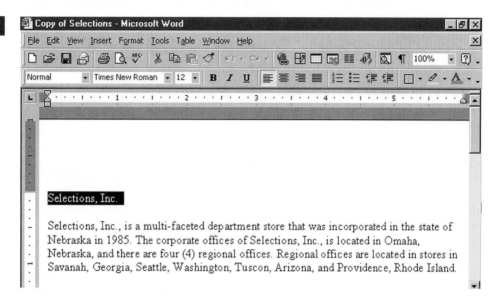

**3** Click the Font drop-down list arrow. Font formats appear on the drop-down palette in alphabetical order by font name.

**FIGURE 2.2**

**TIP** Fonts listed are controlled, to some extent, by the printer you are connected to and the fonts installed on your computer. The fonts you see may be different from those shown here.

**4** Choose Mead Bold. The selected text automatically reformats with the new font.

**TROUBLESHOOTING** If Mead Bold does not appear on your Font list, select a similar font or follow the direction of your instructor.

**5** Click the Font Size drop-down list arrow. A list of numbers appears on a palette, with the current font size highlighted.

**6** Select 24. The title appears much larger.

**7** Click the Italics *I* button on the Formatting toolbar. The title appears slanted and the Italics button is lighter in color and depressed.

**8** Choose Format, Font.

**FIGURE 2.3**

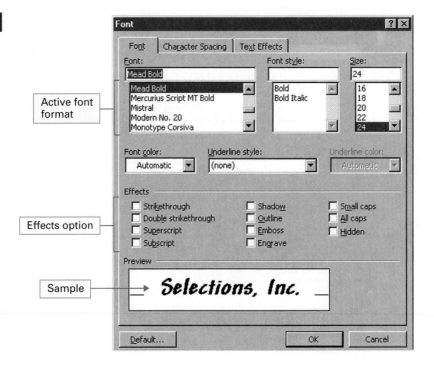

**9** Click the Font color drop-down list arrow. A palette of colors appears.

**10** Click Blue and choose OK. The title text is reformatted in blue print.

**TIP** You can also select a font color by clicking the Font Color drop-down list arrow on the Formatting toolbar.

**11** Click the white space to the right of the title to deselect the title text.

## Copying and Moving Text

Office 2000 offers three different techniques for moving and copying text:

- Click the Cut ✂, Copy 📋, or Paste 📋 button on the Standard toolbar.
- Choose Edit, Cut/Copy/Paste.
- Press (CTRL) + X for Cut, (CTRL) + C for Copy, or (CTRL) + V for Paste.

When you use the Cut command to move text or the Copy command to copy text, Office 2000 applications place the selected text or information on the Clipboard, where it stays until you paste it where you want it. While other Windows applications store only one snippet of information on the Clipboard, Office 2000 applications enable you to store multiple snippets of information on the Clipboard and then choose the snippet or snippets to place when you paste. The Office Clipboard is pictured in Figure 2.4.

**FIGURE 2.4**

The icons identify the application from which the snippet was copied. You can paste all snippets at the current cursor location by clicking the Paste All button. You can click the snippet you want to insert and it automatically appears at the insertion point. Notice that the Office Clipboard can hold up to 12 items.

## Check Point

Use the techniques described for moving and copying text to adjust text in the *Copy of Selections.doc* so that it appears as shown in Figure 2.5. Then save changes to the document.

**FIGURE 2.5**

## Copying Text Formats

Formatting text by applying enhancements, color, and font styles can be tedious—especially when you want to format text in several different locations and maintain consistency of format. You're in luck! Office 2000 applications are equipped with a Format Painter that's designed to help you copy text format and apply the format to additional text.

### TASK 2: To Copy Text Formats Using the Format Painter

**1** Select the formatted title text, *Selections, Inc.*

**2** Click the Format Painter button on the Standard toolbar.

> **TIP** Double-click the Format Painter to apply the format to text in multiple places in a file or to text in other files. Positioning the insertion point in a word is usually sufficient to copy the text format, but when multiple fonts and character settings are contained in a paragraph or in a word, select the character that contains the format you want to copy.

**FIGURE 2.6**

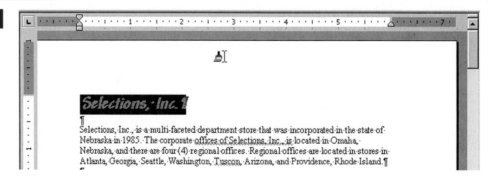

**3** Scroll to the bottom of the document page until the *Regional Offices* text appears on the screen.

**4** Click and drag the paintbrush across the text *Regional Offices*. The text is reformatted with the font and enhancements applied to the title, and the Format Painter is turned off.

> **TROUBLESHOOTING** If only a portion of the text is reformatted, select any formatted word, click the Format Painter again, and paint the additional characters.

## Using Undo and Redo

The Undo feature in all Office 2000 applications reverses actions; the Redo feature restores actions that were reversed. Using Undo and Redo is quite simple. Office 2000 applications offer keyboard, mouse, and menu procedures, as shown in Table 2.3.

**Table 2.3**

| Command | Procedures |
|---|---|
| Undo | Click the Undo button on the Standard toolbar. |
|  | Choose Edit, Undo. |
|  | Press (CTRL) + Z. |
| Redo | Click the Redo button on the Standard toolbar. |
|  | Choose Edit, pause to display all commands, select Redo. |
|  | Press (CTRL) + Y. |

Each of these actions reverses the last action, but Office 2000 applications enable you to reverse numerous actions in succession. In addition, you can click the drop-down list arrow beside the Undo or Redo button and select the action you want to reverse. All actions down to and including the action you select will be reversed.

## Aligning Text

Among the buttons you'll find on the Formatting toolbars in Word, Excel, and PowerPoint are buttons that control text alignment. You can use these alignment buttons on the Formatting toolbar to adjust the position of text in document paragraphs, table or worksheet cells, database forms, and presentation slides. You can also access alignment commands using the keyboard; menu commands for setting alignment vary among the applications. Table 2.4 identifies procedures for aligning text in Word, Excel, and PowerPoint.

**Table 2.4**

| Command | Procedures |
|---|---|
| **Align Left** | Click the Align Left ▤ button.<br>Press (CTRL) + L. |
| **Center** | Click the Center ▤ button.<br>Press (CTRL) + E. |
| **Align Right** | Click the Align Right ▤ button.<br>Press (CTRL) + R. |
| **Justify** | Click the Justify ▤ button.<br>Press (CTRL) + J. |

 **Check Point**

Use the procedures identified in Table 2.4 to align the document title on the right. Undo the action and center the title. Save changes to your work.

## Using Proofing Tools

Proofing tools built into Office 2000 applications make it easy to locate text, replace text, and spell-check your files. There is also a tool that enables you to enter frequently mistyped text and have the Office application automatically correct your error! The procedures for using these tools are consistent among all Office 2000 applications.

### Running the Spelling Checker

When you first opened the copy of *Selections.doc*, you saw red, wavy underlines below misspelled words in the document. Unless the spell-as-you-go feature is turned off, the Spell Check feature runs continuously as you work in Office 2000 applications. The Spell Check feature locates words that don't appear in the Office 2000 dictionary and highlights them for you so that you can determine whether they are correct or need to be changed.

> **TIP** Words that the Office application underlines as you work can be corrected quite easily. Simply point to the misspelled word and right-click. Office 2000 lists suggested spellings for the word not recognized. Choose the correct spelling of the word, choose Ignore All, or choose Add to add the word to the dictionary.

**TASK 3:** <u>To Spell Check a File</u>

**1** Press (CTRL) + (HOME) and then click the Spelling  button on the Standard toolbar.

> **TIP** The button is named Spelling and Grammar in Word 2000.

**FIGURE 2.7**

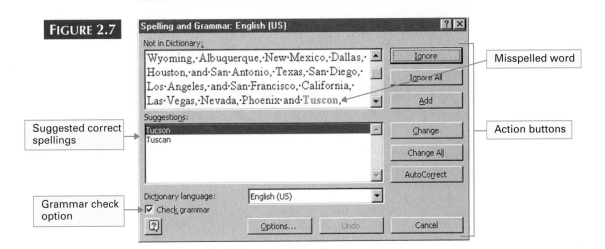

Suggested correct spellings

Grammar check option

Misspelled word

Action buttons

**2** Choose Tucson in the Suggestions list and click Change. The correct spelling of the city Tucson replaces the misspelled word and the next error is highlighted.

**3** Click Change to correct the grammar error.

**4** Continue checking the file, correcting errors that appear, until Word tells you the spelling and grammar check is complete.

**FIGURE 2.8**

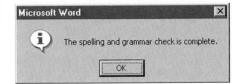

**5** Choose OK and save changes to the file.

## Finding and Replacing Text

The Find and Replace features enable you to locate text if it appears in a file and replace text with substitute text. These features are powerful tools for navigating and editing large files.

## TASK 4: To Find and Replace Text

**1** Choose Edit, Find.

> **TROUBLESHOOTING** In Access, the Find command is available only when an object is open. Find does not appear on the Edit menu when the database window is active.

**2** Type **thirty-four** in the Find what text box and choose Find Next. The Office 2000 application highlights the first occurrence of the phrase.

**FIGURE 2.9**

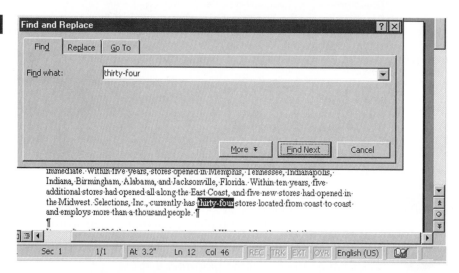

> **TROUBLESHOOTING** Word searches the document for the phrase beginning at the insertion point. As a result, you may find a different occurrence of the phrase.

**3** Click the Replace tab. *Thirty-four* appears in the Find what text box.

**4** Type **forty-four** in the Replace with text box and click Replace All. A message window tell you how many replacements were made.

**5** Click OK, close the dialog box, and save your changes to the document.

## Break Point

If necessary, you can save your file, exit the application, and continue this project later.

# Adding Art in Office 2000

Adding art to Office 2000 files dresses them up and makes them more inviting. Each Office 2000 application offers such a variety of methods for adding art to your files that it's sometimes difficult to decide which feature you want to use. You can add clip art images, scanned images or picture files from other sources, WordArt, and manual drawings to files in all Office 2000 applications. Each art type has a complete set of tools that enable you to edit and manipulate the art object. As a result, we'll just whet your appetite with a few little tips and tricks and then let you explore features that you need most on your own.

## Inserting Clip Art

All Office 2000 applications share a common Clip Gallery that contains a variety of different images you can add to your files. The first time you access the Clip Gallery, the Office 2000 application takes a few moments to build the gallery and then presents *thumbnails*—very small copies—of the images.

**TASK 5:   To Insert Clip Art**

**1** Create a new blank document in Word.

**2** Choose Insert, Picture, Clip Art.

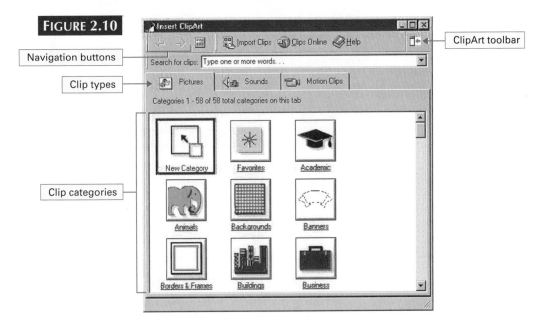

**FIGURE 2.10**

Navigation buttons

Clip types

Clip categories

ClipArt toolbar

**TROUBLESHOOTING** The clip categories may vary, depending on the categories that were installed during set up of PowerPoint 2000 and clips that have been downloaded from the Web.

 **Web Tip**

You can find additional clip art images on the Web by clicking the Clips On-line button or go directly to the Microsoft Web site at http://cgl.microsoft.com/clipgallerylive. You'll be reminded about copyright laws governing clips found in the gallery and also be asked to accept a licensing agreement before you'll see any clips.

**3** Scroll the list of categories and click Seasons. A list of season-related images displays.

**4** Click an image that represents the current season.

**FIGURE 2.11**

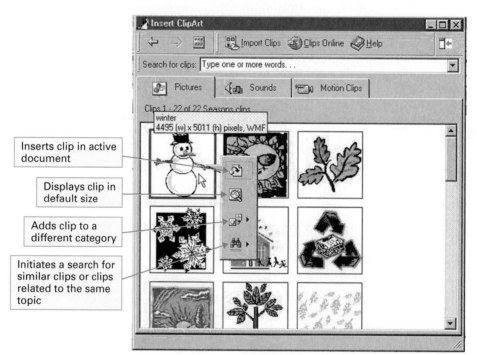

**5** Choose Insert Clip and then close the Insert ClipArt dialog box. The image appears at the top of the new document and the insertion point is blinking to the right of the clip.

## Moving and Sizing Clip Art Images

After you insert a Clip Art image into a file, you can size the image so that it fits the space you want it to occupy and move the image to position it more precisely. Before you can move most Clip Art images, you have to change the image layout settings.

## TASK 6:   To Move and Size Clip Art Images

**1** Click the image.

**FIGURE 2.12**

Handles for sizing

> **TIP**   The Picture toolbar often appears when a picture is selected. You can use tools on the toolbar to format your image.

**2** Point to a corner handle and drag the handle to size the image. The pointer appears as a two-headed diagonal arrow when it's positioned on a corner handle.

> **TIP**   To prevent the object size from becoming distorted, you can size an object's height and width together and maintain the object's proportion. Simply hold down the (SHIFT) key while you drag a corner handle.

**3** Point to the center of the selected image and right-click. The shortcut menu appears.

**4** Choose Format Picture. The Format Object dialog box opens.

**5** Click the Layout tab. The In line with text option is active and limits the movement of the graphic, as shown in Figure 2.13.

**FIGURE 2.13**

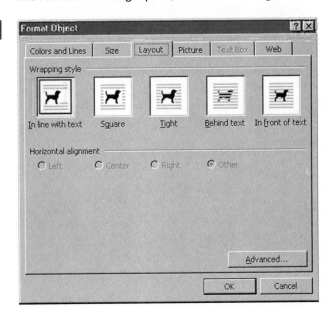

**6** Choose Square and then click Advanced.

**FIGURE 2.14**

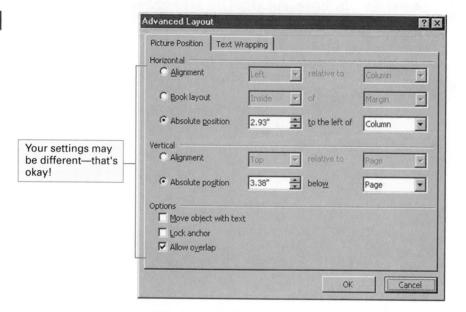

Your settings may be different—that's okay!

**7** Clear the Move object with text option and choose OK twice. The image appears with white handles on all corners and sides.

**8** Point to the center of the image, click, and drag it to a different location on the page. As you drag, the pointer appears as a four-headed arrow. You can drop the image anywhere on the document page and the text will flow to accommodate it.

**9** Close the document without saving it.

## Creating WordArt

***WordArt*** is a feature that enables you to dress up your files by creating graphic text, shaping it on curves and flows. WordArt is easy to create and can be positioned in a file to fit the size and shape you need. You can use WordArt to create a letterhead for your Selections, Inc., stationery.

**TASK 7: To Create WordArt**

**1** Click ☐ to create a new blank document.

**2** Choose Insert, Picture, WordArt. Each WordArt style is preformatted for shape, size, and color, as shown in Figure 2.15.

FIGURE 2.15

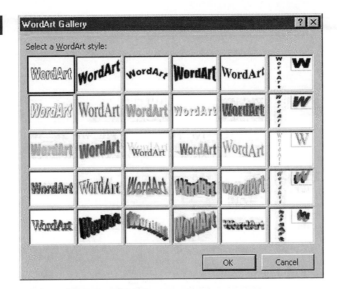

**3**  Double-click the shadowed vertical style in the lower right corner of the dialog box.

FIGURE 2.16

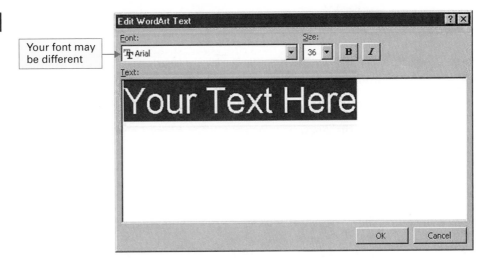

Your font may be different

**4**  Type **Selections, Inc.**

**5**  Select Mead Bold from the Font drop-down list and choose OK.

> **TROUBLESHOOTING** If Mead Bold is not available on your computer, use a similar font or the font identified by your instructor.

FIGURE 2.17

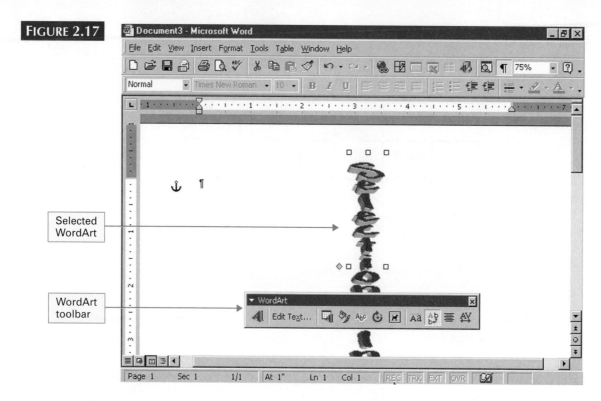

Selected WordArt

WordArt toolbar

**6** Click the WordArt Gallery button on the WordArt toolbar, select a horizontal format, and choose OK.

**7** Click a white area of the page to deselect the WordArt.

**8** Save the document using the file name *Letterhead.doc*.

## Creating and Manipulating Drawings

When you want to add shapes, lines, text boxes, and arrows to your Office 2000 files, you will find quite a sophisticated set of drawing tools that enable you to enhance your slides with original *freehand* creations. Even if you're no artist, you'll find the tools on the Drawing toolbar easy to use. Simply select the tool that represents the shape you want to draw, position the pointer where you want to start the drawing, and click and drag the pointer to the point where you want the shape to end. Then, while the shape is still selected, you can move, size, and edit the shape as needed.

> **TIP** The Drawing Toolbar is not available in Access.

**TASK 8:** To Create and Manipulate Drawings

**1** Click the Drawing button on the Standard toolbar. The Drawing toolbar appears as last positioned.

> **TROUBLESHOOTING** If the Drawing button is hidden, click the More Buttons drop-down arrow at the end of the Standard toolbar, select Add or Remove Buttons, and click Drawing on the button list.

**2** Dock the toolbar at the bottom of the window, if necessary.

**3** Click the Rectangle ▢ button. The pointer appears as a large plus sign ✛ called a ***crosshair***.

**4** Position the crosshair just above and to the left of the WordArt object, and then click and drag diagonally to a position just below and to the right of the WordArt. The selected rectangle conforms to the shape and 3-D effect of the WordArt but hides the text.

**5** Choose Draw, Order, Send to Back. The rectangle moves behind the WordArt and the text is visible.

**FIGURE 2.18**

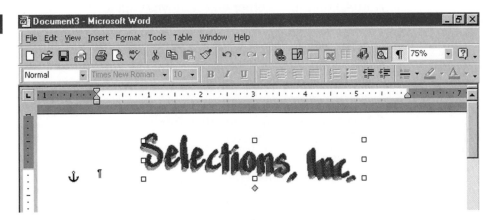

**6** Click the Fill 🖌▾ button drop-down list arrow and select the color Indigo.

**7** Click 🖌▾ again and select Fill Effects.

**FIGURE 2.19**

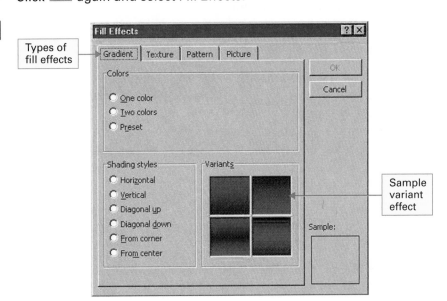

Types of fill effects

Sample variant effect

**8** Set color, gradient, and texture options to customize your drawing, then choose OK.

**9** Click the Select Objects ![pointer] button on the Drawing toolbar. Click and drag a dashed line around the WordArt object and rectangle. Both objects are selected.

FIGURE 2.20

**10** Choose Draw, Group. One set of selection handles appears; the two objects are now considered one object so that when you move the rectangle or WordArt object, the other object moves with it.

**11** Click the Text Box ![icon] button on the Drawing toolbar and drag the crosshair to create a narrow box at the bottom of the page. The style, color, and format of the previously set shape appears with the insertion point positioned at the left end of the textbox.

**12** Type **1500 Woodmen Tower, 30th Floor, Omaha, Nebraska 68102** in the text box, and then format the text box using tools on the Drawing toolbar as follows:

- Choose No 3-D from the 3-D palette.
- Choose No Line from the Line Style dialog box.
- Choose No Fill from the Fill Color palette.
- Italicize and right-align text in the text box.
- Select a color for the text from the Font Color palette.

**13** Click the Drawing ![icon] button to hide the Drawing toolbar and save your changes to the document.

## Inserting, Sizing, and Positioning Image Files

As you continue to work with Office 2000 applications, you will begin to acquire images from a variety of sources—from the Internet, scanned images from friends and relatives, and from graphics collections you purchase. When you want to use one of these saved images in an Office 2000 file, you can simply insert it using basically the same techniques you used to insert a clip art image.

**TASK 9:** To Insert, Size, and Position File Images

**1** Press (CTRL) + (HOME) to position the insertion point at the top of the document.

**2** Choose Insert, Picture, From File. The Insert Picture dialog box opens.

**3** Open the disk drive and folder containing the Selections, Inc., logo file you downloaded from the SELECT Web site.

 **Web Tip**

If you have not yet downloaded the file from the Web site, ask your instructor where to find the file.

**4** Double-click *Selections Logo*. The logo appears on screen in a default format.

**5** Size and position the logo so that it appears to the left of the Selections WordArt object.

> **TROUBLESHOOTING** You may need to adjust the logo settings to be able to position the graphic freely. Refer to the instructions found in "Moving and Sizing Clip Art Images" earlier in this project.

**6** Save changes to the file and print a copy of your letterhead.

**7** Close the document and exit Word.

 **Web Tip**

Interested in stories about famous people, places, and things? Explore the Entertainment area of http://www.geocities.com.

# Summary and Exercises

## Summary

- Navigating text allows you to move from character to character, paragraph to paragraph, screen to screen, or page to page.
- By selecting text, you can apply enhancements to text, change fonts, or move or copy text.
- Inserting and deleting text is the same in all Office 2000 applications, and Word allows you to switch to Overtype mode to replace text as you type.
- Enhancing and formatting text is made easy using the buttons on the Formatting toolbar.
- Text can be cut, copied, and moved within or among all Office 2000 applications.
- Office 2000 makes it easy to maintain text format consistency by using Format Painter.
- Using the Undo or Redo features enables you to reverse the last action, and you can reverse numerous and selected actions in Office 2000.
- Text can be aligned left or right, centered, or justified on the left and right.
- Proofing tools are used to locate text, replace text, and spell-check files.
- The AutoCorrect feature corrects commonly misspelled words and allows you to enter your own words to be automatically corrected.
- Clip art images, scanned images, WordArt, and manual drawings allow you to dress up files in all Office 2000 applications.
- The ClipArt Gallery contains graphics on a number of topics and allows you to search by topic for related images.
- A sophisticated set of drawing tools enable you to create original freehand art.
- When a shape or object is inserted, you can move, size, and edit the selected item as needed.

## Key Terms

| | | |
|---|---|---|
| align | Insert mode | proofing |
| attributes | justify | Redo |
| crosshair | keyboard | Replace |
| Delete | mouse | Spelling Checker |
| Enhance | navigating | thumbnail |
| font | Overtype mode | Tools |
| Format | Page Down | Undo |
| freehand | Page Up | WordArt |
| Home | Paste | |

# Study Questions

## Multiple Choice

1. Moving from character to character, paragraph to paragraph, screen to screen or page to page is called
   a. scrolling.
   b. skipping.
   c. navigating.
   d. keystroking.

2. You can change the appearance of text by changing the font, size, and
   a. art.
   b. attributes.
   c. paragraph.
   d. selection.

3. To move up one screen, the key that is used in all applications is
   a. (PRT SC).
   b. (↑).
   c. (CTRL) + (HOME).
   d. (PGUP).

4. Before you can move most ClipArt images, you must change which settings?
   a. Image Layout
   b. Graphic Format
   c. Image Size
   d. Format Object

5. To create a letterhead that arches over the top of a page, you would choose which feature?
   a. Headers
   b. ClipArt
   c. TextFont
   d. WordArt

6. Clearing which option restores free placement of a graphic?
   a. allow overlap
   b. lock anchor
   c. move object with text
   d. none of the above

7. To change the pattern of the inside of a rectangle in freehand drawing, select
   a. Line Color.
   b. Format Object.
   c. Fill Effects.
   d. Insert Text.

## Short Answer

1. What must you do before you can apply, enhance, or change the text font or move or copy text?

2. List the three ways to delete text.

3. Which buttons can you use to reverse the last action or selected actions?

4. What are the first three steps of adding a ClipArt picture to a file?

5. If you would like the text to type over the graphic, which layout should you select?

6. Which feature would you use to draw a map with lines, arrows, and boxes?

7. What steps would you follow to insert a graphic from the Internet?

8. What are the three options you can choose from ClipArt?

9. What are the very small copies of images in the Clip Gallery called?

## Fill in the Blank

1. You can use the keyboard or the _____ to move within a file.

2. _____ mode allows you to replace existing text as you type new text in Word.

3. Double-click the _____ button to copy a text format to multiple places.

4. Misspelled words are located and corrected using _____.

5. _____ is a feature that enables you to dress up files by creating graphic text.

6. Office 2000 applications share a common _____ that contains a variety of different images you can add to your files.

7. _____ appear on selected images, which allow you to resize or drag the object.

8. _____ buttons control the categories displayed and enable you to move back and forward among clips in the ClipArt Gallery.

## For Discussion

1. Discuss several different ways of enhancing and formatting text.

2. Describe the steps you would follow to move and resize a ClipArt image.

# Projects for Microsoft Excel 2000

# Introducing Excel 2000

While a graduate student in a finance class at Harvard in 1978, Dan Bricklin watched his professor "run the numbers." As the class explored different corporate investment scenarios, the professor would continually erase and replace columns of numbers on the chalkboard at the front of the room. Dan envisioned a computer program that would recalculate numbers automatically, greatly decreasing the time required to explore financial models. With the help of MIT student Bob Frankston, Dan developed VisiCalc, the first electronic spreadsheet.

Today's electronic spreadsheets have revolutionized the use of personal computers for performing calculations. Electronic spreadsheet applications such as Microsoft Excel have many powerful features, but all spreadsheets are based upon the relatively simple concept of storing text and numbers in a two-dimensional grid.

Excel is especially useful for answering *"what if?"* questions by changing numbers to examine alternative scenarios. You may want to know, for example, how the monthly payment on a loan will differ if the term is 5 years and the interest rate is 7 percent, versus a loan with a term of 4 years at 7 percent. By constructing a simple worksheet in Excel, you can quickly answer this question.

## Objectives

After completing this project, you will be able to:

➤ Describe electronic spreadsheets and explain what they are used for

➤ Define common spreadsheet concepts

➤ Explain what steps are required to build an electronic workbook

➤ Launch Microsoft Excel

➤ Identify the Excel user interface

➤ Close a workbook and exit Excel

# Worksheets and Workbooks

The first electronic spreadsheet applications worked with only one two-dimensional worksheet grid at a time. Think of an accountant who keeps financial ledgers on separate ledger sheets. If this accountant were to develop an electronic version of each ledger sheet, a separate electronic file would be required to store each ledger. As electronic spreadsheet software has evolved to incorporate new features, working with multiple worksheets is now commonplace.

In Excel, each ledger sheet can be represented electronically in a separate **worksheet**. An Excel file, called a **workbook**, contains one or more worksheets, and you can link data from one worksheet in a workbook to other worksheets in the same workbook. Thus, Excel allows you to create three-dimensional solutions.

As with the other Office 2000 applications, you can create a worksheet by entering data into a blank workbook, or by using one of Excel's many templates. A **template** is a special workbook file containing specific data—such as headings, initial values, and other supporting information—that you can use to create workbooks.

## Where Data Resides and What Kind of Data Worksheets Contain

When you use Excel it is important that you identify where data resides in an Excel workbook, and what kind of data Excel contains. For simplicity, let us refer to these concepts as the where and the what. When you first launch Excel, you may notice that the screen looks different than the other Office applications such as Word. In Word, you create documents. In Excel, you create workbooks, which are composed of one or more worksheets.

## Where Data Resides in a Worksheet

You create an Excel worksheet by entering data into the worksheet's two-dimensional grid. The horizontal and vertical dimensions of each worksheet each have a name. **Columns** are the vertical worksheet dimension, and are designated by a letter, which appears at the top of the column. **Rows** represent the horizontal dimension. Each row is designated by a number, which appears to the left of the row.

The intersection of a column and a row is a **cell**, which is identified by an **address**. For example, the cell at the intersection of column C and row 20 has the address C20. The data you enter into a worksheet is al-

ways entered into a specific cell. Each Excel worksheet contains 256 columns and 65,536 rows, for a total of over 16 million cells (16,777,216)! As you can see, each worksheet is a very large two-dimensional grid.

## What Kind of Data Excel Worksheets Contain

You create an Excel worksheet by entering data into specific cells. The kind of data you enter into a cell depends upon whether the entry will act as a label, as a number used in a calculation, or as an expression that will perform a calculation. **Text** is any combination of numbers, spaces, and nonnumeric characters. You normally enter text as a **label** that describes the data within the worksheet. Regardless of what you enter, text will be stored as data in a cell.

**Numbers** in Excel are the values you will use to perform calculations. A number can contain only the following characters:

$$0\ 1\ 2\ 3\ 4\ 5\ 6\ 7\ 8\ 9\ +\ -\ (\ )\ ,\ /\ \$\ \%\ .\ E\ e$$

Excel ignores leading plus signs (+) and treats a single period as a decimal. All other combinations of numbers and nonnumeric characters are treated as text. You can also enter dates and times in Excel by typing a number, a character such as /, -, or :. Excel treats all date and time entries as numbers, which can be used in calculations.

A **formula** is a sequence of values, cell references, names, functions, or operators in a cell that produces a new value from existing values. A formula always begins with an equal sign (=). Formulas often contain **functions**, which are predefined formulas that perform calculations by using specific values, called arguments, in a particular order, or structure. Where you enter data in Excel and the kind of data workbooks contain are listed in Figure O.1. Your screen may not appear as shown, depending on your settings.

# Planning Excel Workbooks for Timely, Useful, and Accurate Information

Planning and designing electronic workbooks is deceptively simple: The data displayed in a workbook is only as good as the structure of the worksheet, which will usually contain formulas that calculate results and link information. To maintain **data integrity**, or consistently accurate results, consider following a simple seven-step design process to minimize the risk of introducing errors into your workbooks, thereby insuring timely, relevant, and useful information. This process is shown in Figure O.2.

## Determine the Workbook's Purpose

Since electronic worksheets consist of a matrix (a matrix is a two-dimensional representation of data) of cells that can contain text, numbers, formulas, and functions, you should carefully determine the workbook's scope and purpose. In addition to performing simple and complex calculations, electronic worksheets can be used as databases to sort and filter data. Before de-

**FIGURE O.1**

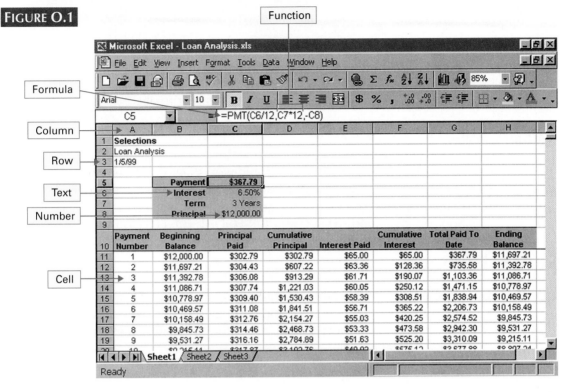

**FIGURE O.2**

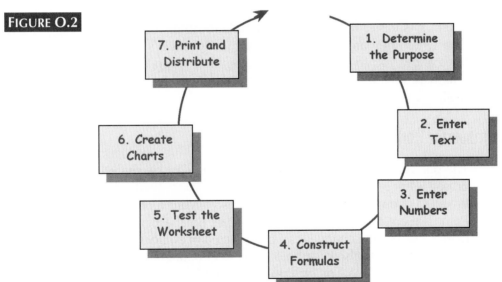

**Seven steps for producing timely, relevant, and useful information in electronic workbooks**

signing a worksheet, the user should have a clear idea of what task the work-sheet is to accomplish.

## Enter Text

Text entries provide the basic structure of an electronic worksheet. The labels give meaning to the numbers residing in the worksheet's cells. Text can be formatted to provide the worksheet with a particular look.

## Enter Numbers

Numbers are the data upon which calculations are performed. Numbers are entered according to the text labels that define the overall worksheet structure. Numbers can be formatted with leading characters, as currency, dates, percentages, or in a number of other standard formats.

## Construct Formulas

Formulas are what give an electronic worksheet its power. Formulas, which always begin with an equal sign (=), can include one or more of Excel's functions. Formulas can also include conditional statements (IF-THEN) and Boolean logic (GREATER THAN OR EQUAL TO, LESS THAN, and so on).

## Test the Worksheet

Since any of three data types can be entered into an electronic worksheet, and a formula can contain complex functions and expressions, it is important to test a worksheet thoroughly before using it. Excel includes auditing tools for isolating potential problems in a worksheet.

## Create Charts

Often, it is easier to understand the relationships that exist among numeric data when they are represented graphically. Excel's powerful charting features allow you to create the most common graph types, and dynamically link them to your data. If the underlying data changes, the charts will automatically reflect the changes.

## Print and Distribute the Workbook

The data represented in an Excel workbook can be shared with other Microsoft Office applications. For instance, sales results by region can be linked to or embedded in either a Microsoft Word report, a Microsoft PowerPoint presentation, or a Microsoft Access database. By using the tools together, last-minute changes can be reflected in all documents where the data appears. You can also distribute your Excel data electronically by sending a workbook via e-mail or by publishing workbook data to the World Wide Web. By saving Excel 2000 data in HTML format, your worksheet formats are retained when the data is viewed in Microsoft Internet Explorer or a similar Web browser.

# Launching Excel 2000

You can launch Excel the same way you launch other Office applications. You can use the Start menu, Documents list or the Office Shortcut bar.

**TASK 1:**    <u>To Launch Microsoft Excel</u>

**1**  Click the Start **Start** button.

**2**  Choose Programs from the Start menu and select Microsoft Excel, as shown in Figure O.3.

**FIGURE O.3**

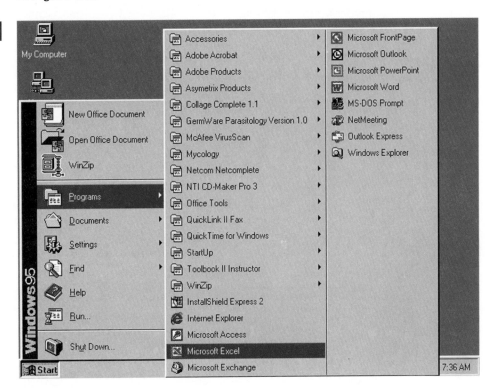

**3**  Choose Customize from the Tools menu.

**4**  Click the Options tab.

**5**  Select the options shown in Figure O.4. This will turn off Excel's customization features and display the Standard and Formatting toolbars in their entirety.

**FIGURE O.4**

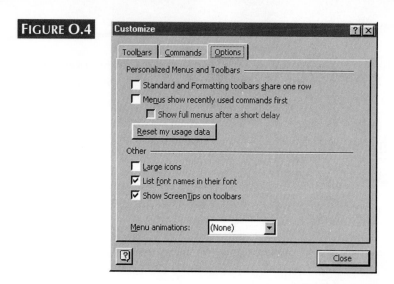

**6** Click the Close button. Excel will display the default workbook Book1.

## The Excel 2000 User Interface

After you launch Excel as described in the previous task, your screen should look similar to Figure O.5. You will recognize some elements if you have used other Office applications. Some of the items on the interface are unique to Excel. Table O.1 describes each of these elements.

**FIGURE O.5**

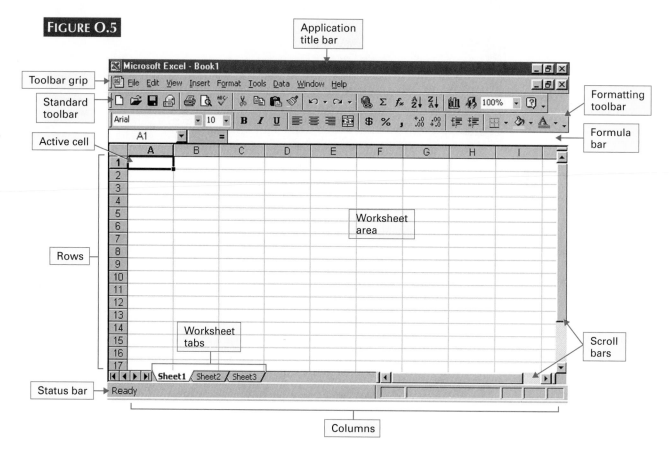

**Table O.1**

| Element | Description |
| --- | --- |
| **Application title bar** | Displays the name of the Office application, name of the active workbook, and the Minimize, Maximize, Restore, and Close buttons. |
| **Worksheet area** | The entire worksheet and all its elements, including cells, gridlines, row and column headings, scroll bars, and sheet tabs. |
| **Standard Toolbar** | Toolbar containing shortcuts to common commands and tasks. |
| **Formatting Toolbar** | Toolbar containing shortcuts to the most common formatting commands. |
| **Formula bar** | Displays the constant value or formula used in the active cell. Also used to enter or edit values or formulas. |
| **Sheet tabs** | Displays the name of a sheet. Click the sheet tab to make a sheet active. |
| **Rows** | Horizontal dimension of Excel's two-dimensional grid. |
| **Columns** | Vertical dimension of Excel's two-dimensional grid. |
| **Active cell** | The cell currently in use. The active cell can receive data. |
| **Status bar** | Displays information about a selected command or an operation in progress. The right side of the status bar shows whether keys such as (CAPS LOCK), (SCROLL LOCK), or (NUM LOCK) are turned on. |
| **Scroll bars** | Horizontal and vertical bars for moving within a worksheet. |

**TASK 2:** <u>To Close Your Workbook and Exit Microsoft Excel</u>

**1** Click the Close button ✕ for the Worksheet area.

**2** Choose Exit from the File menu or click the Close button ✕ in the application window to exit Microsoft Excel.

# Summary and Exercises

## Summary

- Microsoft Excel is an electronic spreadsheet application that allows you to develop powerful tools for performing calculations.
- Spreadsheets are often used to conduct a "what if?" analysis.
- An Excel workbook is composed of one or more worksheets, which provides three-dimensional capabilities.
- Data in an Excel worksheet is located in rows, columns, and cells.
- Excel workbooks contain text, numbers, dates, times, formulas, and functions.
- By following seven steps for designing workbooks, you minimize the potential for error.
- You can launch Excel the same way you launch other Office applications.

## Key Terms

| | |
|---|---|
| active cell | row |
| address | scroll bars |
| application title bar | sheet tabs |
| cell | Standard toolbar |
| column | status bar |
| data integrity | template |
| Formatting toolbar | text |
| formula | "what if?" |
| formula bar | workbook |
| function | worksheet |
| label | worksheet area |
| number | |

## Study Questions

### Multiple Choice

1. The intersection of a row and a column is a
   a. function.
   b. address.
   c. cell.
   d. row.

2. Which Excel interface object is used to modify the contents of a cell?
   a. status bar
   b. Standard toolbar
   c. Formatting toolbar
   d. formula bar

3. The vertical dimension of an Excel worksheet is called a
   a. cell.
   b. column.
   c. address.
   d. row.

4. An Excel worksheet contains approximately how many cells?
   a. 256
   b. 16,000
   c. one hundred thousand
   d. 16 million

5. Which kind of Excel data actually performs calculations?
   a. labels
   b. numbers
   c. dates/times
   d. formulas

## Short Answer

1. What is the cell currently in use called?

2. How do you identify a particular cell?

3. Rows are arranged along which dimension?

4. What kind of data defines the structure of a worksheet?

5. What symbol always precedes a formula?

## Fill in the Blank

1. An Excel formula will often contain a _____ to perform a calculation.

2. All data is entered into worksheet _____.

3. An Excel workbook will always contain at least one _____.

4. Excel is often used to conduct a _____ analysis.

5. The five kinds of data contained in Excel worksheets are _____, _____, _____, _____, and _____.

## For Discussion

1. How do worksheets differ from a workbook?

2. What is a function and how does it differ from a formula?

# Designing Worksheets and Workbooks

To use Excel effectively you must know how to plan, create, save, and print worksheets. In this project you will enter text and numbers into cells, and then create formulas with functions to perform calculations.

## Objectives

After completing this project, you will be able to:

➤ Design a workbook

➤ Navigate within worksheets and workbooks

➤ Enter text as labels

➤ Use the fill handle to complete a data series

➤ Adjust column width

➤ Create a folder and save a workbook

➤ Enter numbers into cells

➤ Enter formulas and functions into cells

➤ Preview and print worksheets

➤ Close a workbook and exit Excel

## Running Case

Travis Traylor of the Selections, Inc. knows that Microsoft Excel is made to perform calculations and conduct "what-if" analyses, and therefore is often used to list financial or numeric data in order to make business decisions. He wants you to help him analyze sales data using Excel.

# The Challenge

Selections, Inc., is a multifaceted department store with four regional offices. Travis Traylor, manager of accounting and finance, has asked you to create a workbook listing the sales figures for four fiscal quarters for each region. He further specified that the workbook should be flexible enough so that he can "drill down" to specific department totals in each region, yet also see the annual sales by department for all sales regions. He wants to meet with you after you design the workbook so that he can review your progress and approve your design.

# The Strategy

Since an Excel workbook can contain multiple worksheets, you will want to design this workbook so that it provides both summary and detail information. You will develop a prototype workbook listing the departmental sales for the north region, and then meet with Mr. Traylor before adding additional worksheets to the workbook. Since you are merely seeking his approval for the workbook's design, you will not need to be concerned with formatting this workbook. The worksheet you will create in this project is shown in Figure 1.1.

**FIGURE 1.1**

Microsoft Excel - Selections.xls

| | A | B | C | D | E | F |
|---|---|---|---|---|---|---|
| 1 | Selections Inc. | | | | | |
| 2 | Quarterly Sales | | | | | |
| 3 | | | | | | |
| 4 | Department | 1st Qtr. | 2nd Qtr. | 3rd Qtr. | 4th Qtr. | Total |
| 5 | Clothing | 405112 | 321670 | 401934 | 393714 | 1522430 |
| 6 | Cosmetics | 373211 | 34812 | 29718 | 38248 | 475989 |
| 7 | Watches & Jewelry | 45213 | 21397 | 18923 | 44971 | 130504 |
| 8 | Electronics and Computers | 211396 | 189201 | 174916 | 193712 | 769225 |
| 9 | Appliances | 48761 | 39675 | 36582 | 38619 | 163637 |
| 10 | Furniture | 23819 | 18912 | 21975 | 24187 | 88893 |
| 11 | Housewares | 34907 | 26585 | 39638 | 33935 | 135065 |
| 12 | China and Crystal | 33185 | 32081 | 41972 | 18381 | 125619 |
| 13 | Knives and Cutlery | 12954 | 9273 | 10593 | 11976 | 44796 |
| 14 | Books & Magazines | 36719 | 37383 | 38121 | 29753 | 141976 |
| 15 | Bed and Bath | 21082 | 18910 | 19718 | 17544 | 77254 |
| 16 | Total | 1246359 | 749899 | 834090 | 845040 | 3675388 |
| 17 | | | | | | |
| 18 | | | | | | |
| 19 | | | | | | |

**Regional sales worksheet**

# The Setup

Launch Microsoft Excel, and make sure that you select the Excel settings listed in Table 1.1. This will ensure that your screen matches the illustrations and that the tasks in this project function as described.

**Table 1.1**

| Location | Make these settings: |
|---|---|
| **Office Shortcut Bar** | Right-click the Office icon on the shortcut bar and click Exit. |
| **Office Assistant** | Hide the Assistant. |
| **Tools, Customize** | Click the Options tab and deselect the option to show recently used menu commands first. Deselect the option to display the Standard and Formatting toolbars on one row. |
| **Tools, Options** | Click the Edit tab and select Move selection after Enter. |
| **View, Formula Bar** | Display the formula bar. |
| **View, Status Bar** | Display the status bar. |
| **View, Normal** | View the workbook in Normal view. |
| **Maximize** | Maximize the application and workbook windows. |

# Designing a Workbook

You will recall from "Introducing Excel 2000" that before you enter data into worksheet cells, you need an overall plan for the workbook. To design a workbook you will want to think about how the data will be used for reporting and how often it may need to be updated. For example, Mr. Traylor indicated that he wants to be able to see departmental sales for each sales region, summarized by fiscal quarter. In addition, he wants to see a summary for each department across all sales regions.

Your best strategy will be to use five worksheets—four for each sales region and one for the summary of sales across regions. Some data will remain constant across sales regions, such as the names of the departments. Other data, namely the sales figures, will vary by region. The overall structure of the four regional worksheets will be similar, in that the departments will most likely appear in the same order.

After you design each regional worksheet you can determine how best to list the total sales by department in a fifth worksheet. You will want your workbook to be flexible enough to accept changes and revision without jeopardizing the accuracy of the sales totals. In Project 2 you will learn how to link data between worksheets. For now, think in terms of how best to organize the regional worksheets.

You may want to initially plan the structure using a legal pad. Your proposed worksheet might resemble the one shown in Figure 1.2, which lists total sales by department for four fiscal quarters.

**FIGURE 1.2**

Selections Inc.
Quarterly Sales

| Department | 1st Qtr. | 2nd Qtr. | 3rd Qtr. | 4th Qtr. | Total |
|---|---|---|---|---|---|
| Clothing | 405112 | 321670 | 401934 | 393714 | ? |
| Cosmetics | 373211 | 34812 | 29718 | 38248 | ? |
| Watches & Jewelry | 45213 | 21397 | 18923 | 44971 | ? |
| Electronics and Computers | 211396 | 189201 | 174916 | 193712 | ? |
| Appliances | 48761 | 39675 | 36582 | 38619 | ? |
| Furniture | 23819 | 18912 | 21975 | 24187 | ? |
| Housewares | 34907 | 26585 | 39638 | 33935 | ? |
| China and Crystal | 33185 | 32081 | 41972 | 18381 | ? |
| Knives and Cutlery | 12954 | 9273 | 10593 | 11976 | ? |
| Books & Magazines | 36719 | 37383 | 38121 | 29753 | ? |
| Bed and Bath | 21082 | 18910 | 19718 | 17544 | ? |
| Total | ? | ? | ? | ? | ? |

To design an electronic worksheet using this structure, begin by entering the text data to define the overall structure. Then enter the sales data as numbers. Finally, construct formulas every place you see a question mark symbol (?) to calculate the sales totals.

## Web Tip

You will recall that Dan Bricklin came up with the idea of the electronic spreadsheet, making what you will do in this project possible. Did you know that Dan received an award for his work? Visit the site http://www.acm.org/awards/fellows_citations/bricklin.html for more information.

## Navigating in a Workbook

As you work in Excel you will need to move within a worksheet and among worksheets in the workbook. As you add text, numbers, dates, times, and formulas into cells, you will need to first select a specific cell to make it the *active cell*. The active cell has the focus, as indicated by its thick border. In Figure 1.3, cell A1 is the active cell. Cell A1 is also called the *home cell*, since it is the uppermost left cell in the worksheet. The workbook shown in Figure 1.3 contains three worksheets by default. You will use Sheet1 in this project.

FIGURE 1.3

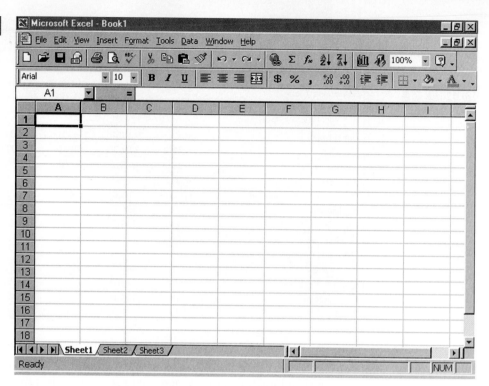

**An Excel workbook with the home cell active in Sheet 1**

To move between cells on a worksheet, click any cell or use the arrow keys. When you move to a cell, it becomes the active cell. To see a different area of the sheet, use the scroll bars.

> **TIP** You can also use the Go To dialog box to move to a specific cell. Press the (F5) key and enter the cell reference in the Reference: text box, and click OK.

## Navigating in a Worksheet Using Keystrokes

Using the scroll bars or clicking the left mouse button are effective methods for navigating in a relatively small worksheet, but at times you will want to move large distances. Excel supports a number of keystrokes you can use to quickly change the active cell. Table 1.2 lists keystrokes you can use to navigate within a worksheet.

**Table 1.2**

| To move: | Use these keystrokes: |
| --- | --- |
| One cell to the right | → or TAB |
| One cell to the left | ← or SHIFT + TAB |
| One cell down | ↓ or ENTER |
| One cell up | ↑ or SHIFT + ENTER |
| To the home cell | CTRL + HOME |
| Down one screen | PGDN |
| Up one screen | PGUP |
| Right one screen | ALT + PGDN |
| Left one screen | ALT + PGUP |
| Last column of the worksheet | CTRL + → |
| Last row of the worksheet | CTRL + ↓ |
| First column of the worksheet | CTRL + ← |
| First row of the worksheet | CTRL + ↑ |

**TIP** You can move around and zoom on your worksheet or chart sheet by using the Microsoft IntelliMouse pointing device. For more information, open the Help system, search for Intellimouse, and choose the first topic in the list.

## Navigating Among Worksheets in a Workbook

To navigate among the sheets in a workbook, simply click the appropriate worksheet tab. Depending upon how Excel is configured on your computer, you may see more than three worksheet tabs. You can use the controls shown in Figure 1.4 to display the tabs for the worksheets in a workbook. As you navigate through the sheets in a workbook, keep in mind that only one sheet is the *active sheet*, or the worksheet with the focus. Once a sheet is active, you can enter text, numbers, dates, and formulas into any of its cells.

**TIP** You can also right-click the tab scrolling buttons to select a specific sheet.

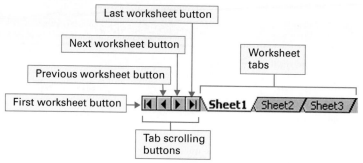

**FIGURE 1.4**

Last worksheet button

Next worksheet button

Previous worksheet button

First worksheet button

Worksheet tabs

Sheet1 / Sheet2 / Sheet3 /

Tab scrolling buttons

**Worksheet navigation buttons and sheet tabs**

## Web Tip

Worksheet tabs are an effective tool for workbook navigation. For more information, visit the site http://support.microsoft.com/support/Office/ InProdHlp/contents/Excel/tocxlmain9hhc8.asp

## Entering Text in a Worksheet

When you are creating a workbook, the text you enter into specific cells defines the overall structure. In Microsoft Excel, text is any combination of numbers, spaces, and nonnumeric characters, and text entries often serve as labels that define a worksheet's structure. You will now enter text as labels to create the worksheet prototype shown in Figure 1.2.

**TASK 1:** To Enter Text as Labels

**1** Select cell A1 of Sheet1 and type **Selections, Inc.** Notice that the mode in the status bar changes to Enter since you are in the process of entering data. Press (ENTER) to complete your entry.

> **TIP** As you enter text in a cell, it will spill over to the next cell if the column is not wide enough to display the entire entry, if the adjacent cell is empty.

**2** Type **Quarterly Sales** in cell A2 and press (ENTER).

**3** Enter the following text as labels into rows 4 through 16 of column A. Press (ENTER) after you type each label.

**Department**
**Clothing**
**Cosmetics**

**Watches & Jewelry**
**Electronics and Computers**
**Appliances**
**Furniture**
**Housewares**
**China and Crystal**
**Knives and Cutlery**
**Books & Magazines**
**Bed and Bath**

Your worksheet should now look like Figure 1.5.

FIGURE 1.5

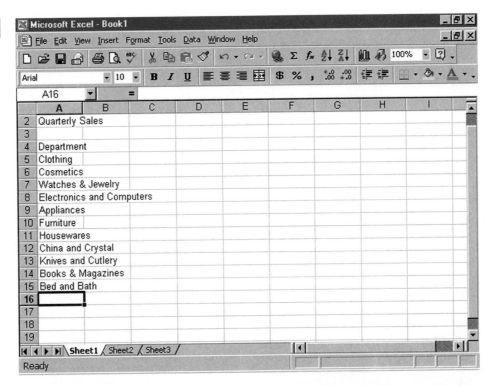

**TROUBLESHOOTING** Data in column A spills over into the adjacent cells in column B for some rows, since these cells do not yet contain data. Once they contain data, the entries will be truncated.

4   Select cell B4 and type **1st Qtr.** and press ⟨ENTER⟩ and select cell B4 again.

**TROUBLESHOOTING** If you make a mistake and need to edit the contents of the cell, highlight the cell and type the correct entry, or highlight the cell, click to edit the cell contents on the formula bar, and press ⟨ENTER⟩.

# Filling in Data Based on Adjacent Cells

Excel has numerous features that make entering data into a worksheet an easy task. One very useful feature is filling in data based upon the contents of adjacent cells. In this next task you will see how you can use the **fill handle**, which is the small rectangle in the lower right corner of the active cell, to complete a data series.

**TASK 2:** To Use the Fill Handle to Complete a Data Series

**1** Move the mouse pointer over the small rectangle in the lower-right corner of cell B4 until it changes to a small cross, as shown in Figure 1.6.

**FIGURE 1.6**

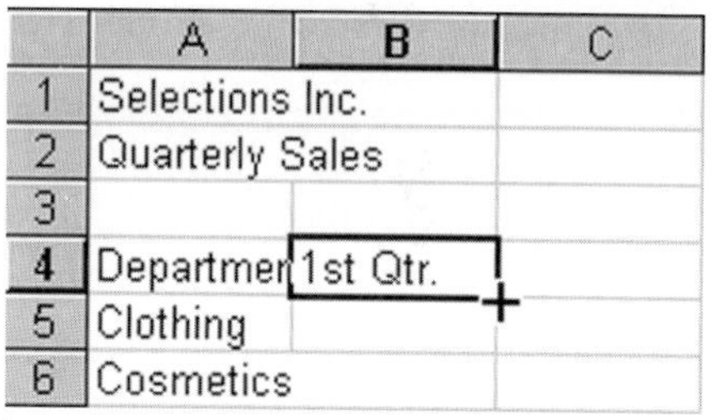

|   | A | B | C |
|---|---|---|---|
| 1 | Selections Inc. | | |
| 2 | Quarterly Sales | | |
| 3 | | | |
| 4 | Departmen | 1st Qtr. | |
| 5 | Clothing | | |
| 6 | Cosmetics | | |

**2** Click the left mouse button and drag the selection to the right through cell E4, as shown in Figure 1.7. Notice the **cell tip**, or descriptive label, that appears as you drag the selection.

**FIGURE 1.7**

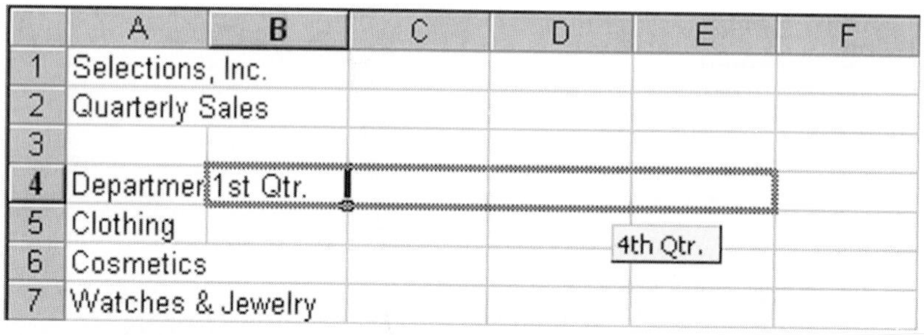

|   | A | B | C | D | E | F |
|---|---|---|---|---|---|---|
| 1 | Selections, Inc. | | | | | |
| 2 | Quarterly Sales | | | | | |
| 3 | | | | | | |
| 4 | Departmen | 1st Qtr. | | | | |
| 5 | Clothing | | | | 4th Qtr. | |
| 6 | Cosmetics | | | | | |
| 7 | Watches & Jewelry | | | | | |

**3** Release the left mouse button. Excel used the entry in cell B4 to determine the appropriate data series for the adjacent cells. Notice that cells C4 through E4 are shaded, as shown in Figure 1.8. This indicates that the range of cells from B4 to E4 is selected, with cell B4 as the active cell. Any time you select multiple cells, the selection will appear as shaded.

**FIGURE 1.8**

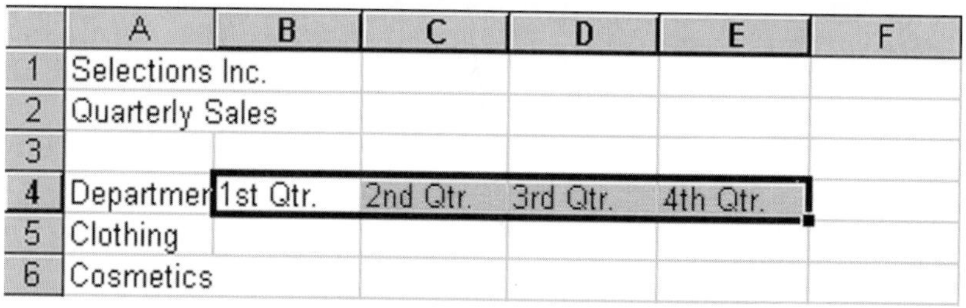

|   | A | B | C | D | E | F |
|---|---|---|---|---|---|---|
| 1 | Selections Inc. | | | | | |
| 2 | Quarterly Sales | | | | | |
| 3 | | | | | | |
| 4 | Departmen | 1st Qtr. | 2nd Qtr. | 3rd Qtr. | 4th Qtr. | |
| 5 | Clothing | | | | | |
| 6 | Cosmetics | | | | | |

**4** Click outside the selected range to deselect it.

> **TIP** When you refer to a range of adjacent cells, list the first cell in the range, a colon character to indicate an adjacent range, and the last cell in the range.

## Adjusting Column Width and Entering Additional Text

As you enter data into a worksheet, you will often need to adjust the width of one or more columns. By default, all columns have a width of 8.43. The displayed column width equals the width of the digits 0 through 9 of the standard font. As you can see, the data in cell A4 is truncated, or cut off, since there is data in the adjacent cell. You can easily remedy this situation by changing the column width.

**TASK 3:** To Change the Width of Worksheet Columns

**1** Move the insertion point to the border between the headings for columns A and B. The insertion point's icon will change to a double-headed arrow to indicate that you can resize the column, as shown in Figure 1.9.

**FIGURE 1.9**

**2** Double-click the left mouse button. The column will resize to display the contents of the widest entry, as shown in Figure 1.10.

**FIGURE 1.10**

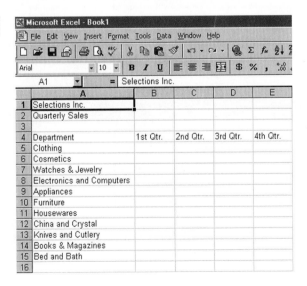

**3** Point to the border between columns B and C. Click and drag the width of column B to 12.00, as shown in Figure 1.11.

FIGURE 1.11

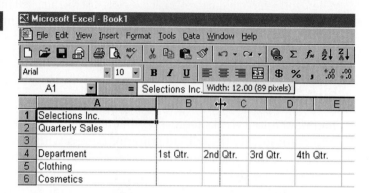

**4** Click the heading for column C. The entire column is selected, as shown in Figure 1.12.

FIGURE 1.12

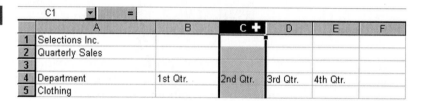

**5** Depress the (SHIFT) key and click the heading for column E. This will select the range of columns from C to E (Figure 1.13).

FIGURE 1.13

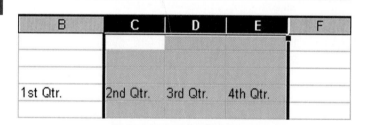

**6** Select any of the column borders in the selection, and then click and drag the column widths to 12.00, as shown in Figure 1.14.

FIGURE 1.14

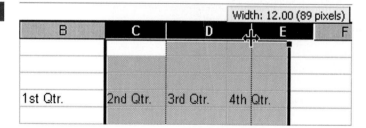

**7** Release the mouse button. Columns C through E have now been resized.

## TASK 4:   To Enter Additional Text Labels and Adjust Column Width

**1** Select cell F4, type **Total**, and press ENTER.

**2** Using the click-and-drag method of resizing a column described in the preceding task, change the width of this column to 12.00.

> **TROUBLESHOOTING** Depending upon your screen resolution, you may need to use the horizontal scroll bar to display additional worksheet columns before resizing column F.

**3** Select cell A16, type **Total**, and press ENTER. Your worksheet will now appear as shown in Figure 1.15.

**FIGURE 1.15**

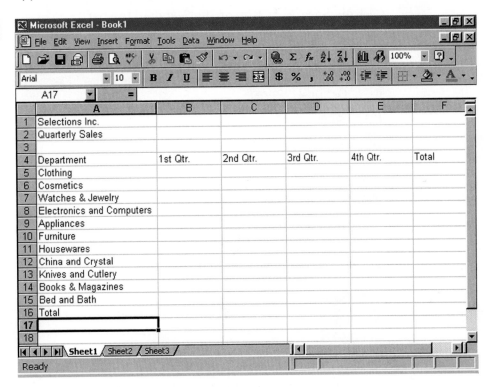

## Check Point

You have not yet saved your workbook. Where does your data currently reside?

## Saving Your Workbook

At this point you should probably save your workbook. As you know, everything you have done so far resides in memory, and if the computer were to lose power, you would have to recreate this workbook! Therefore, we're going to pause and save our workbook.

It is often customary to create a folder to store files related to a specific project. In the steps that follow you will create a folder on a floppy disk and save your workbook in that folder.

### TASK 5: To Create a Folder and Save Your Workbook

**1** Click the Save 🖫 button on the Standard toolbar.

**2** The Save As dialog box appears, as shown in Figure 1.16.

**FIGURE 1.16**

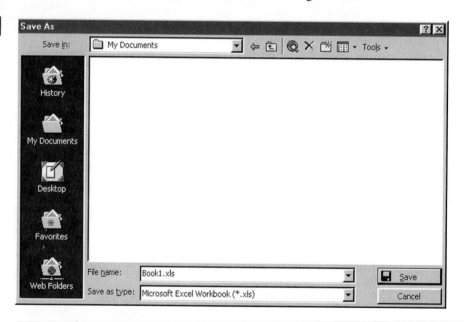

**TIP** Since you have not saved your workbook yet, Excel displays the Save As dialog box so that you can specify the file name, file location, and file type for your workbook. Depending on your operating system, your screen may differ.

**3** Place a blank, formatted floppy disk in the 3½-inch drive on your computer.

**TROUBLESHOOTING** If you do not have access to a floppy drive, use the local or network drive your instructor specifies.

**4** Select the appropriate drive from the Save in: drop-down list, as shown in Figure 1.17.

**FIGURE 1.17**

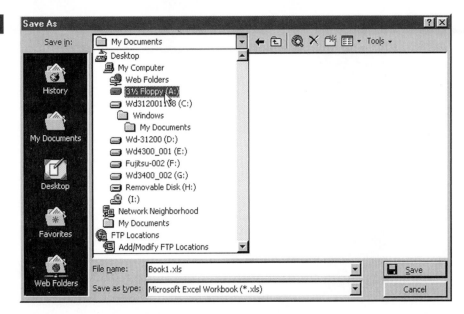

> **TROUBLESHOOTING** The drives listed will be specific to your computer or network.

**5** Click the Create New Folder button near the upper-right corner of the Save As dialog box, as shown in Figure 1.18.

**FIGURE 1.18**

**6** Type **Selections** as the name of the folder you will create, as shown in Figure 1.19. Click OK to create the folder.

**FIGURE 1.19**

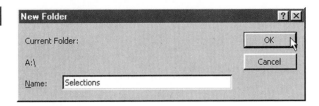

**7** The default file name *Book1.xls* appears highlighted in the File name: box. Type **Selections** as the file name for your workbook, as shown in Figure 1.20.

FIGURE 1.20

TIP You do not need to add a period (.) and xls as the file name extension .xls. Since the Save as type: list box indicates that the file will be saved as an Excel workbook, the file name extension will be added automatically.

**8** Click the Save button. Your workbook is now saved, as indicated by the file name that appears in Excel's title bar.

## Check Point

At this point you should recognize that you have defined the structure for one regional worksheet, and saved the workbook in a folder that you have created. You are now ready to enter numbers into the worksheet, and then define formulas to perform calculations.

## Break Point

If necessary, you can exit Excel and continue this project later.

## Entering Numbers

You will recall that numbers are the data upon which calculations are performed. In Microsoft Excel, a number can contain only the following characters:

0 1 2 3 4 5 6 7 8 9 + - ( ) , / $ % . E e

Excel ignores leading plus signs (+) and treats a single period as a decimal. All other combinations of numbers and nonnumeric characters are treated as text.

The worksheet design shown in Figure 1.2 displays four columns of sales figures as numbers. You will enter these into columns B through E of your workbook.

## TASK 6:  To Enter Numbers

**1** Launch Excel and open the *Selections.xls* workbook if necessary.

**2** Type **405112** in cell B5 and press (ENTER).

**3** Enter the following numbers in columns B through E of your worksheet. When you are finished, your screen should resemble the worksheet shown in Figure 1.21.

| Row | Column B | Column C | Column D | Column E |
|-----|----------|----------|----------|----------|
| B5  | 405112   | 321670   | 401934   | 393714   |
| B6  | 373211   | 34812    | 29718    | 38248    |
| B7  | 45213    | 21397    | 18923    | 44971    |
| B8  | 211396   | 189201   | 174916   | 193712   |
| B9  | 48761    | 39675    | 36582    | 38619    |
| B10 | 23819    | 18912    | 21975    | 24187    |
| B11 | 34907    | 26585    | 39638    | 33935    |
| B12 | 33185    | 32081    | 41972    | 18381    |
| B13 | 12954    | 9273     | 10593    | 11976    |
| B14 | 36719    | 37383    | 38121    | 29753    |
| B15 | 21082    | 18910    | 19718    | 17544    |

**FIGURE 1.21**

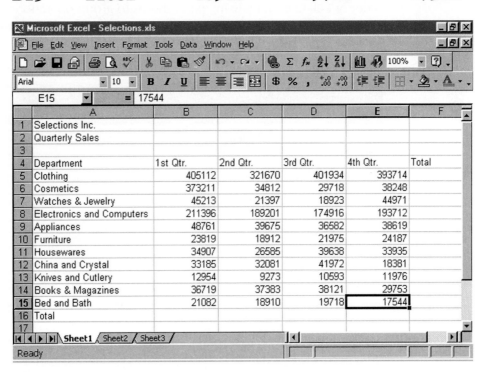

**4** Save your workbook.

# Creating Formulas

Your prototype worksheet is almost complete! You need to add formulas in row 16 and column F to add together the sales figures.

## About Formulas

As you learned in the Introduction to Excel, a **formula** uses existing values to calculate new ones. Formulas often contain **functions**, which essentially are predefined formulas that perform calculations by using specific values, called **arguments**. Both formulas and functions are therefore mathematical or logical statements that perform calculations. Formulas always begin with an equal sign (=).

The order of the elements in a formula determines the final result of the calculation. Formulas in Microsoft Excel follow a specific **syntax**, or order, that includes an equal sign (=) followed by the elements to be calculated (the **operands**), which are separated by calculation operators. Each operand can be a value that does not change (such as a number entered in a cell), a cell or range reference, a label, a name, or a worksheet function. For example, the formula =SUM(B5:B15) will total the range of cells from B5 to B15, inclusive. The equal sign is followed by the function name (SUM), which requires an argument, a cell range in this case (B5:B15).

Excel performs the operations from left to right—according to the order of **operator precedence**—starting with the equal sign (=). You can control the order of calculation by using parentheses to group operations that should be performed first. Many formulas use arithmetic operators. Table 1.3 lists the arithmetic operators recognized by Excel.

**Table 1.3**

| Operator | Purpose | Formula (using cell references) | Result (A1 = 2, A2 = 4) |
|---|---|---|---|
| + (plus sign) | Addition | = A1 + A2 | 6 |
| – (minus sign) | Subtraction<br>Negation | = A1 – A2<br>= –A2 | –2<br>–4 |
| * (asterisk) | Multiplication | = A1 * A2 | 8 |
| / (forward slash) | Division | = A1 / A2 | .5 |
| % (percent sign) | Percent | = A1% | .02 |
| ^ (caret) | Exponentiation | = A1 ^ A2 | 16 |

Although you can enter formulas in Excel using numeric values, most formulas make extensive use of cell references. A **cell reference** is the address of a specific cell that you want to include in a formula or function. By using cell references, the formula will calculate based upon the values in cells, so that if you change a cell's value, the result of the calculation will change as well. This capability is what gives Excel such power as an analytical tool.

## About Functions

Formulas often contain functions, since functions both simplify creating formulas and also improve the accuracy of the results. Excel includes over 200 functions!

Functions include elements called arguments, which provide the necessary values required by the specific function. A function's arguments are enclosed in parentheses, and for functions requiring more than one argument, the arguments are separated from one another with a comma.

Functions in Excel are classified according to a specific type of calculation. The most common classifications include Financial, Date & Time, Math & Trig, Statistical, Lookup & Reference, and Logical. In addition, Excel supports user-defined functions. Some of the more common Excel functions are listed in Table 1.4.

**Table 1.4**

| Function | Purpose | Example (using cell references) | Result (A1 = 2, A2 = 4, A3 = 6) |
| --- | --- | --- | --- |
| **=SUM(argument)** | Calculates the sum of a range of values | =SUM(A1:A3) | 12 |
| **=MIN(argument)** | Returns the minimum value in a range | =MIN(A1:A3) | 2 |
| **=MAX(argument)** | Returns the maximum value in a range | =MAX(A1:A3) | 6 |
| **=AVERAGE(argument)** | Calculates the arithmetic mean of a range of values | =AVERAGE(A1:A3) | 4 |
| **=PMT(argument)** | Calculates the payment of a loan based upon periodic payments and a constant interest rate | =PMT(A1,A2,-A3) | $12.15 |
| **=IF(argument)** | Returns a value based upon a logical test | =IF(A1>0,"Positive") | Positive |
| **=COUNT(argument)** | Counts the number of cells in a range that have a numeric value | =COUNT(A1:A3) | 3 |

 **Check Point**

Based upon the functions listed in Table 1.4, which function is most appropriate for the worksheet you are designing?

Compare the functions in Table 1.4 with the worksheet design shown in Figure 1.2, and you will see that you should use the SUM function in each formula you will create. Although the following formula would return a correct result:

$$=B5+B6+B7+B8+B9+B10+B11+B12+B13+B14+B15,$$

you should use functions for simplicity and accuracy whenever possible. You can enter a formula in a cell by typing directly in the cell, inserting a function using the *formula palette*, or by using the pointing method. If the formula will include the SUM function, you can use Excel's **AutoSum** feature. Once you create a formula, it can be copied to other worksheet cells.

**TASK 7:** To Enter Formulas Using a Variety of Methods

**1** Click cell B16 to make it the active cell.

**2** Type **=SUM(B5:B15)**, press (ENTER), and select B16 again.

> **TIP** As you type a formula directly in a cell, the word *Enter* appears in the Status bar to indicate that you are using data entry mode.

The result shown in Figure 1.22 is displayed.

**FIGURE 1.22**

Microsoft Excel - Selections.xls

File   Edit   View   Insert   Format   Tools   Data   Window   Help

Arial        ▼  10  ▼   B   I   U

B16        ▼        =   =SUM(B5:B15)

|    | A | B | C |
|----|---|---|---|
| 1 | Selections Inc. | | |
| 2 | Quarterly Sales | | |
| 3 | | | |
| 4 | Department | 1st Qtr. | 2nd Qtr. |
| 5 | Clothing | 405112 | 321670 |
| 6 | Cosmetics | 373211 | 34812 |
| 7 | Watches & Jewelry | 45213 | 21397 |
| 8 | Electronics and Computers | 211396 | 189201 |
| 9 | Appliances | 48761 | 39675 |
| 10 | Furniture | 23819 | 18912 |
| 11 | Housewares | 34907 | 26585 |
| 12 | China and Crystal | 33185 | 32081 |
| 13 | Knives and Cutlery | 12954 | 9273 |
| 14 | Books & Magazines | 36719 | 37383 |
| 15 | Bed and Bath | 21082 | 18910 |
| 16 | | 1246359 | |
| 17 | | | |

**3** Select cell C16.

**4** Click the Insert Function $f_x$ button on the Standard toolbar.

**5** The Paste Function dialog box appears. Select All as the function category, and select SUM as the function name, as shown in Figure 1.23.

**FIGURE 1.23**

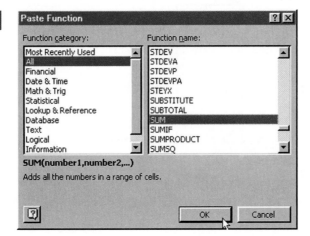

**6** Click OK. When the formula palette shown in Figure 1.24 appears, click OK, as the range appearing in the highlighted text box is correct. The results of the calculation are now displayed. Notice that the formula palette displays the results of the calculation.

**FIGURE 1.24**

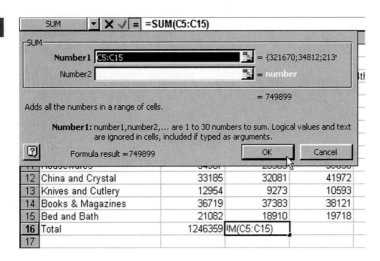

**7** Select cell D5 and click and drag the selection through cell D16, as shown in Figure 1.25.

**FIGURE 1.25**

| | B | C | D | E |
|---|---|---|---|---|
| 2 | | | | |
| 3 | | | | |
| 4 | 1st Qtr. | 2nd Qtr. | 3rd Qtr. | 4th Qtr. |
| 5 | 405112 | 321670 | 401934 | 393714 |
| 6 | 373211 | 34812 | 29718 | 38248 |
| 7 | 45213 | 21397 | 18923 | 44971 |
| 8 | 211396 | 189201 | 174916 | 193712 |
| 9 | 48761 | 39675 | 36582 | 38619 |
| 10 | 23819 | 18912 | 21975 | 24187 |
| 11 | 34907 | 26585 | 39638 | 33935 |
| 12 | 33185 | 32081 | 41972 | 18381 |
| 13 | 12954 | 9273 | 10593 | 11976 |
| 14 | 36719 | 37383 | 38121 | 29753 |
| 15 | 21082 | 18910 | 19718 | 17544 |
| 16 | 1246359 | 749899 | ✛ | |
| 17 | | | | |

**TIP** You have just selected an adjacent range in Excel. In Project 2 you will learn more about selecting ranges.

**8** Click the AutoSum ∑ button on the Standard toolbar. Excel creates a formula with a SUM function and displays the results of the calculation.

**9** Select cell D16 and click the Copy button on the Standard toolbar. The formula in cell C16 is placed on the Clipboard.

**10** Select cell E16 and click the Paste button on the Standard toolbar. The formula is pasted in cell E16 and the results of the calculation are displayed, as shown in Figure 1.26.

**FIGURE 1.26**

| 13 | 12954 | 9273 | 10593 | 11976 |
|---|---|---|---|---|
| 14 | 36719 | 37383 | 38121 | 29753 |
| 15 | 21082 | 18910 | 19718 | 17544 |
| 16 | 1246359 | 749899 | 834090 | 845040 |
| 17 | | | | |
| 18 | | | | |

Sheet1 / Sheet2 / Sheet3 /

**11** Using any of the methods shown here, enter a formula in cell F5 that sums the range B5:E5.

**12** Using the fill handle, drag this formula from F5 down the worksheet through cell F16. Excel automatically creates a formula that sums the values in each row, as shown in Figure 1.27.

**FIGURE 1.27**

| | F5 | ▼ | = | =SUM(B5:E5) | | |
|---|---|---|---|---|---|---|
| | B | C | D | E | F | G |
| 1 | | | | | | |
| 2 | | | | | | |
| 3 | | | | | | |
| 4 | 1st Qtr. | 2nd Qtr. | 3rd Qtr. | 4th Qtr. | Total | |
| 5 | 405112 | 321670 | 401934 | 393714 | 1522430 | |
| 6 | 373211 | 34812 | 29718 | 38248 | 475989 | |
| 7 | 45213 | 21397 | 18923 | 44971 | 130504 | |
| 8 | 211396 | 189201 | 174916 | 193712 | 769225 | |
| 9 | 48761 | 39675 | 36582 | 38619 | 163637 | |
| 10 | 23819 | 18912 | 21975 | 24187 | 88893 | |
| 11 | 34907 | 26585 | 39638 | 33935 | 135065 | |
| 12 | 33185 | 32081 | 41972 | 18381 | 125619 | |
| 13 | 12954 | 9273 | 10593 | 11976 | 44796 | |
| 14 | 36719 | 37383 | 38121 | 29753 | 141976 | |
| 15 | 21082 | 18910 | 19718 | 17544 | 77254 | |
| 16 | 1246359 | 749899 | 834090 | 845040 | 3675388 | |
| 17 | | | | | | |

**13** Press (CTRL) + (HOME) to return to the home cell.

**14** Save your workbook.

## Previewing and Printing Worksheets

Before you print a worksheet, you should preview it to make sure it will print as you expect. By using Excel's **Print Preview**, you can see exactly how your worksheet will appear in printed form. In addition to being able to see the entire worksheet on the screen, Print Preview allows you to zoom in on selected areas of the workbook and print directly from the Preview screen. Once you preview the worksheet, you can send a copy to the printer. For more control over how your worksheet is printed, select Print from the File menu to open the Print dialog box.

**TASK 8:    To Preview and Print Worksheets**

**1** Click the Print Preview 🔍 button on the Standard toolbar. The Print Preview displays the worksheet, as shown in Figure 1.28.

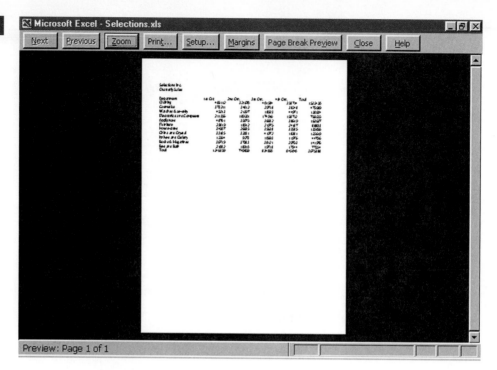

FIGURE 1.28

**2** Click the insertion point, which now appears as a magnifying glass near the top of the Preview window. Excel zooms the preview.

**3** When you are finished previewing the worksheet, click the Close button in the upper-right corner of the Print Preview window. This closes the preview.

> **TROUBLESHOOTING** Make sure you do not click the Close button on the title bar, or you will close Excel.

**4** Choose Print from the File menu.

**5** In the Print dialog box, verify the printer attached to your computer or network, and click OK. The worksheet prints.

# Closing Your Workbook

When you are finished with your workbook, it is a good idea to save it one last time before closing it and exiting Excel. If you have made changes to your workbook and attempt to close Excel, you will be prompted to save your changes.

## TASK 9:   To Save and Close Your Workbook

**1**   Click the Save button 🖫 on the Standard toolbar to update your workbook.

**2**   Click the Close button ☒ in the workbook window, or select Close from the File menu.

**3**   Click the Close button ☒ in the application window to exit Excel.

> **TIP**   You can also exit Excel by simply closing Excel, and save any changes you have made to any open workbooks when you are prompted to do so.

You are now ready to meet with Mr. Traylor to have him approve your design. In the next project you will modify this workbook by adding additional regional sheets, a summary sheet, and formulas to link the worksheets.

## Summary

- It is generally a good idea to plan your workbook before entering data into Excel.
- You can navigate within a worksheet using the mouse, the scroll bars, or keyboard shortcuts.
- To navigate among worksheets in a workbook, use the sheet tabs or the navigation buttons.
- You can enter text in a worksheet by selecting the appropriate cell and typing an entry.
- You can use the fill handle to fill data in cells based upon the value in an adjacent cell.
- You can easily adjust column widths to display the entire contents of all cells.
- When you first save a workbook, you can specify the file name, location, and file type in the Save As dialog box.
- Enter numbers in a cell by selecting the cell and typing a valid entry.
- You can use a variety of methods to enter formulas with functions into worksheet cells.
- You should always preview a worksheet before printing it.
- Consider saving your workbook prior to closing it and exiting Excel. Excel will prompt you to save your workbook upon closing if it contains any updated information.

## Key Terms and Operations

### Key Terms

| | |
|---|---|
| active cell | formula palette |
| active sheet | function |
| argument | home cell |
| AutoSum | operand |
| cell reference | operator precedence |
| cell tip | Print Preview |
| fill handle | syntax |
| formula | |

### Operations

| | |
|---|---|
| adjust column width | enter text |
| close a workbook | preview a workbook |
| create a workbook | print a workbook |
| enter formulas | save a workbook |
| enter numbers | use functions |

# Study Questions

## Multiple Choice

1. To return to the home cell from anywhere in a worksheet, press
   a. (CTRL) + (→).
   b. (PGDN).
   c. (CTRL) + (HOME).
   d. (PGUP).

2. Which Excel function calculates the total for a range of values?
   a. MIN
   b. PMT
   c. MAX
   d. SUM

3. If cell A1 is 10, cell A2 is 20, and cell A3 is 30, what value is returned by the formula =SUM(A2:A3)?
   a. 30
   b. 40
   c. 50
   d. 60

4. When you highlight a cell, =A1*2 is displayed in the formula bar. This cell contains what kind of operator?
   a. arithmetic
   b. division
   c. exponentiation
   d. multiplication

5. If the data in a cell appears truncated, what should you do to find the optimum column width?
   a. Edit the data so it is not so long.
   b. Adjust the width of all columns in the worksheet.
   c. Double-click the right border of the column displaying the truncated data.
   d. Construct a formula to calculate the optimum width.

6. When you type a formula containing a function, what must the function contain?
   a. cell references
   b. a range, indicated as such by the colon character
   c. the letters SUM
   d. one or more arguments

7. Which of the following is a valid reference to an adjacent range?
    a. A1:A1
    b. B3;C3
    c. A1:A10
    d. B1-E1

8. Cell A10 contains the following data:
    SUM(B10:LL10)
   Excel will treat this data as:
    a. text.
    b. a formula.
    c. a function.
    d. a date.

9. By default, an Excel workbook contains how many worksheets?
    a. 1
    b. 3
    c. 5
    d. 8

10. When you highlight a cell, =(D211/A7)*(C41/2) is displayed in the formula bar. This cell contains what kind of data?
    a. text
    b. a formula
    c. numbers
    d. a function

## Short Answer

1. A cell contains both letters and numbers. What kind of data does it contain?

2. What is the address of the home cell?

3. Write a formula that totals the values in cell A1 to A5.

4. What is the default name for a workbook?

5. Approximately how many functions does Excel contain?

6. What are text entries in cells called when they define a worksheet's structure?

7. PMT is what kind of function?

8. What do functions always contain?

9. What should you do before printing a worksheet?

10. What should you do before closing Excel?

## Fill in the Blank

1. A _____ is a predefined formula.

2. Arguments are contained inside _____.

3. All functions require _____.

4. When you save a workbook for the first time, the _____ dialog box appears.

5. The _____ function calculates the arithmetic mean for a range of values.

6. You can use Excel's _____ to fill in a data series based upon the value in an existing cell.

7. The _____ displays the results of a function as you are building it.

8. An Excel formula always begins with _____.

9. Formulas often contain _____ to perform specific calculations.

10. Cell A1 is called the _____.

## For Discussion

1. List two reasons why you should use functions in formulas whenever possible.

2. How do functions differ from formulas?

3. How do text, numbers, and formulas differ?

4. How does the fill handle simplify data entry?

5. List three methods for navigating within worksheets.

# Hands-On Exercises

## 1. Creating a Sales Summary

The Java Bar is a coffee and espresso shop located in the Selections, Inc. retail stores. Angie Stover has asked you to create a simple worksheet summarizing the first quarter sales on a weekly basis. In this exercise you will create the worksheet shown in Figure 1.29.

**FIGURE 1.29**

Microsoft Excel - Java Sales.xls

File  Edit  View  Insert  Format  Tools  Data  Window  Help

Arial   10   **B** *I* U

D11   =   =AVERAGE(D5:D8)

|    | A | B | C | D | E | F |
|----|---|---|---|---|---|---|
| 1 | Java Coffee Bar | | | | | |
| 2 | First Quarter Sales | | | | | |
| 3 | | | | | | |
| 4 | | January | February | March | Total | Average |
| 5 | Week 1 | 8560 | 7080 | 7813 | 23453 | 7817.667 |
| 6 | Week 2 | 10341 | 11985 | 9812 | 32138 | 10712.67 |
| 7 | Week 3 | 9481 | 10845 | 10691 | 31017 | 10339 |
| 8 | Week 4 | 12901 | 7609 | 9814 | 30324 | 10108 |
| 9 | | | | | | |
| 10 | Total | 41283 | 37519 | 38130 | | |
| 11 | Average | 10320.75 | 9379.75 | 9532.5 | | |
| 12 | | | | | | |

**Sales summary worksheet for the Selections, Inc. Java Bar**

1. Launch Excel if it is not currently running, or create a new worksheet by selecting New from the File menu.

2. Enter the text labels shown in Figure 1.29.

3. Enter the numeric data shown in the range B5:D8.

4. Enter a SUM function in cell E5 to total the Week 1 data for the quarter.

5. Use the fill handle to copy this formula through cell E8.

6. Create a formula containing a SUM function in cell B10. Copy this formula through cell D10.

7. Type **=AVERAGE(B5:D5)** in cell F5. Copy this formula through cell F8.

8. Type **=AVERAGE(B5:B8)** in cell B11. Copy this formula through cell D11.

9. Create a folder on your floppy disk named Java Bar.

10. Save your workbook to the Java Bar folder as *Java Sales.xls*. Close the workbook.

 **Web Tip**

Do you like coffee? You can order Starbucks coffee directly from the Web. For more information, visit http://www.starbucks.com.

## 2. Adding an Additional Worksheet to the Java Bar Workbook

Angie Stover likes the workbook you created, and now wants you to enter data for the second quarter of operations. In this exercise you will copy the existing data, paste it to a new worksheet, and change the appropriate information. Your completed worksheet appears in Figure 1.30.

**FIGURE 1.30**

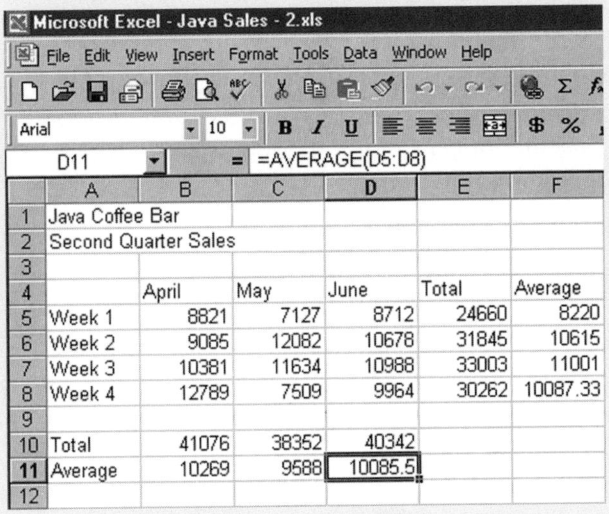

*Microsoft Excel - Java Sales - 2.xls*

D11 = =AVERAGE(D5:D8)

| | A | B | C | D | E | F |
|---|---|---|---|---|---|---|
| 1 | Java Coffee Bar | | | | | |
| 2 | Second Quarter Sales | | | | | |
| 3 | | | | | | |
| 4 | | April | May | June | Total | Average |
| 5 | Week 1 | 8821 | 7127 | 8712 | 24660 | 8220 |
| 6 | Week 2 | 9085 | 12082 | 10678 | 31845 | 10615 |
| 7 | Week 3 | 10381 | 11634 | 10988 | 33003 | 11001 |
| 8 | Week 4 | 12789 | 7509 | 9964 | 30262 | 10087.33 |
| 9 | | | | | | |
| 10 | Total | 41076 | 38352 | 40342 | | |
| 11 | Average | 10269 | 9588 | 10085.5 | | |
| 12 | | | | | | |

1. Launch Excel if it is not currently running.

2. Open the *Java Sales.xls* workbook you created in the previous exercise. If you do not have a copy, ask your instructor how to obtain this file.

3. Copy the range A1:F11 in Sheet1.

4. Select Sheet2 to make it the active worksheet.

5. Make cell A1 the active cell, and paste the data you just copied to the Office Clipboard.

6. Highlight the range B5:D5, and Choose Clear, Contents from the Edit menu to clear the contents of these cells. Enter the data shown in Figure 1.31.

**FIGURE 1.31**

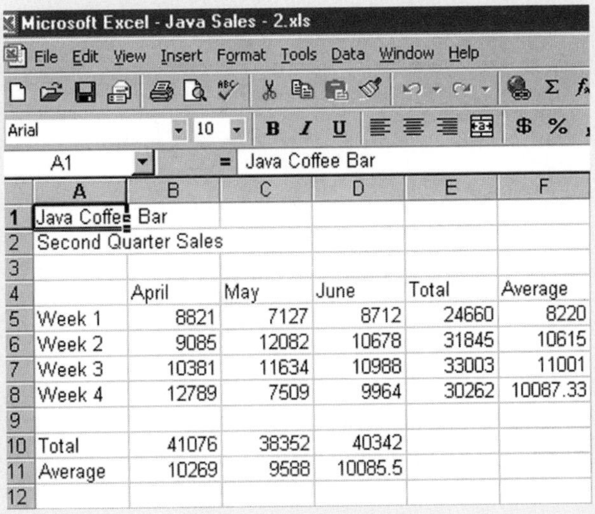

*Microsoft Excel - Java Sales - 2.xls*

A1 = Java Coffee Bar

| | A | B | C | D | E | F |
|---|---|---|---|---|---|---|
| 1 | Java Coffee Bar | | | | | |
| 2 | Second Quarter Sales | | | | | |
| 3 | | | | | | |
| 4 | | April | May | June | Total | Average |
| 5 | Week 1 | 8821 | 7127 | 8712 | 24660 | 8220 |
| 6 | Week 2 | 9085 | 12082 | 10678 | 31845 | 10615 |
| 7 | Week 3 | 10381 | 11634 | 10988 | 33003 | 11001 |
| 8 | Week 4 | 12789 | 7509 | 9964 | 30262 | 10087.33 |
| 9 | | | | | | |
| 10 | Total | 41076 | 38352 | 40342 | | |
| 11 | Average | 10269 | 9588 | 10085.5 | | |
| 12 | | | | | | |

7. Save your workbook to the Java folder on your diskette as *Java Sales–2.xls*.

## On Your Own Exercises

### 1. Creating a List of Web Sites

If you enter a fully registered URL into an Excel worksheet, it will be formatted as a hyperlink you can follow by simply clicking it. Search the Web for three financial or investment sites. Create a workbook listing three financial or investment sites. Enter the name of the site in column A, and the URL in column B. Create a folder on your disk named *Investments*. Save the workbook to your Investments folder with the name *Financial Sites.xls*.

### 2. Creating a Class Schedule

Create a workbook listing your current class schedule. Enter the day, time, name of each class, and credit hours. Create a folder on your disk named *Personal*. Save the workbook to your Personal folder as *Class Schedule.xls*.

### 3. Creating a Time Card

Many students work while attending school. Create a workbook listing your time card for one week. Include the days, total hours worked, hourly rate, and gross pay. Save the workbook to your Personal folder as *Time Card.xls*.

### 4. Creating an Address List in Excel

Excel is often used to store lists of structured information, such as an address list. Create an address list that stores the first name, last name, address, city, zip code, and phone number for three personal contacts. Save the workbook to your Personal folder. Name the workbook *Addresses.xls*.

### 5. Calculating the Minimum Value in a Range

Ask your instructor or lab assistant where the file named *January Sales.xls* is located.

 **Web Tip**

If you cannot obtain a copy from your instructor, visit the SELECT Web site at http://www.prenhall.com/select to download a copy.

Modify the worksheet so that it calculates the minimum value for each department. Save your updated worksheet to the Personal folder on your disk. Name the updated workbook *January – Update 1.xls*.

## 6. Conducting a "What-If" Analysis

Open the workbook named *Utility Costs.xls* from your network or disk.

 **Web Tip**

If you cannot obtain a copy from your instructor, visit the SELECT Web site at http://www.prenhall.com/select to download a copy.

Modify the worksheet so that it calculates all utility costs if the price of electricity and natural gas is increased by 10% and 15%, respectively. Save your updated workbook to your Personal folder as *Updated Utility Costs.xls*.

# Modifying Worksheets and Workbooks

**N**ow that you have created the Selections, Inc. Sales Summary workbook, you can modify it so that it is easier to use and provides more information. In this project you will enhance the functionality of the workbook by adding worksheets for additional sales regions, deleting worksheets you no longer need, and repositioning the worksheets in the workbook. In addition, you will move, copy, and delete data, and create formulas that share information among worksheets in the Sales Summary workbook.

## Objectives

After completing this project, you will be able to:

➤ Open an Excel workbook

➤ Insert worksheets into a workbook

➤ Delete worksheets from a workbook

➤ Change the position of worksheets in a workbook

➤ Edit worksheets by copying and moving data

➤ Edit worksheets by revising data

➤ Enter additional text and number data into a workbook

➤ Create 3-D formulas that link information among worksheets

## Running Case

Mr. Traylor is pleased with the progress you have made so far. He enthusiastically accepted your initial design, and now wants you to finish defining the structure of your workbook to include quarterly sales for the remaining sales regions, and a summary of sales for all regions.

# The Challenge

The regional worksheets need to be in order by region (North, South, East, West), with the summary worksheet appearing first in the workbook. The summary sales worksheet must contain formulas that dynamically list the regional sales data, so if the figures change for one or more regions, the changes are automatically reflected in the summary. When you are finished updating the workbook, Mr. Traylor will review your changes and approve the next phase of design.

# The Strategy

You can easily add worksheets to the workbook and then enter the appropriate data, create formulas, and modify the workbook structure by deleting any extra worksheets and ordering the remaining ones.

You can create 3-D linking formulas to dynamically include all regional sales data in the Sales Summary worksheet. Your workbook will look similar to the one shown in Figure 2.1 after you complete this project.

**FIGURE 2.1**

Microsoft Excel - Selections.xls

File  Edit  View  Insert  Format  Tools  Data  Window  Help

B6 = =North!F6

| | A | B | C | D | E | F |
|---|---|---|---|---|---|---|
| 1 | Selections Inc. | | | | | |
| 2 | Quarterly Sales | | | | | |
| 3 | | North Region | South Region | East Region | West Region | Total |
| 4 | | | | | | |
| 5 | Department | | | | | |
| 6 | Clothing | 1522430 | 1246050 | 1108983 | 1235508 | 5112971 |
| 7 | Cosmetics | 475989 | 111833 | 99529 | 110637 | 797988 |
| 8 | Watches & Jewelry | 130504 | 122476 | 109002 | 121277 | 483259 |
| 9 | Electronics & Computers | 769225 | 687746 | 612091 | 683707 | 2752769 |
| 10 | Appliances | 163637 | 136685 | 121648 | 135501 | 557471 |
| 11 | Furniture | 88893 | 109848 | 97762 | 108692 | 405195 |
| 12 | Housewares | 135065 | 84728 | 75405 | 83941 | 379139 |
| 13 | China & Crystal | 125619 | 74138 | 65982 | 73330 | 339069 |
| 14 | Knives & Cutlery | 44796 | 152278 | 135526 | 153605 | 486205 |
| 15 | Books & Magazines | 141976 | 88851 | 79075 | 88632 | 398534 |
| 16 | Bed & Bath | 77254 | 85061 | 75702 | 84421 | 322438 |
| 17 | Total | 3675388 | 2899694 | 2580705 | 2879251 | 12035038 |

**Sales Summary** / North / South / East / West /

Ready

# The Setup

Launch Microsoft Excel and make sure that you select the Excel settings listed in Table 2.1. This will ensure that your screen matches the illustrations and that the tasks in this project function as described.

**Table 2.1**

| Location | Make these settings: |
|----------|---------------------|
| **Office Shortcut Bar** | Right-click the Office icon on the shortcut bar and click Exit. |
| **Office Assistant** | Hide the Assistant. |
| **Tools, Customize** | Click the Options tab and deselect the option to show recently used menu commands first. Deselect the option to display the Standard and Formatting toolbars on one row. |
| **Tools, Options** | Click the Edit tab and select Move selection after Enter. |
| **View, Formula Bar** | Display the formula bar. |
| **View, Status Bar** | Display the status bar. |
| **View, Normal** | View the workbook in Normal view. |
| **Maximize** | Maximize the application and workbook windows. |

## Opening a Workbook

Before you can modify your workbook, you must open it. To open an existing workbook you must specify the file name and location.

### TASK 1:  To Open an Excel Workbook

**1** Select Open from the File menu.

**2** In the File Open dialog box, select drive A.

> **TROUBLESHOOTING** If you saved your workbook to another location at the conclusion of Project 1, select the appropriate drive letter.

**3** Open the Selections folder by double-clicking it, highlight the *Selections.xls* file, and click Open, as shown in Figure 2.2. Depending on your settings, your screen may differ slightly.

**FIGURE 2.2**

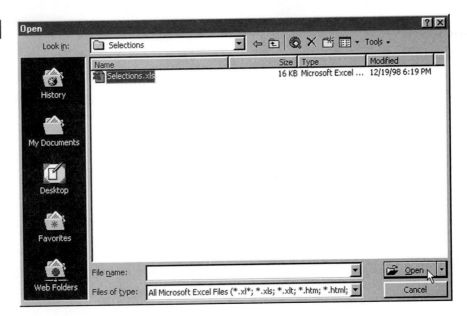

**4** Excel opens your workbook.

# Working with Worksheets

You will recall from "Introduction to Excel 2000" that an Excel workbook contains one or more worksheets. A workbook with multiple worksheets is useful for a variety of reasons. First, multiple worksheets allow you to keep related but distinct business data in one electronic file. Second, most workbooks contain data for multiple entities, and will often contain charts or graphics as additional worksheets. Finally, Excel supports **linking formulas**, whereby you can link data among worksheets to create three-dimensional data models and solutions. A **3-D workbook** has multiple worksheets containing one or more linking formulas.

You can easily add, delete, rename, and reposition worksheets in a workbook. You will recall that each worksheet is represented by a sheet tab, which you can select to edit or print the worksheet.

 **Web Tip**

Are you new to Microsoft Excel, but know how to use Lotus 1-2-3? The site http://www.microsoft.com/TechNet/Excel/TechNote/lotusex1.asp has information about how Excel and Lotus differ.

# Editing a Workbook by Inserting Worksheets

Adding worksheets to a workbook is a common task. When you add worksheets to an existing workbook, they will be inserted into the workbook immediately before the current worksheet. Once you enter a worksheet, you can easily rename its tab and change its position.

## TASK 2: To Insert Worksheets into the Current Workbook

**1** Select Worksheet from the Insert menu. Excel adds a worksheet named Sheet4, as shown in Figure 2.3.

**FIGURE 2.3**

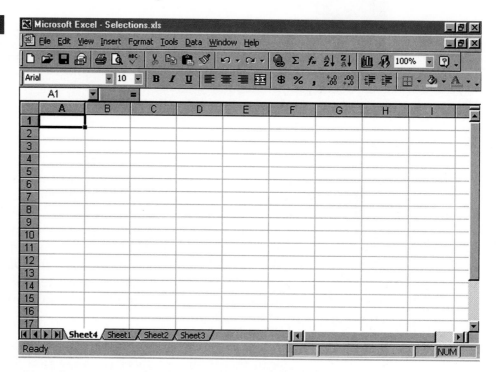

**2** Right-click the Sheet4 tab, as shown in Figure 2.4.

**FIGURE 2.4**

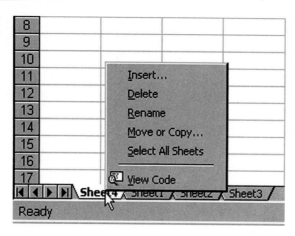

**3** Choose Insert from the shortcut menu.

**4** Select Worksheet from the Insert dialog box, as shown in Figure 2.5.

FIGURE 2.5

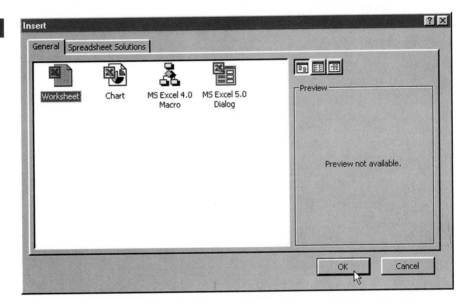

**TROUBLESHOOTING** If you do not see an icon representing a general worksheet, make sure the General tab is active.

**5** Click OK. Sheet5 is now added to the workbook.

**6** Using either method just shown, add an additional worksheet to the workbook.

## Renaming Worksheets

Excel provides two methods for renaming worksheets using the worksheet tabs. You can either double-click a worksheet tab and type a new name, or right-click the worksheet tab and select Rename from the menu.

**TASK 3: To Rename Worksheets**

**1** Place the insertion point directly over the Sheet1 worksheet tab.

**2** Right-click.

**3** Select Rename from the shortcut menu.

**4** Type **North**. The worksheet tab is renamed, as shown in Figure 2.6.

FIGURE 2.6

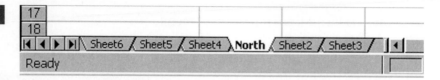

**5** Double-click the Sheet2 tab.

**6** Type **South** as the worksheet name.

**7** Rename the Sheet3, Sheet4, and Sheet5 tabs **East**, **West**, and **Sales Summary**, respectively. Your worksheet appears as shown in Figure 2.7.

FIGURE 2.7

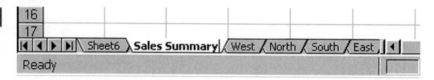

**8** Press (ENTER) to accept the last tab name. Save the workbook.

> **TIP** You cannot revert to a previous worksheet tab name using Undo.

## Deleting Worksheets

As you might expect, there will be times when you will need to delete worksheets from a workbook. This is a destructive task, and once you delete a worksheet and then save the workbook, there is no way to recover the deleted sheet. Before deleting a worksheet, Excel will verify your intent to do so.

**TASK 4: To Delete a Worksheet**

**1** Select the Sheet6 tab by clicking it.

**2** Select Delete Sheet from the Edit menu, as shown in Figure 2.8.

**FIGURE 2.8**

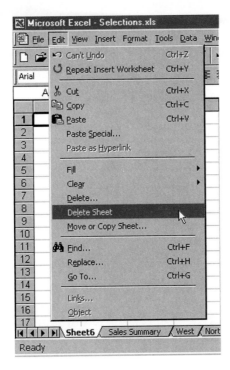

③ The dialog box shown in Figure 2.9 appears. Click OK to permanently delete the worksheet.

**FIGURE 2.9**

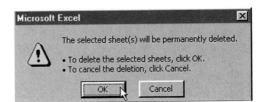

④ The worksheet has now been deleted from the workbook. Save your changes.

> **TIP** You can also delete a worksheet by right-clicking the worksheet tab and selecting Delete from the shortcut menu. If you ever inadvertently delete a worksheet that you need, close the file without saving the workbook, and then reopen the file.

## Repositioning Worksheets in a Workbook

In Excel, you can easily change the position of a worksheet in a workbook. You may need to do this when the order of the worksheets represents some logical order, such as fiscal quarters, days, or months. At other times, a specific order is desired to assist users in navigating among worksheets using the controls.

**TASK 5:** To Change the Order of Worksheet Tabs

**1** Click the West worksheet tab to select it.

**2** Hold down the left mouse button and drag the worksheet tab to the right of the East worksheet. Notice the icon next to the mouse pointer indicating that a move operation is in progress, and the pointer displaying the new worksheet position, as shown Figure 2.10.

**FIGURE 2.10**

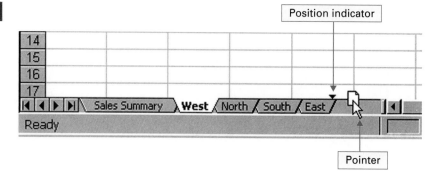

Position indicator

Pointer

**3** Release the left mouse button. The worksheet tabs are now reordered, as shown in Figure 2.11.

**FIGURE 2.11**

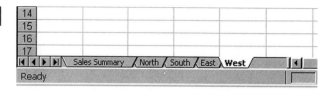

**TIP** You can also change the position of worksheets by selecting Move or Copy Sheet from the Edit menu, or by right-clicking the worksheet tab and selecting Move or Copy.

**4** Save the workbook.

## Check Point

Can you remember two methods for renaming worksheets and the procedure for changing their position in a workbook? You can rename worksheet tabs by double-clicking and right-clicking. You can quickly reposition worksheets in a workbook using drag-and-drop.

## Editing Worksheet Data

When you are constructing electronic workbooks, you often must enter additional data or change the location of existing data in worksheets. Editing is distinct from formatting: editing includes changing workbook data by copying, moving, or revising text, numbers, and formulas. Formatting, which you will learn in Project 3, changes the way workbook data appears for display and printing, without changing the underlying data.

## Editing Worksheets by Copying and Moving Data

When constructing a 3-D workbook it is often possible to enter data in one location and then copy it to additional locations. For example, the column headings in the range B4 to F4 and the department headings in A4 to A16 will be the same for the regional worksheets. The department headings will also appear in the Sales Summary worksheet.

### Copying Worksheet Data

You can easily complete the structure of your workbook by copying the existing text labels. Before copying data, you must **select**, or highlight, the data you want to copy. The data you select is a **range** consisting of one or more cells. The ranges you select can include **adjacent cells**, which is a continuous range, or **non-adjacent cells**, which is a selection of more than one continuous range.

A new feature in Office 2000 is the **Office Clipboard**. The Office Clipboard differs from the Windows Clipboard in that the Office Clipboard holds up to 12 items, where the Windows Clipboard holds only one item. When using the Office Clipboard, you can store up to 12 items from any Office application. Each item appears on the Office Clipboard, which you can display as a toolbar.

> **TIP**  For copy operations in Excel, you must work with a single adjacent range. For formatting procedures, you can work with non-adjacent selections.

**TASK 6:** <u>To Copy Ranges</u>

**1**  Click the North worksheet tab to make it the active sheet.

**2**  Click cell B4 and drag the selection through cell F4, as shown in Figure 2.12.

**FIGURE 2.12**

| 1R x 5C ▼ | = | 1st Qtr. | | | |
|---|---|---|---|---|---|
| A | B | C | D | E | F |
| 1 Selections Inc. | | | | | |
| 2 Quarterly Sales | | | | | |
| 3 | | | | | |
| 4 Department | 1st Qtr. | 2nd Qtr. | 3rd Qtr. | 4th Qtr. | Total |
| 5 Clothing | 405112 | 321670 | 401934 | 393714 | 1522430 |
| 6 Cosmetics | 373211 | 34812 | 29718 | 38248 | 475989 |

**3** Click the Copy 🖺 button on the Standard toolbar. You will notice a marquee surrounding the selection, indicating that data is now on the Office Clipboard. In addition, the status bar instructs you to select a destination for the copy procedure, as shown in Figure 2.13.

**FIGURE 2.13**

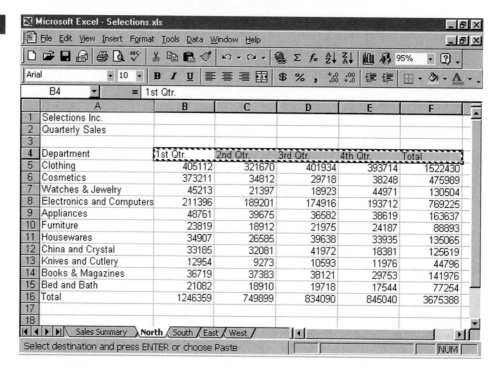

**4** Click the South worksheet tab and select cell B4. This indicates the upper-left cell of the selection that will be pasted into this worksheet.

**5** Press the (SHIFT) key and click the West worksheet tab. The range of worksheets shown in Figure 2.14 is now selected.

**FIGURE 2.14**

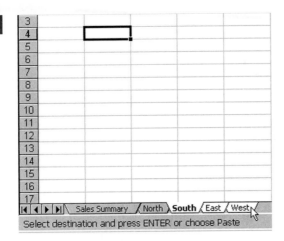

Select destination and press ENTER or choose Paste

**6** Click the Paste 📋 button on the Standard toolbar. The range has been pasted into each selected worksheet.

**7** Click the North worksheet tab, highlight the range A4 to A16, and click the Copy 📋 button. The Clipboard toolbar appears.

**8** Click the South worksheet tab and place the insertion point in cell A4.

**9** Press (SHIFT), click the West worksheet tab, and click the Paste 📋 button.

**10** Click the Sales Summary worksheet tab, select cell A4, and click Paste 📋.

**11** Click the Sales Summary worksheet tab, press the (CTRL) key, and click the South, East, and West worksheet tabs, respectively. The non-adjacent range of worksheets shown in Figure 2.15 is now selected.

**FIGURE 2.15**

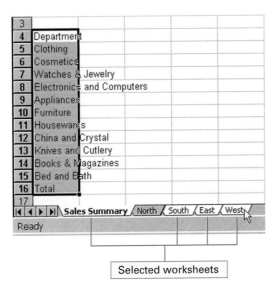

Selected worksheets

**12** Double-click the border between columns A and B. Column A for each worksheet is resized.

## Check Point

What does this double-click procedure do? It resizes column A in each selected worksheet to display the widest entry.

**13** Select cell A1, press the (SHIFT) key, and click the Sales Summary worksheet tab to deselect the highlighted range in the selected worksheets.

**14** Save the workbook.

### TASK 7: To Copy an Additional Range

**1** Select the range A1 to A2 in the North worksheet.

**2** Copy the range to the Clipboard.

> **TIP** The selected data is added to the Office Clipboard.

**3** Select the Sales Summary worksheet tab and place the insertion point in cell A1.

**4** Press the (CTRL) key and click the South, East, and West worksheet tabs.

**5** Paste the selection into the destination cells.

**6** Select cell A1, press the (SHIFT) key, and click the Sales Summary worksheet tab.

**7** Hide the Office Clipboard and save the workbook.

> **TIP** If you make a mistake while copying and pasting data, you can reverse your actions using Undo, as follows:
> - To undo recent actions one at a time, click Undo ↰.
> - To undo several actions at once, click the arrow next to Undo ↰ and select from the list. Microsoft Excel reverses the selected action and all actions above it.
> - To cancel an entry in a cell or the formula bar before you press (ENTER), press (ESC).
>
> If you change your mind, click Redo ↱.

## Break Point

If necessary you can save your file, exit Excel, and continue this project later.

## Moving Worksheet Data

Although you have successfully copied text labels, the structure of the workbook is not quite complete. To make the data on each worksheet easier to understand, you should add a text label for each regional worksheet, and for the Sales Summary sheet as well. To make room for this entry, you will need to move the existing worksheet data. You will add data to this row when you enter the remaining sales figures.

**TASK 8:   To Move Ranges**

**1**   Launch Excel if it is not currently running, and open the *Selections.xls* workbook.

**2**   Click the Sales Summary worksheet tab, press the (SHIFT) key, and click the West worksheet tab to select all worksheets in the workbook.

**3**   Highlight the range A4 to F16, as shown in Figure 2.16.

> **TIP**   The word *Group* in the title bar indicates that your actions will be applied to multiple worksheets.

**FIGURE 2.16**

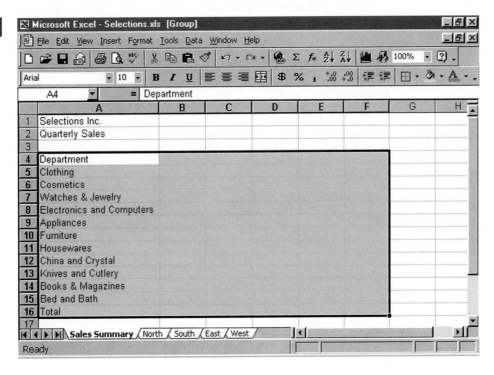

**4**   Point to any border of the selection and click with the left mouse button.

**5**   Drag the selection down one row, as shown in Figure 2.17. As you drag, notice the shaded border surrounding the selection you are moving, and the verification of the range you are currently moving.

**FIGURE 2.17**

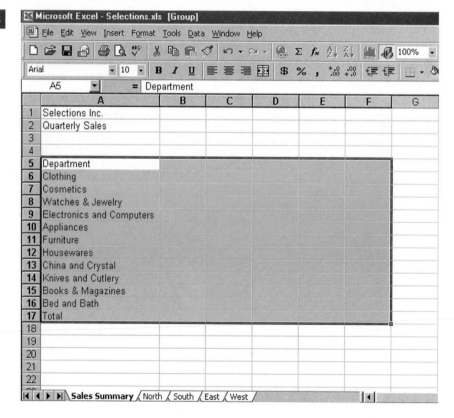

| 3 | | | | |
|---|---|---|---|---|
| 4 | Department | | A5:F17 | |
| 5 | Clothing | | | |
| 6 | Cosmetics | | | |
| 7 | Watches & Jewelry | | | |
| 8 | Electronics and Computers | | | |
| 9 | Appliances | | | |
| 10 | Furniture | | | |
| 11 | Housewares | | | |
| 12 | China and Crystal | | | |
| 13 | Knives and Cutlery | | | |
| 14 | Books & Magazines | | | |
| 15 | Bed and Bath | | | |
| 16 | Total | | | |
| 17 | | | | |
| 18 | | | | |
| 19 | | | | |

**6** Drop the selection in its new location by releasing the mouse button. The range of cells has been moved, as shown in Figure 2.18. The range A4:F16 on each of the selected worksheets appears in this new location.

**FIGURE 2.18**

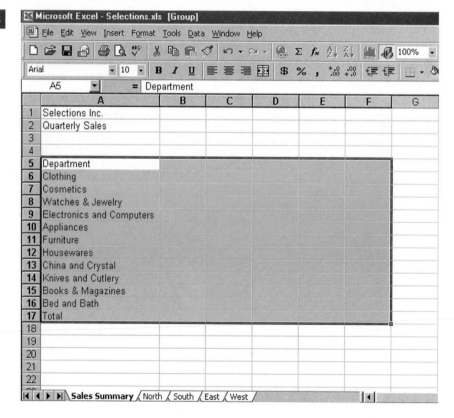

**7** Select cell A1, press the (SHIFT) key, and click the Sales Summary worksheet tab to deselect the worksheet selection.

**8** Save the workbook.

# Editing Worksheets by Revising Existing Data

Another common workbook editing task is revising existing worksheet data. To edit existing data you highlight the cell and either type a new value and press (ENTER), or use the formula bar to change the existing data. In your workbook for Selections, Inc., the product descriptions are inconsistent in the use of the word *and* in the description, a problem that can quickly be remedied.

**TASK 9:   To Revise Existing Worksheet Data**

**1** Select cell A9 of the Sales Summary worksheet.

**2** Press the (SHIFT) key and click the West worksheet tab to select all worksheets in the workbook. Release the (SHIFT) key after making the selection.

## Check Point

Why in this case are you selecting each worksheet in the workbook? Because the text labels requiring revision appear on every worksheet.

**3** Select Replace from the Edit menu. The Replace dialog box appears.

**4** Type **and** in the Find What: text box and **&** in the Replace with: text box, as shown in Figure 2.19.

**FIGURE 2.19**

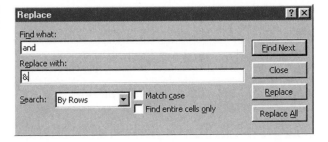

**5** Click the Replace All button. The replacement is made for each worksheet in the workbook.

**6** Click the North worksheet tab and select cell A1 to verify the changes. The worksheet appears, as shown in Figure 2.20.

**FIGURE 2.20**

| | A | B | C | D | E | F | G | H | I |
|---|---|---|---|---|---|---|---|---|---|
| 1 | Selections Inc. | | | | | | | | |
| 2 | Quarterly Sales | | | | | | | | |
| 3 | North Region | | | | | | | | |
| 4 | | | | | | | | | |
| 5 | Department | 1st Qtr. | 2nd Qtr. | 3rd Qtr. | 4th Qtr. | Total | | | |
| 6 | Clothing | 405112 | 321670 | 401934 | 393714 | 1522430 | | | |
| 7 | Cosmetics | 373211 | 34812 | 29718 | 38248 | 475989 | | | |
| 8 | Watches & Jewelry | 45213 | 21397 | 18923 | 44971 | 130504 | | | |
| 9 | Electronics & Computers | 211396 | 189201 | 174916 | 193712 | 769225 | | | |
| 10 | Appliances | 48761 | 39675 | 36582 | 38619 | 163637 | | | |
| 11 | Furniture | 23819 | 18912 | 21975 | 24187 | 88893 | | | |
| 12 | Housewares | 34907 | 26585 | 39638 | 33935 | 135065 | | | |
| 13 | China & Crystal | 33185 | 32081 | 41972 | 18381 | 125619 | | | |
| 14 | Knives & Cutlery | 12954 | 9273 | 10593 | 11976 | 44796 | | | |
| 15 | Books & Magazines | 36719 | 37383 | 38121 | 29753 | 141976 | | | |
| 16 | Bed & Bath | 21082 | 18910 | 19718 | 17544 | 77254 | | | |
| 17 | Total | 1246359 | 749899 | 834090 | 845040 | 3675388 | | | |
| 18 | | | | | | | | | |
| 19 | | | | | | | | | |

**7** Save the workbook.

# Entering Additional Text and Number Data

You are now ready to complete the workbook structure by entering the remaining text labels. Then you will enter sales figures for the South, East, and West sales regions. Once these tasks are complete, you will be ready to enter the remaining formulas.

## TASK 10: To Enter Additional Text and Numeric Data

**1** Type **North Region, South Region, East Region, West Region,** and **Total** in cells B3 through F3 of the *Sales Summary* worksheet.

> **TIP** Remember that you can use ⬚ TAB ⬚ or the right directional arrow to move one cell to the right as you enter data into a worksheet.

**2** Select columns B through F and change the column widths to 11.00.

**3** Select cell A3 of the North worksheet, and type **North Region** as the text label.

**4** Type **South Region, East Region** and **West Region** in cell A3 of the South, East, and West worksheets, respectively.

**5** Change the column widths of columns B through F of the South, East, and West worksheets to 11.00.

## Checkpoint

How can you change all column widths simultaneously? First select the worksheets, then the columns, and then change the width of one column in the selection.

**6**  Using Figure 2.21 as a guide, enter the sales figures for the South region into the South worksheet.

FIGURE 2.21

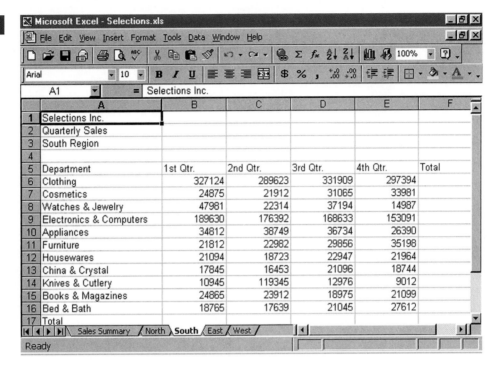

Microsoft Excel - Selections.xls

| | A | B | C | D | E | F |
|---|---|---|---|---|---|---|
| | A1 | = | Selections Inc. | | | |
| 1 | Selections Inc. | | | | | |
| 2 | Quarterly Sales | | | | | |
| 3 | South Region | | | | | |
| 4 | | | | | | |
| 5 | Department | 1st Qtr. | 2nd Qtr. | 3rd Qtr. | 4th Qtr. | Total |
| 6 | Clothing | 327124 | 289623 | 331909 | 297394 | |
| 7 | Cosmetics | 24875 | 21912 | 31065 | 33981 | |
| 8 | Watches & Jewelry | 47981 | 22314 | 37194 | 14987 | |
| 9 | Electronics & Computers | 189630 | 176392 | 168633 | 153091 | |
| 10 | Appliances | 34812 | 38749 | 36734 | 26390 | |
| 11 | Furniture | 21812 | 22982 | 29856 | 35198 | |
| 12 | Housewares | 21094 | 18723 | 22947 | 21964 | |
| 13 | China & Crystal | 17845 | 16453 | 21096 | 18744 | |
| 14 | Knives & Cutlery | 10945 | 119345 | 12976 | 9012 | |
| 15 | Books & Magazines | 24865 | 23912 | 18975 | 21099 | |
| 16 | Bed & Bath | 18765 | 17639 | 21045 | 27612 | |
| 17 | Total | | | | | |

Sales Summary / North \ **South** / East / West /

Ready

**7**  Enter the data shown in Figure 2.22 into the East worksheet.

FIGURE 2.22

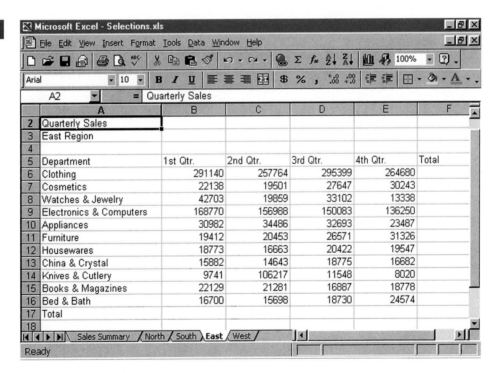

Microsoft Excel - Selections.xls

| | A | B | C | D | E | F |
|---|---|---|---|---|---|---|
| | A2 | = | Quarterly Sales | | | |
| 2 | Quarterly Sales | | | | | |
| 3 | East Region | | | | | |
| 4 | | | | | | |
| 5 | Department | 1st Qtr. | 2nd Qtr. | 3rd Qtr. | 4th Qtr. | Total |
| 6 | Clothing | 291140 | 257764 | 295399 | 264680 | |
| 7 | Cosmetics | 22138 | 19501 | 27647 | 30243 | |
| 8 | Watches & Jewelry | 42703 | 19859 | 33102 | 13338 | |
| 9 | Electronics & Computers | 168770 | 156988 | 150083 | 136250 | |
| 10 | Appliances | 30982 | 34486 | 32693 | 23487 | |
| 11 | Furniture | 19412 | 20453 | 26571 | 31326 | |
| 12 | Housewares | 18773 | 16663 | 20422 | 19547 | |
| 13 | China & Crystal | 15882 | 14643 | 18775 | 16682 | |
| 14 | Knives & Cutlery | 9741 | 106217 | 11548 | 8020 | |
| 15 | Books & Magazines | 22129 | 21281 | 16887 | 18778 | |
| 16 | Bed & Bath | 16700 | 15698 | 18730 | 24574 | |
| 17 | Total | | | | | |
| 18 | | | | | | |

Sales Summary / North / South \ **East** / West /

Ready

**8**  Enter the data shown in Figure 2.23 into the West worksheet.

FIGURE 2.23

| | A | B | C | D | E | F |
|---|---|---|---|---|---|---|
| 1 | Selections Inc. | | | | | |
| 2 | Quarterly Sales | | | | | |
| 3 | West Region | | | | | |
| 4 | | | | | | |
| 5 | Department | 1st Qtr. | 2nd Qtr. | 3rd Qtr. | 4th Qtr. | Total |
| 6 | Clothing | 338246 | 294546 | 301605 | 301111 | |
| 7 | Cosmetics | 25720 | 22284 | 28228 | 34405 | |
| 8 | Watches & Jewelry | 49612 | 22693 | 33798 | 15174 | |
| 9 | Electronics & Computers | 196077 | 179390 | 153236 | 155004 | |
| 10 | Appliances | 35995 | 39407 | 33380 | 26719 | |
| 11 | Furniture | 22553 | 23372 | 27130 | 35637 | |
| 12 | Housewares | 21811 | 19041 | 20851 | 22238 | |
| 13 | China & Crystal | 18451 | 16732 | 19169 | 18978 | |
| 14 | Knives & Cutlery | 11317 | 121373 | 11791 | 9124 | |
| 15 | Books & Magazines | 25710 | 24318 | 17242 | 21362 | |
| 16 | Bed & Bath | 19403 | 17938 | 19123 | 27957 | |
| 17 | Total | | | | | |

Sheet tabs: Sales Summary / North / South / East / **West**

**9** Save the workbook.

## Constructing Linking Formulas with 3-D References

You are almost finished designing the text, numbers, and formulas for the *Selections, Inc.* workbook. You do, however, have a few more formulas to create. You will first enter the necessary formulas containing the SUM function to total the sales figures by quarter and also by department for each sales region. After these are complete, you will add linking formulas to the workbook. Linking formulas are formulas containing 3-D references, which display data from one part of the workbook in another.

**TASK 11:** To Create Formulas Containing the SUM Function on Multiple Worksheets Simultaneously

**1** Select cell F6 of the South worksheet.

**2** Press the (SHIFT) key and click the West worksheet tab to select three worksheets.

**3** Type **=SUM(B6:E6)** in the cell.

**4** Click the Enter Formula ✓ button on the formula bar to accept the formula, as shown in Figure 2.24.

**FIGURE 2.24**

| SUM | ▼ | X | ✓ | = | =sum(B6:E6) |
| --- | --- | --- | --- | --- | --- |

| | B | | D | E | F | G |
| --- | --- | --- | --- | --- | --- | --- |
| 1 | | Enter | | | | |
| 2 | | | | | | |
| 3 | | | | | | |
| 4 | | | | | | |
| 5 | 1st Qtr. | 2nd Qtr. | 3rd Qtr. | 4th Qtr. | Total | |
| 6 | 327124 | 289623 | 331909 | 297394 | =sum(B6:E6) | |
| 7 | 24875 | 21912 | 31065 | 33981 | | |

**5** Use the fill handle to copy the formula through row 16, as shown in Figure 2.25.

**FIGURE 2.25**

| F6 | ▼ | | = | =SUM(B6:E6) |
| --- | --- | --- | --- | --- |

| | B | C | D | E | F | G |
| --- | --- | --- | --- | --- | --- | --- |
| 1 | | | | | | |
| 2 | | | | | | |
| 3 | | | | | | |
| 4 | | | | | | |
| 5 | 1st Qtr. | 2nd Qtr. | 3rd Qtr. | 4th Qtr. | Total | |
| 6 | 327124 | 289623 | 331909 | 297394 | 1246050 | |
| 7 | 24875 | 21912 | 31065 | 33981 | | |
| 8 | 47981 | 22314 | 37194 | 14987 | | |
| 9 | 189630 | 176392 | 168633 | 153091 | | |
| 10 | 34812 | 38749 | 36734 | 26390 | | |
| 11 | 21812 | 22982 | 29856 | 35198 | | |
| 12 | 21094 | 18723 | 22947 | 21964 | | |
| 13 | 17845 | 16453 | 21096 | 18744 | | |
| 14 | 10945 | 119345 | 12976 | 9012 | | |
| 15 | 24865 | 23912 | 18975 | 21099 | | |
| 16 | 18765 | 17639 | 21045 | 27612 | | |
| 17 | | | | | | |

**6** Release the mouse button, select the range B6:F17 and click the AutoSum button.

**7** Select cell A1 and click North worksheet tab.

**8** Save your workbook.

## TASK 12: Creating 3-D References

**1** Select the range F6:F16 in the North worksheet.

**2** Click Copy 🖹.

**3** Click the Sales Summary worksheet tab.

**4** Place the insertion point in cell B6.

**5** Choose Paste Special from the Edit menu, as shown in Figure 2.26.

FIGURE 2.26

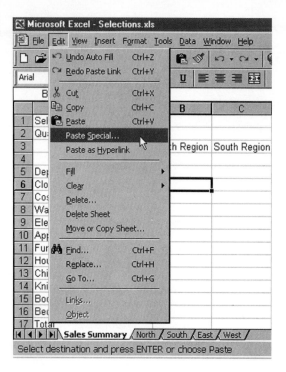

**6** The Paste Special dialog box appears. Click the Paste Link button, as shown in Figure 2.27.

FIGURE 2.27

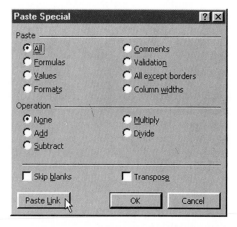

**TROUBLESHOOTING** Make sure you click the Paste Link button to create a linking formula!

**7** Repeat the procedure outlined in the preceding steps to create linking formulas between column F of the South, East, and West worksheets, respectively.

**TROUBLESHOOTING** Make sure you select Paste Special from the Edit menu and click the Paste Link button to create the linking formulas.

**8** When you are finished, the worksheet should display the values shown in Figure 2.28.

**TROUBLESHOOTING**  If your values differ, check the formulas and values you have entered for errors.

FIGURE 2.28

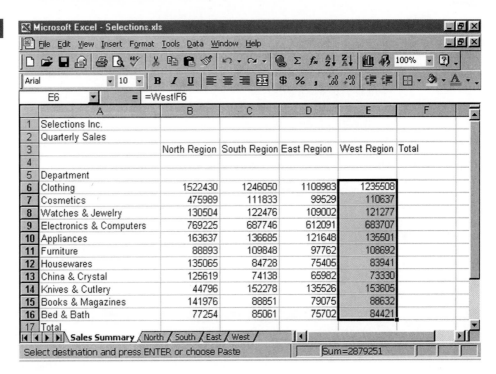

| | A | B | C | D | E | F |
|---|---|---|---|---|---|---|
| 1 | Selections Inc. | | | | | |
| 2 | Quarterly Sales | | | | | |
| 3 | | North Region | South Region | East Region | West Region | Total |
| 4 | | | | | | |
| 5 | Department | | | | | |
| 6 | Clothing | 1522430 | 1246050 | 1108983 | 1235508 | |
| 7 | Cosmetics | 475989 | 111833 | 99529 | 110637 | |
| 8 | Watches & Jewelry | 130504 | 122476 | 109002 | 121277 | |
| 9 | Electronics & Computers | 769225 | 687746 | 612091 | 683707 | |
| 10 | Appliances | 163637 | 136685 | 121648 | 135501 | |
| 11 | Furniture | 88893 | 109848 | 97762 | 108692 | |
| 12 | Housewares | 135065 | 84728 | 75405 | 83941 | |
| 13 | China & Crystal | 125619 | 74138 | 65982 | 73330 | |
| 14 | Knives & Cutlery | 44796 | 152278 | 135526 | 153605 | |
| 15 | Books & Magazines | 141976 | 88851 | 79075 | 88632 | |
| 16 | Bed & Bath | 77254 | 85061 | 75702 | 84421 | |
| 17 | Total | | | | | |

Cell E6 = =West!F6

Sheet tabs: Sales Summary / North / South / East / West

Status bar: Select destination and press ENTER or choose Paste    Sum=2879251

**9**  Save the workbook.

Notice the syntax for the formula displayed in Figure 2.28. The formula begins with an equal sign, as all formulas do, but the cell reference is preceded by the name of the worksheet, followed by an exclamation point. This formula is a dynamic link; if the value in cell F6 of the West workbook changes, the correct value will be displayed here.

## Web Tip

In the previous task you linked data between Excel worksheets. For future reference, you can also share information between Excel and Access. If you do not need to update the data between applications, you can paste data between applications. See http://www.microsoft.com/ACCESSDEV/Articles/BuildApp/bapp11part1.htm#Integrating for more information.

## Entering Formulas to Sum the Sales Summary Data

To complete your workbook, you need to create formulas containing the SUM function in cells F6:F16 and B17:F17. You can complete this task by creating one formula in each range, and then use the fill handle to replicate it.

## TASK 13: Creating Formulas to Sum the Sales Summary Data

**1** Place the insertion point in cell F6 of the Sales Summary worksheet.

**2** Type **=SUM(B6:E6)**, and click the Enter Formula button to accept the formula.

> **TIP** In Excel, formulas are not case sensitive. You may enter formulas with upper or lower case letters.

**3** Using the fill handle, copy this formula through cell F16.

**4** Type **=SUM(B6:B16)** in cell B17 and press (ENTER).

**5** Use the fill handle to copy this formula through cell F17.

**6** Chance the width of columns B through F to 12.00.

**7** Select cell A1 and save the workbook. Your screen should now appear as shown in Figure 2.29.

**FIGURE 2.29**

Microsoft Excel - Selections.xls

File  Edit  View  Insert  Format  Tools  Data  Window  Help

Arial    10    B  I  U

A1    =    Selections Inc.

|  | A | B | C | D | E | F |
|---|---|---|---|---|---|---|
| 1 | Selections Inc. | | | | | |
| 2 | Quarterly Sales | | | | | |
| 3 | | North Region | South Region | East Region | West Region | Total |
| 4 | | | | | | |
| 5 | Department | | | | | |
| 6 | Clothing | 1522430 | 1246050 | 1108983 | 1235508 | 5112971 |
| 7 | Cosmetics | 475989 | 111833 | 99529 | 110637 | 797988 |
| 8 | Watches & Jewelry | 130504 | 122476 | 109002 | 121277 | 483259 |
| 9 | Electronics & Computers | 769225 | 687746 | 612091 | 683707 | 2752769 |
| 10 | Appliances | 163637 | 136685 | 121648 | 135501 | 557471 |
| 11 | Furniture | 88893 | 109848 | 97762 | 108692 | 405195 |
| 12 | Housewares | 135065 | 84728 | 75405 | 83941 | 379139 |
| 13 | China & Crystal | 125619 | 74138 | 65982 | 73330 | 339069 |
| 14 | Knives & Cutlery | 44796 | 152278 | 135526 | 153605 | 486205 |
| 15 | Books & Magazines | 141976 | 88851 | 79075 | 88632 | 398534 |
| 16 | Bed & Bath | 77254 | 85061 | 75702 | 84421 | 322438 |
| 17 | Total | 3675388 | 2899694 | 2580705 | 2879251 | 12035038 |

Sales Summary / North / South / East / West /

Ready

**8** Close the workbook and exit Excel.

# Summary and Exercises

## Summary

- Modifying a workbook's structure includes adding worksheets, deleting worksheets, and repositioning worksheets.
- You can rename worksheet tabs to identify each worksheet's contents.
- Editing includes additions and changes to the data contained in workbooks.
- 3-D linking formulas display results from one cell in another worksheet cell.

## Key Terms and Operations

### Key Terms

adjacent cells
Enter Formula button
linking formulas
non-adjacent cells
Office Clipboard

range
row header
select
selection
3-D workbook

### Operations

change the position of
   worksheets
copy ranges using the Office
   Clipboard
create formulas to total linked
   data
delete worksheets

insert linking formulas
insert worksheets into a
   workbook
move ranges
open a workbook
revise ranges

## Study Questions

### Multiple Choice

1. A workbook contains five worksheets. Which key would you press to select the first, third, and fifth worksheet in the workbook?
   a. (ENTER)
   b. (SHIFT)
   c. (DEL)
   d. (CTRL)

2. Which menu adds worksheets to a workbook?
   a. the Edit menu
   b. a shortcut menu
   c. the Insert menu
   d. b and c

3. Which statement is false?
   a. Once you delete a worksheet from a workbook, it cannot be restored.
   b. You can restore a deleted worksheet using the Undo menu.
   c. If you delete a worksheet from a workbook but do not update the file, you can open the old version and retain the deleted worksheet.
   d. Deleting worksheets is considered a destructive command.

4. You can easily reposition a worksheet in a workbook using
   a. the View menu.
   b. clicking and dragging.
   c. the File menu.
   d. a and b.

5. You can edit the contents of a cell using
   a. the View menu.
   b. the status bar.
   c. the formula bar.
   d. the (CTRL) key.

6. 3-D references always contain all but which of the following?
   a. an equal (=) sign
   b. an exclamation point (!)
   c. an ampersand (&)
   d. the sheet name

7. A linking formula creates which kind of link?
   a. dynamic
   b. static
   c. fixed
   d. movable

8. What happens if you delete a worksheet from a workbook and update the file?
   a. The workbook is irretrievably lost.
   b. The workbook can be restored using Undo.
   c. The worksheet is saved to a backup file.
   d. The workbook is renamed.

9. A selection that contains data from cell A1 to A5, and also from cell C10 to D10, is called a(n)
   a. adjacent selection.
   b. range.
   c. non-adjacent selection.
   d. linking formula.

10. 3-D references will always begin with
    a. an exclamation point.
    b. an asterisk.
    c. an ampersand.
    d. an equals sign.

## Short Answer

1. When you change the location of data in a worksheet, are you editing or formatting?

2. Which method quickly changes the location of a worksheet in a workbook?

3. 3-D references always include which character after the sheet name?

4. What does it mean if you see an exclamation point and a worksheet name in a formula?

5. Can a deleted worksheet be restored using Undo?

6. How can you quickly change the contents of a cell?

7. If you delete a worksheet but do not save the file, can you retrieve the worksheet?

8. To create a 3-D reference, which option under the Edit menu do you select?

9. What is a link?

10. How do you rename a worksheet tab without using a menu?

## Fill in the Blank

1. A _____ formula dynamically links data from one worksheet cell to another.

2. A linking formula contains the _____ character between the worksheet name and cell reference.

3. You can easily rename a worksheet tab by _____ and typing a new name.

4. To insert a worksheet into a workbook, select _____ from the Insert menu.

5. A selection of cells is called a _____.

6. In a(n) _____ range, the cell range is continuous.

7. In a(n) _____ range, the selection includes multiple ranges.

8. To select a non-adjacent range of worksheets, press the _____ key while you add each worksheet to the selection.

9. To select an adjacent range of worksheets, press the _____ key as you click each worksheet tab.

10. You can change the position of a worksheet in a workbook by _____ the worksheet tab to a new location.

## For Discussion

1. How does an adjacent selection differ from a non-adjacent selection?

2. How does editing differ from formatting?

3. Why might you want to select multiple worksheets when modifying workbooks?

4. What happens to the data in a 3-D reference if the source data changes?

5. How do linking formulas differ from other formulas you have created?

# Hands-On Exercises

## Web Tip

If you cannot obtain a copy of these files from your instructor, visit the SELECT Web site at http://www.prenhall.com/select.

## 1. Adding a Worksheet to the Java Sales Workbook

Angie Stover has asked you to add a summary worksheet to the Java Sales workbook you created in Project 1. Using the procedures you learned in this project, create the structure of the Sales Summary worksheet. The additional worksheet is shown in Figure 2.30.

**FIGURE 2.30**

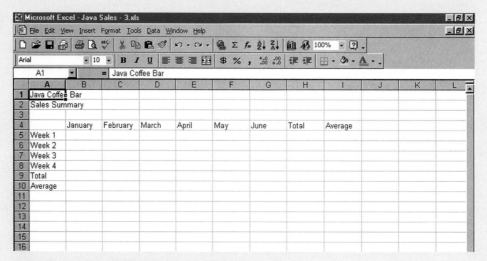

**Sales Summary worksheet for Java Sales**

1. Launch Excel if it is not currently running.
2. Open the *Java Sales—2.xls* workbook in the Java Bar folder on your disk.
3. Rename the Sheet3 tab as *Sales Summary*.
4. Reposition the Sales Summary worksheet so it appears at the first sheet in the workbook.
5. Add the text labels shown in Figure 2.30.
6. Save the workbook as *Java Sales—3.xls.*

## 2. Adding Linking Formulas to the Sales Summary Worksheet

In this exercise you will link formulas to the Sales Summary worksheet that you added to the Java Sales workbook in the previous exercise. When you finish adding these formulas, the Sales Summary worksheet appears as shown in Figure 2.31.

**FIGURE 2.31**

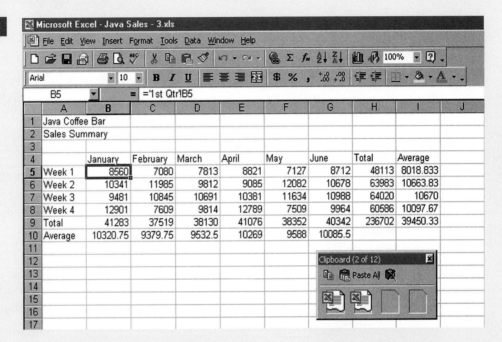

1. Open the *Java Sales—3.xls* workbook, if it is not currently open.
2. Choose Toolbars from the View menu, and select Clipboard.
3. Copy the range the range B5:D8 in the 1st Qtr worksheet. The selection appears on the Office Clipboard, as shown in Figure 2.32.

**FIGURE 2.32**

TIP   As you add copy additional items, they will be added to the Office Clipboard.

4. Use Paste Special, Paste Link to paste this data beginning in cell B5 of the Sales Summary worksheet.
5. Repeat this procedure to paste the sales figures from April, May, and June to the Sales Summary worksheet. Make sure you create linking formulas!

6. Create the necessary formulas to calculate the total and average weekly and monthly data.

7. Save the workbook as *Java Sales—4.xls*.

8. Close the workbook.

# On Your Own Exercises

## 1. Summarizing a List of Web Sites

Open the *Financial Sites.xls* workbook you created in Project 1. Edit the workbook so it contains four additional sites. Save the workbook to the Investments folder with the name *Financial Sites 2.xls*.

## 2. Creating a Class Schedule

Open the *Class Schedule.xls* workbook you created in Project 1. Add a summary page at the beginning of the workbook that summarizes your class schedule by day. Include linking formulas to list the class data. Save the workbook as *Class Schedule—By Day.xls*.

## 3. Create a Time Card

Open the *Time Card.xls* workbook. Add payroll data from an additional week, and then create a worksheet that summarizes the gross pay information for each week. Save the workbook as *Time Cards—Weekly Summary.xls*.

## 4. Creating an Address List in Excel

Open the *Address.xls* workbook. Add three professional contacts. Then create two additional worksheets for listing the personal versus professional contacts on two separate worksheet plys. Save the workbook as *Updated Addresses.xls*.

## 5. Calculating the Minimum Value in a Range

Open the file *January—update1.xls* you created in Project 1.

## Web Tip

If you cannot obtain a copy from your instructor, visit the SELECT Web site at http://www.prenhall.com/select to download a copy.

Modify the worksheet so that it summarizes the minimum value for each department on a separate worksheet in the workbook. Save the updated workbook as *January—Update 2.xls*.

## 6. Modifying a "What-If" Analysis

Open the workbook named *Updated Utility Costs.xls* from your network or floppy disk.

Modify the worksheet so that it displays a summary of the 10% and 15% utility price increase estimates. Save the updated workbook to your Personal folder as *Summary of Updated Utility Costs.xls*.

# Formatting Worksheets and Workbooks

**N**ow that you have completed the structure of the Selections Sales Summary workbook, it is time to enhance its appearance by applying formats to the cells. Cell formats make it easier to interpret the data in a worksheet, and include tasks such as changing the format of numeric data, adding borders around specific cells, and applying shading to highlight important elements.

## Objectives

After completing this project, you will be able to:

➤ Apply number formats

➤ Apply font formats

➤ Change cell alignment

➤ Create and apply styles

➤ Work with rows and columns

➤ Format cells with borders and shading

➤ Use the Web Page Preview

## Running Case

When you complete this project, the Selections Sales Summary workbook will be ready to publish to the company's corporate Intranet. Mr. Traylor has reviewed your most recent revisions to the Selections, Inc. Sales Summary workbook. He agrees that the structure is sound, and now wants you to format the workbook so it is more visually appealing. Specifically, Mr. Traylor wants all currency values to be displayed as such, with no decimal places.

# The Challenge

For consistency with current reports, Mr. Traylor wants each regional worksheet to look like accounting "green bar" paper, and the Sales Summary sheet to utilize shading, borders, and font styles appropriate for the Web.

# The Strategy

Excel includes numerous features and tools for simplifying formatting. Since the four regional worksheets share a common structure, you can apply formats to the North worksheet, and then copy these formats to each additional regional worksheet. For the Sales Summary worksheet, you will want to think about fonts, borders, and shading options that will display well in a Web browser. Using the Web preview, you can see how your formats will display in a browser. Figure 3.1 displays the Sales Summary worksheet, and Figure 3.2 the North regional sales worksheet, as they will appear prior to exporting to the Web.

**FIGURE 3.1**

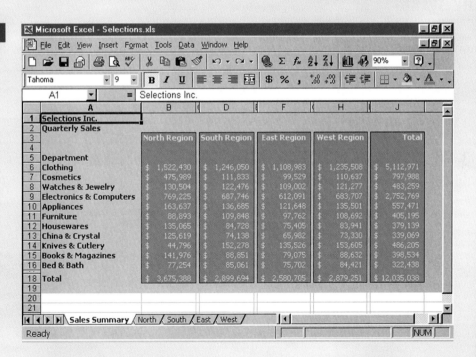

FIGURE 3.2

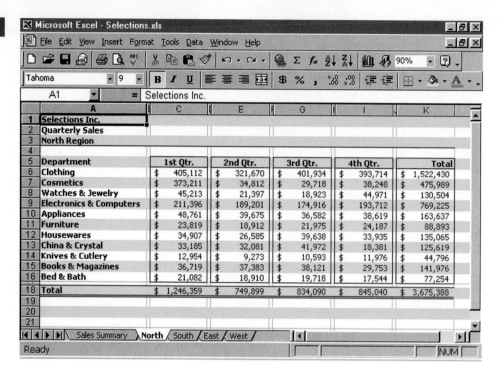

# The Setup

Launch Microsoft Excel and select the Excel settings listed in Table 3.1. This will ensure that your screen matches the illustrations and that the tasks in this project function as described.

### Table 3.1

| Location | Make these settings: |
|---|---|
| **Office Shortcut Bar** | Right-click the Office icon on the shortcut bar and click Exit. |
| **Office Assistant** | Hide the Assistant. |
| **Tools, Customize** | Click the Options tab and deselect the option to show recently used menu commands first. Deselect the option to display the Standard and Formatting toolbars on one row. |
| **Tools, Options** | Click the Edit tab and select Move selection after Enter. |
| **View, Formula Bar** | Display the formula bar. |
| **View, Status Bar** | Display the status bar. |
| **View, Normal** | View the workbook in Normal view. |
| **Maximize** | Maximize the application and workbook windows. |
| **File, Open** | Open the *Selections.xls* workbook. |

## About Worksheet Formats

The formats you apply to Excel worksheets communicate much to those who view your data. Using appropriate formats portrays excellence and professionalism. Bad formatting is like bad Web page design—it can send the wrong message.

Formatting in Excel is a simple task. To make text stand out, you can format all of the text in a cell or only selected characters. To distinguish between different types of information in a worksheet, you can apply borders to cells, shade cells with a background color, or shade cells with a color pattern. You can use number formats to change the appearance of numbers, including dates and times, without changing the number behind the appearance. Finally, if your data is in a list, there are several ways to quickly format the list by using AutoFormats, styles, and the Format Painter button.

## Formatting Numbers

Since the primary data in Excel workbooks tend to be numbers, let's start enhancing the Selections workbook by changing the number formats. **Number formats** change the appearance of numbers, including dates and times, without changing the underlying data. You can apply some number formats using tools such as the Currency Style button, which formats a selection in **currency style**. Currency style formats a number with a dollar sign and two places to the right of the decimal point.

**TASK 1:**   To Apply Number Formats

**1** Click the Sales Summary worksheet tab if it is not currently the active sheet.

**2** Select the range B6:F17.

**3** Click the Currency Style button $ on the Formatting toolbar. The values are displayed in currency style, as shown in Figure 3.3.

FIGURE 3.3

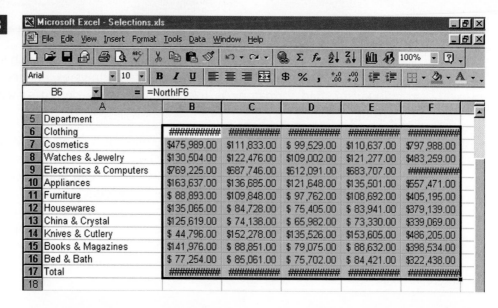

| | A | B | C | D | E | F |
|---|---|---|---|---|---|---|
| 5 | Department | | | | | |
| 6 | Clothing | ########## | ########## | ########## | ########## | ########## |
| 7 | Cosmetics | $475,989.00 | $111,833.00 | $ 99,529.00 | $110,637.00 | $797,988.00 |
| 8 | Watches & Jewelry | $130,504.00 | $122,476.00 | $109,002.00 | $121,277.00 | $483,259.00 |
| 9 | Electronics & Computers | $769,225.00 | $687,746.00 | $612,091.00 | $683,707.00 | ########## |
| 10 | Appliances | $163,637.00 | $136,685.00 | $121,648.00 | $135,501.00 | $557,471.00 |
| 11 | Furniture | $ 88,893.00 | $109,848.00 | $ 97,762.00 | $108,692.00 | $405,195.00 |
| 12 | Housewares | $135,065.00 | $ 84,728.00 | $ 75,405.00 | $ 83,941.00 | $379,139.00 |
| 13 | China & Crystal | $125,619.00 | $ 74,138.00 | $ 65,982.00 | $ 73,330.00 | $339,069.00 |
| 14 | Knives & Cutlery | $ 44,796.00 | $152,278.00 | $135,526.00 | $153,605.00 | $486,205.00 |
| 15 | Books & Magazines | $141,976.00 | $ 88,851.00 | $ 79,075.00 | $ 88,632.00 | $398,534.00 |
| 16 | Bed & Bath | $ 77,254.00 | $ 85,061.00 | $ 75,702.00 | $ 84,421.00 | $322,438.00 |
| 17 | Total | ########## | ########## | ########## | ########## | ########## |
| 18 | | | | | | |

**TROUBLESHOOTING** You will notice that some cells display a series of pound signs (#). This indicates that these columns are too narrow to display the values in the cells as formatted. You can remedy this problem by either changing the cell format or adjusting the column width.

## Modifying Formats

When you apply formats, you may need to modify the results. By modifying the formats you just applied to the selected range, the values will display without resizing the columns.

TASK 2: To Modify Number Formats

**1** With the range B6:F17 of the Sales Summary worksheet selected, choose Cells from the Format menu.

**2** Click the Number tab in the Format Cells dialog box, if it is not active.

**3** The format displays values with two places to the right of the decimal point. Click the down arrow at the bottom of the text box displaying the decimal value twice. The value changes to 0, as shown in Figure 3.4.

**FIGURE 3.4**

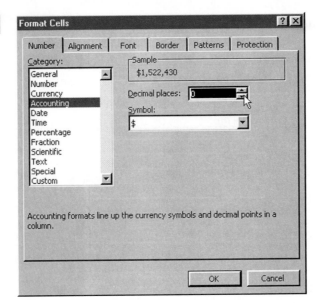

④ Click OK. Your worksheet now looks similar to the one displayed in Figure 3.5.

**FIGURE 3.5**

| | A | B | C | D | E | F |
|---|---|---|---|---|---|---|
| 5 | Department | | | | | |
| 6 | Clothing | $ 1,522,430 | $ 1,246,050 | $ 1,108,983 | $ 1,235,508 | $ 5,112,971 |
| 7 | Cosmetics | $ 475,989 | $ 111,833 | $ 99,529 | $ 110,637 | $ 797,988 |
| 8 | Watches & Jewelry | $ 130,504 | $ 122,476 | $ 109,002 | $ 121,277 | $ 483,259 |
| 9 | Electronics & Computers | $ 769,225 | $ 687,746 | $ 612,091 | $ 683,707 | $ 2,752,769 |
| 10 | Appliances | $ 163,637 | $ 136,685 | $ 121,648 | $ 135,501 | $ 557,471 |
| 11 | Furniture | $ 88,893 | $ 109,848 | $ 97,762 | $ 108,692 | $ 405,195 |
| 12 | Housewares | $ 135,065 | $ 84,728 | $ 75,405 | $ 83,941 | $ 379,139 |
| 13 | China & Crystal | $ 125,619 | $ 74,138 | $ 65,982 | $ 73,330 | $ 339,069 |
| 14 | Knives & Cutlery | $ 44,796 | $ 152,278 | $ 135,526 | $ 153,605 | $ 486,205 |
| 15 | Books & Magazines | $ 141,976 | $ 88,851 | $ 79,075 | $ 88,632 | $ 398,534 |
| 16 | Bed & Bath | $ 77,254 | $ 85,061 | $ 75,702 | $ 84,421 | $ 322,438 |
| 17 | Total | $ 3,675,388 | $ 2,899,694 | $ 2,580,705 | $ 2,879,251 | $12,035,038 |
| 18 | | | | | | |

⑤ Save the workbook.

## Copying Formats

Once you define the formats for a range of cells, you can copy these formats to other cells in the worksheet or workbook. The ***Format Painter*** is one tool you can use to quickly copy formats from one cell to others.

**TASK 3:**   To Copy Cell Formats Using the Format Painter

① Select cell B6 in the Sales Summary worksheet.

② Click the Format Painter button 🖌 on the Formatting toolbar.

**3** Select cells B6:F17 of the North worksheet, as shown in Figure 3.6.

**FIGURE 3.6**

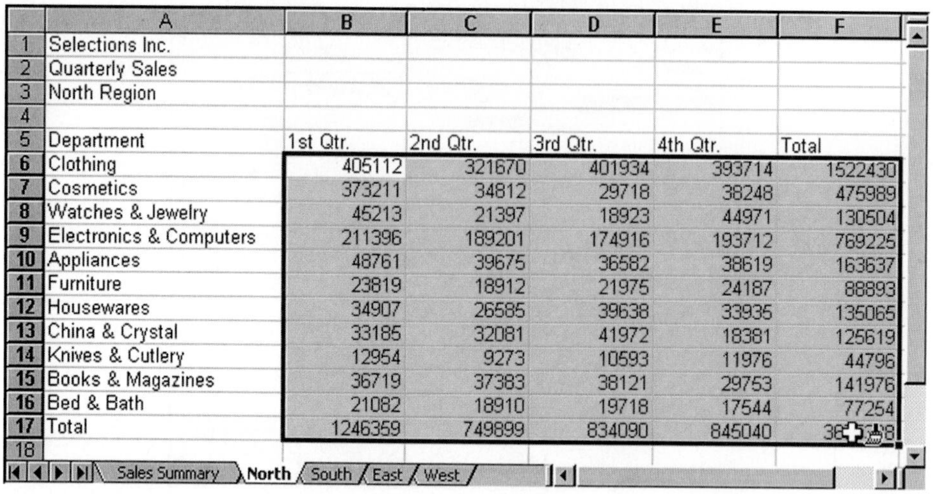

| | A | B | C | D | E | F |
|---|---|---|---|---|---|---|
| 1 | Selections Inc. | | | | | |
| 2 | Quarterly Sales | | | | | |
| 3 | North Region | | | | | |
| 4 | | | | | | |
| 5 | Department | 1st Qtr. | 2nd Qtr. | 3rd Qtr. | 4th Qtr. | Total |
| 6 | Clothing | 405112 | 321670 | 401934 | 393714 | 1522430 |
| 7 | Cosmetics | 373211 | 34812 | 29718 | 38248 | 475989 |
| 8 | Watches & Jewelry | 45213 | 21397 | 18923 | 44971 | 130504 |
| 9 | Electronics & Computers | 211396 | 189201 | 174916 | 193712 | 769225 |
| 10 | Appliances | 48761 | 39675 | 36582 | 38619 | 163637 |
| 11 | Furniture | 23819 | 18912 | 21975 | 24187 | 88893 |
| 12 | Housewares | 34907 | 26585 | 39638 | 33935 | 135065 |
| 13 | China & Crystal | 33185 | 32081 | 41972 | 18381 | 125619 |
| 14 | Knives & Cutlery | 12954 | 9273 | 10593 | 11976 | 44796 |
| 15 | Books & Magazines | 36719 | 37383 | 38121 | 29753 | 141976 |
| 16 | Bed & Bath | 21082 | 18910 | 19718 | 17544 | 77254 |
| 17 | Total | 1246359 | 749899 | 834090 | 845040 | 36⊡⊡8 |
| 18 | | | | | | |

Sales Summary \ **North** / South / East / West /

**TIP** Notice the appearance of the insertion point, which now includes an icon of a paintbrush. The next cell you select will receive the formats of the cell that was active when you chose the Format Painter.

**4** Release the left mouse button. The currency format you copied is now applied to this range.

**5** Click the Format Painter button again.

**TIP** You can also double-click the Format Painter to apply a format to multiple selections.

**6** Select cells B6:F17 of the South worksheet and release the left mouse button.

**7** Using the procedures outlined in the preceding steps, copy these formats to the range B6:F17 of the East and West worksheets, respectively.

**8** Save your changes.

**TIP** You can also copy formats to multiple worksheets by selecting a range of worksheets, as you learned how to do in Project 2.

## Applying Font Formats

In Excel, font formats include the font face, style, size, and color. By changing the format of fonts, you can emphasize areas of the worksheet and categorize groups of data. To apply font formats, select the range of cells that you want to format. You can use the **Select All button**, which is the small rectangular button ▭ immediately above the Row 1 label and to the left of the Column A heading, to select every cell in the worksheet. The **Font box** on the Formatting toolbar displays the name of the current font, and the **Font Size box** displays the current font size. Use these boxes to change these font properties. You can change **cell alignment** using the left, center, and right align buttons on the Formatting toolbar.

## TASK 4:  To Apply Font Formats and Change Cell Alignment

**1** Select the Sales Summary worksheet tab.

**2** Select all worksheets in the workbook.

 **Check Point**

How do you select all worksheets in the workbook? You can select all worksheets by selecting the tab for the first worksheet in a range, pressing the (SHIFT) key, and clicking the last tab in the range of worksheets you want to select.

**3** Press the Select All button, shown in Figure 3.7. This selects every cell in the worksheet range.

| FIGURE 3.7 |
|---|

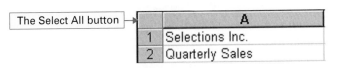

The Select All button ➝

|   | A |
|---|---|
| 1 | Selections Inc. |
| 2 | Quarterly Sales |

**4** Click the drop-down arrow in the Font box to display the current fonts, as shown in Figure 3.8.

**TROUBLESHOOTING**  The fonts displayed depend on your computer's settings. You may see different fonts in this list.

**FIGURE 3.8**

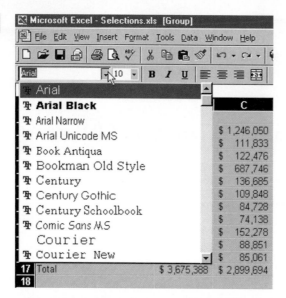

**5** Scroll down the list and select the Tahoma font by clicking it with the left mouse button, as shown in Figure 3.9.

**FIGURE 3.9**

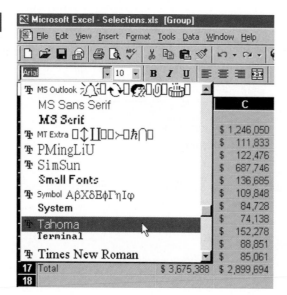

**6** Select 9 as the font size in the Font Size box.

**7** Click the heading in column A to select it, and change the column width to 21.00.

**8** Click the heading for column B, hold down the (SHIFT) key, and click the column F heading to select this range of columns. Change their width to 12.00.

**9** Press the (SHIFT) key and click the Sales Summary worksheet tab to deselect the regional worksheets.

**10** Highlight the range A1:F3 and click the Bold **B** button on the Formatting toolbar.

**11** Highlight the range A5:A17 and click Bold **B**.

**12** Select cells B3:E3 and click the Center Align button on the Formatting toolbar, as shown in Figure 3.10. Select cell F3 and click Right Align ≡.

**FIGURE 3.10**

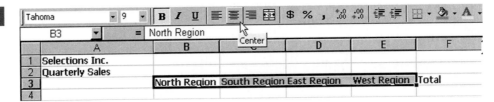

**13** Select the North through West worksheets and change the format of cells B5:F5 to Bold **B**.

**14** Change the alignment of cells B5:E5 to center aligned ≡, and cell F5 to right aligned ≡.

**15** Select cell A1 of the Sales Summary worksheet, and save your changes. The worksheet appears as shown in Figure 3.11.

**FIGURE 3.11**

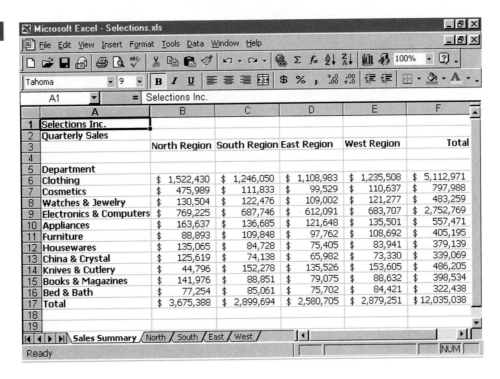

# Creating and Applying Styles

You will recall that Mr. Traylor wants each regional worksheet to look like accounting "green bar" paper. This means that you will need to change the **cell shading**, or the color that fills one or more cells, to green. The easiest way to accomplish this task will be to create a style. An Excel **style** is a collection of cell formats—font sizes, patterns, and alignments—that you apply and save as a group. Once a style is defined, it can be applied to additional cells or ranges.

You can shade the appropriate worksheet cells by first applying shading, and then creating and applying a style.

### TASK 5: Shading Worksheet Cells

**1** Select the North through West worksheets.

**2** Click the row heading for row 1, hold down the (CTRL) key, and select rows 3 and 5, as shown in Figure 3.12.

**FIGURE 3.12**

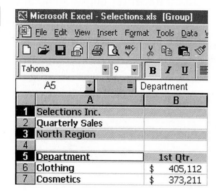

**TIP** By clicking the row heading, you will select a row. Using the (CTRL) key allows you to make a non-adjacent selection of multiple rows.

## Check Point

Why does the word *Group* appear in the title bar? This indicates that the current operation applies to a group of selected worksheets.

**3** Click the drop-down arrow on in the Fill Color button on the Formatting Toolbar.

**TROUBLESHOOTING** Make sure you click the drop-down arrow to see a list of available colors. If you click the button, the current fill color will be applied to the selection.

**4** Choose Light Green in the color list, as shown in Figure 3.13.

**FIGURE 3.13**

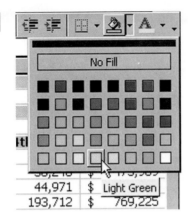

**⑤** Select cell A1. The first three odd rows in the selected worksheets are shaded, as shown in Figure 3.14.

**FIGURE 3.14**

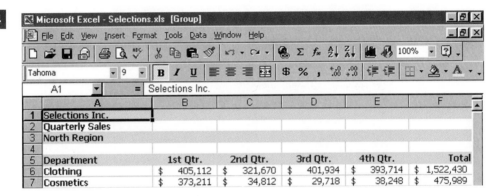

**TIP** The entire rows in the selected worksheets are shaded, since you used the row heading to select the entire row for each row in the selection.

**TASK 6:** To Create and Apply Styles

**①** Click the row heading for row 7.

**②** Click the Fill Color button to apply the Light Green shading to the row.

**TIP** The Fill Color button now displays Light Green as the active color.

**③** Choose Style from the Format menu, as shown in Figure 3.15.

FIGURE 3.15

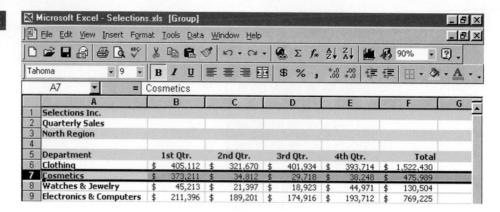

④ The Style dialog box appears. Select the options shown in Figure 3.16, type **GreenBar** as the style name in the name box, and click OK.

FIGURE 3.16

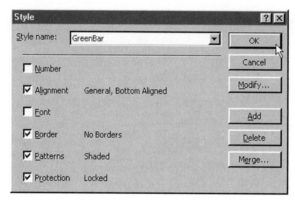

**Naming a style**

⑤ Select the row heading for row 9, press the (CTRL) key, and click the row headers for rows 11, 13, 15, 17, and 19.

⑥ Choose Style from the Format menu, click the drop-down list button on the Style name: text box, and choose GreenBar from the list of available styles by clicking the name with the left mouse button, as shown in Figure 3.17.

FIGURE 3.17

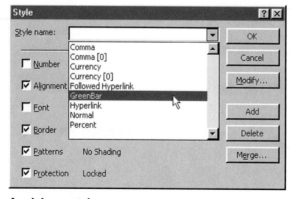

**Applying a style**

⑦ Click OK, and select cell A1. The style has been applied to the selected worksheets, as shown in Figure 3.18.

FIGURE 3.18

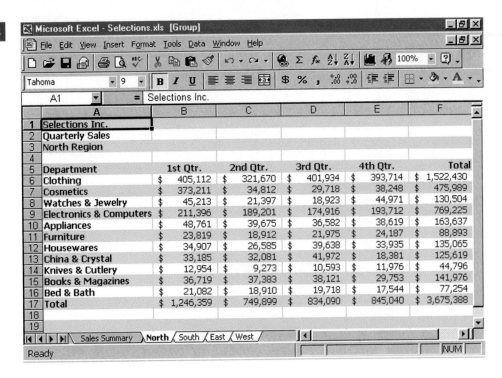

| | | A | B | C | D | E | F |
|---|---|---|---|---|---|---|---|
| 1 | | Selections Inc. | | | | | |
| 2 | | Quarterly Sales | | | | | |
| 3 | | North Region | | | | | |
| 4 | | | | | | | |
| 5 | | Department | 1st Qtr. | 2nd Qtr. | 3rd Qtr. | 4th Qtr. | Total |
| 6 | | Clothing | $ 405,112 | $ 321,670 | $ 401,934 | $ 393,714 | $ 1,522,430 |
| 7 | | Cosmetics | $ 373,211 | $ 34,812 | $ 29,718 | $ 38,248 | $ 475,989 |
| 8 | | Watches & Jewelry | $ 45,213 | $ 21,397 | $ 18,923 | $ 44,971 | $ 130,504 |
| 9 | | Electronics & Computers | $ 211,396 | $ 189,201 | $ 174,916 | $ 193,712 | $ 769,225 |
| 10 | | Appliances | $ 48,761 | $ 39,675 | $ 36,582 | $ 38,619 | $ 163,637 |
| 11 | | Furniture | $ 23,819 | $ 18,912 | $ 21,975 | $ 24,187 | $ 88,893 |
| 12 | | Housewares | $ 34,907 | $ 26,585 | $ 39,638 | $ 33,935 | $ 135,065 |
| 13 | | China & Crystal | $ 33,185 | $ 32,081 | $ 41,972 | $ 18,381 | $ 125,619 |
| 14 | | Knives & Cutlery | $ 12,954 | $ 9,273 | $ 10,593 | $ 11,976 | $ 44,796 |
| 15 | | Books & Magazines | $ 36,719 | $ 37,383 | $ 38,121 | $ 29,753 | $ 141,976 |
| 16 | | Bed & Bath | $ 21,082 | $ 18,910 | $ 19,718 | $ 17,544 | $ 77,254 |
| 17 | | Total | $ 1,246,359 | $ 749,899 | $ 834,090 | $ 845,040 | $ 3,675,388 |
| 18 | | | | | | | |
| 19 | | | | | | | |

**8** Save your changes.

## Web Tip

Did you know that it is common for accountants to use Excel for accounting? Visit http://www.accountingadvisors.com/exlinks.htm for examples of how accountants use Excel.

## Break Point

If necessary you can save your file, exit Excel, and continue this project later.

## Working with Rows and Columns

Your workbook is really taking shape! Before applying borders to selected cells, you can add additional rows and columns to enhance the look of the worksheets even more. By adding **dummy cells**, or cells that don't contain data but merely enhance appearance, you can separate worksheet areas that will be formatted with shading to accentuate the different worksheet areas.

## TASK 7:  To Insert Columns into Worksheets

**1** If necessary, launch Excel and open the *Selections.xls* workbook.

**2** Select the North through West worksheets, if they are not currently selected.

**3** Select column B and choose Columns from the Insert menu, as shown in Figure 3.19.

**FIGURE 3.19**

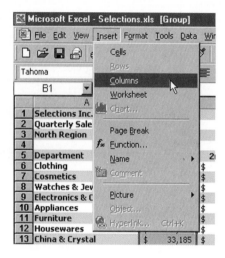

**4** Change the width of the column you just added to 0.5.

**5** Click inside the Zoom Control text box [100%] on the Standard toolbar, type **90** as the view percentage, and press (ENTER).

**6** Change the width of column A to 23.00.

> **TIP** Depending upon your monitor and screen resolution, the contents of Column A appear to spill over into column B at 90% zoom. This is not actually the case, but we are making this change to assist viewing the regional worksheets at this magnification.

**7** Add additional dummy columns between each column displaying the quarterly and total sales figures.

**8** Change the width of the columns you just added to 0.5.

**9** Save your changes. The workbook now looks similar to the one shown in Figure 3.20.

**FIGURE 3.20**

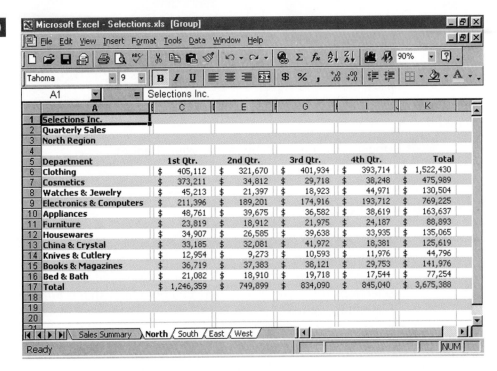

You may wonder what impact these dummy columns have upon the linking formulas in the Sales Summary worksheet. Since these formulas contain relative references to the source data, the formulas are updated automatically. To verify this, you can switch to the Sales Summary worksheet and check the formulas.

> **TIP** To delete a column, highlight the column you want to delete and choose Delete from the Edit menu.

## TASK 8: To Add a Row to the Selected Worksheets and Resize the Row

**1** Select the row heading for row 17.

**2** Choose Rows from the Insert menu. Excel adds a row to the worksheet.

**3** Place the insertion point on the border between the row headings for rows 17 and 18.

**4** Click the left mouse button and resize the row height to 4.50, as shown in Figure 3.21.

FIGURE 3.21

| 12 | Housewares | $ | 34,907 |
| 13 | China & Crystal | $ | 33,185 |
| 14 | Knives & Cutlery | $ | 12,954 |
| 15 | Height: 4.50 (6 pixels) | $ | 36,719 |
| 16 | Bed & Bath | $ | 21,082 |
| 18 | Total | $ | 1,246,359 |
| 19 | | | |

**5**    Update the workbook by saving your changes.

## Adding Borders to Cells

You can further enhance the appearance of Excel worksheets by adding borders to one or more cells. A **cell border** is a format that applies lines of various styles to one or more sides (top, bottom, left, right) of the active cell or selection. You can quickly apply cell borders with the **Borders button** on the Formatting toolbar.

**TASK 9:**    <u>To Apply Borders to Selected Cells</u>

**1**    Highlight the range C5:C16.

**2**    Click the drop-down list arrow on the Borders button ⊞▾ on the Formatting toolbar.

**3**    Choose the Outside Borders option, as shown in Figure 3.22.

FIGURE 3.22

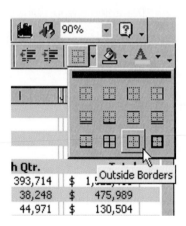

**4**    Highlight cell C5 and apply the Outside Borders.

**5**    Highlight the range C5:C16 and click the Format Painter button 🖌.

**6**    Apply the formats to the range E5:E16.

**7**    Repeat the procedure to apply the format to cells G5:G16 and I5:I16, respectively.

**8**    Highlight cells K5:K16 and apply the Outside Borders option.

**TIP** Since Outside Borders was the last format you applied, it is now the default, and you can simply click the Borders button to apply this format.

**9** Select cell K5 and apply the Outside Borders format. The workbook now appears as shown in Figure 3.23.

**FIGURE 3.23**

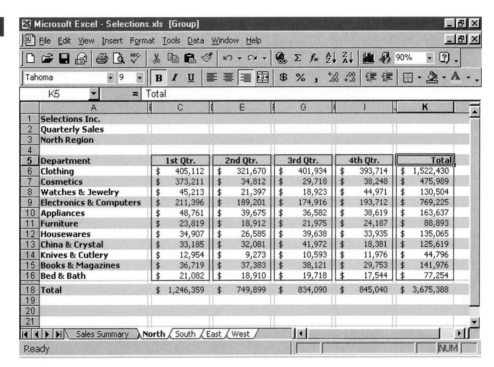

**10** Select cells A18:K18. Apply the Top and Double Bottom Border, shown in Figure 3.24, to the selection.

**FIGURE 3.24**

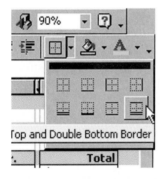

**11** Select the range A3:K3 and apply the Bottom Border style.

**12** Select cell A1.

**13** Save your changes.

**14** Click the Print Preview button. The worksheet appears as shown in Figure 3.25.

FIGURE 3.25

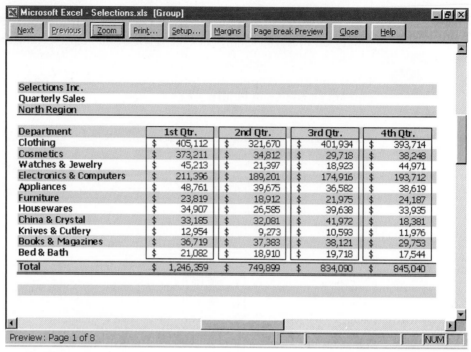

**Print Preview displaying worksheet formats**

**15** Click the Close button in the Print Preview window.

**TROUBLESHOOTING** You will notice that column K does not appear in the preview, and that the message in the status bar indicates that Excel will require 8 pages to print this data. In Project 4 you will learn how to change the page layout to landscape, so each regional worksheet will print on a single page.

## Applying Cell Formats to the Sales Summary Worksheet

The formats you have applied in this project have mostly been for the regional worksheets. Remember that Mr. Traylor wants you to format the Sales Summary worksheet for display on the World Wide Web. In the next task you will apply various formats to the Sales Summary worksheet.

**TASK 10:** To Apply Cell Formats to the Sales Summary Worksheet

**1** Click the Sales Summary worksheet to make it the active sheet.

## Check Point

Have any formats been applied to this worksheet? Yes, you have changed both the font and the number format for this sheet.

**2** Change the zoom magnification for the sheet to 90%.

**3** Change the alignment of cells B3:E3 to Center Align.

**4** Apply dummy columns between each regional column, and also before the Total column. Change the width of these columns to 0.5.

**5** Change the width of column A to 23.00.

**6** Apply a dummy row after row 16, and change the height of this row to 4.50.

**7** Select cells A1:K19 and apply Gray-25% as the shading for the selection.

> **TIP** Remember that you can easily change the fill color and grayscales of a selection by using the Fill Color button on the Formatting toolbar.

**8** Using the (CTRL) key, highlight the non-adjacent selection shown in Figure 3.26. Apply an outside border.

**FIGURE 3.26**

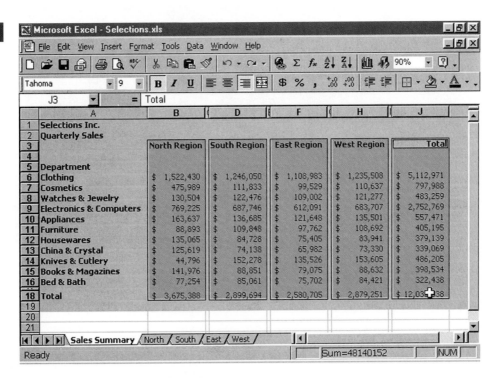

**TROUBLESHOOTING** Make sure you select the following ranges: B3:B18, D3:D18, F3:F18, H3:H18, and J3:J18.

**9** Apply Blue-Gray as the fill color for the selection.

**10** Click the drop-down list arrow on the Font button and select Light Yellow as the font color, as shown in Figure 3.27.

**FIGURE 3.27**

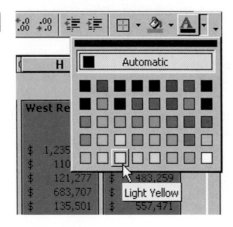

**11** Select cell A1.

**12** Save your changes. The worksheet appears, as shown in Figure 3.28.

**FIGURE 3.28**

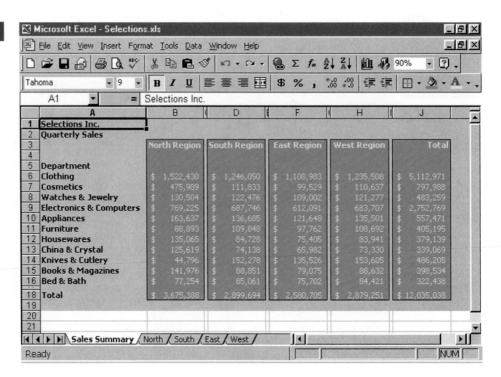

## Using the Web Page Preview

An exciting new feature in Office 2000 is ***Universal Document Viewing***. You can now save Office documents in HTML file format and retain the formatting features of your native Office file. By saving as HTML, you ensure that anyone with a Web browser can view your documents. Editing those documents is not a problem either because Office 2000 allows you to open them again in the original Office program without losing any of the rich functionality of the Office file formats.

**TASK 11:   To Use Excel's Web Page Preview**

**1**   Select Web Page Preview from the File menu. Microsoft Internet Explorer or a similar Web browser generates a preview document for your workbook, as shown in Figure 3.29.

**FIGURE 3.29**

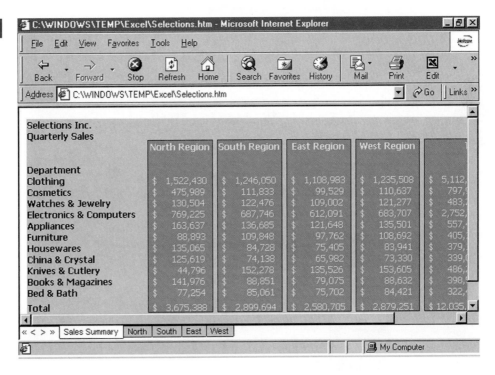

**2**   Click the North tab in the lower-left corner of the browser window. The browser now displays an HTML preview for the North worksheet, as shown in Figure 3.30.

FIGURE 3.30

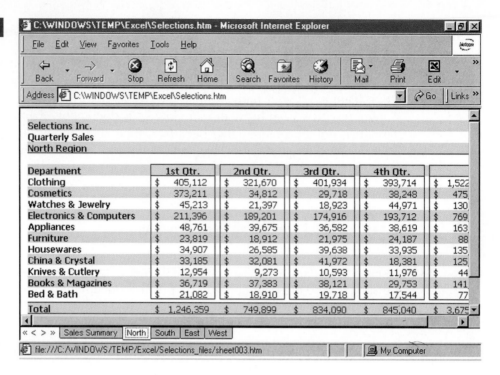

C:\WINDOWS\TEMP\Excel\Selections.htm - Microsoft Internet Explorer

File   Edit   View   Favorites   Tools   Help

Back   Forward   Stop   Refresh   Home   Search   Favorites   History   Mail   Print   Edit

Address   C:\WINDOWS\TEMP\Excel\Selections.htm   Go   Links

Selections Inc.
Quarterly Sales
North Region

| Department | 1st Qtr. | 2nd Qtr. | 3rd Qtr. | 4th Qtr. | |
|---|---|---|---|---|---|
| Clothing | $ 405,112 | $ 321,670 | $ 401,934 | $ 393,714 | $ 1,522 |
| Cosmetics | $ 373,211 | $ 34,812 | $ 29,718 | $ 38,248 | $ 475, |
| Watches & Jewelry | $ 45,213 | $ 21,397 | $ 18,923 | $ 44,971 | $ 130, |
| Electronics & Computers | $ 211,396 | $ 189,201 | $ 174,916 | $ 193,712 | $ 769, |
| Appliances | $ 48,761 | $ 39,675 | $ 36,582 | $ 38,619 | $ 163, |
| Furniture | $ 23,819 | $ 18,912 | $ 21,975 | $ 24,187 | $ 88, |
| Housewares | $ 34,907 | $ 26,585 | $ 39,638 | $ 33,935 | $ 135, |
| China & Crystal | $ 33,185 | $ 32,081 | $ 41,972 | $ 18,381 | $ 125, |
| Knives & Cutlery | $ 12,954 | $ 9,273 | $ 10,593 | $ 11,976 | $ 44, |
| Books & Magazines | $ 36,719 | $ 37,383 | $ 38,121 | $ 29,753 | $ 141, |
| Bed & Bath | $ 21,082 | $ 18,910 | $ 19,718 | $ 17,544 | $ 77, |
| Total | $ 1,246,359 | $ 749,899 | $ 834,090 | $ 845,040 | $ 3,675 |

« < > »   Sales Summary   North   South   East   West

file:///C:/WINDOWS/TEMP/Excel/Selections_files/sheet003.htm   My Computer

**3** Close the browser.

## TASK 12: To Save the Workbook as HTML

**1** Choose Save As Web Page from the File menu.

**2** Accept the default file name and file location in the Save As dialog box by clicking Save, as shown in Figure 3.31.

FIGURE 3.31

Save As

Save in:   Selections   Tools ▾

History

My Documents

Desktop

Favorites

Web Folders

Save:   ⊙ Entire Workbook   ○ Selection: Sheet   Publish...
            □ Add interactivity

Page title:                                          Change Title...

File name:   Selections.htm                         💾 Save

Save as type:   Web Page (*.htm; *.html)            Cancel

**3** Close the workbook and exit Excel.

**TIP** You can verify the HTML document by opening it using your Web browser.

# Summary and Exercises

## Summary

- You can easily apply formats to numbers to make them easier to interpret.
- Font formats include size, style, and weight.
- You can easily change the alignment of data in one or more cells.
- A style is a set of formats that are stored with a name.
- Once you create a style, you can apply it to other selections.
- You can insert, delete, and resize the rows and columns in a worksheet.
- You can format cells by applying borders and shading.
- You can use the Web Page Preview to see how a worksheet will display if exported to the Web.

## Key Terms and Operations

### Key Terms

Borders button
cell alignment
cell border
cell shading
currency style
Font box

Font Size box
Format Painter
number formats
Select All button
style
Universal Document Viewing

### Operations

add borders to cells
apply font formats
apply number formats
apply styles
ahange cell alignment
copy number formats
create styles

insert columns
modify number formats
resize columns
save worksheets as HTML
shade worksheet cells
use Web Page Preview

## Study Questions

### Multiple Choice

1. Which of the following is not considered a number format?
   a. percent
   b. altitude
   c. scientific notation
   d. currency

2. Which cell alignment option is not supported by Excel?
   a. left
   b. center
   c. right
   d. justified

3. You use which menu to add columns to a worksheet?
   a. View
   b. File
   c. Insert
   d. Edit

4. If a range of cells is surrounded by a rectangle, the range contains which of the following?
   a. number formats
   b. shading
   c. text formats
   d. borders

5. Which formatting option changes the color of a cell?
   a. number formats
   b. text formats
   c. borders
   d. shading

6. If you change a cell to display two places to the right of the decimal and a percent symbol, what are you changing?
   a. cell alignment
   b. a number format
   c. a font format
   d. a cell's shading

7. Which screen element contains the tools you can use to change the display of data in cells?
   a. the Drawing toolbar
   b. the Standard toolbar
   c. the Format menu
   d. the formula bar

8. Which button copies formats from a selection to another cell or range?
   a. Copy
   b. Paste
   c. Paste Special
   d. Format Painter

9. Which of the following best describes a style?
   a. the number of decimal places a value displays
   b. the alignment of text in a cell
   c. a set of formatting characteristics
   d. a consistent background for worksheets

10. Which of the following is not a font format?
    a. size
    b. font face
    c. percent
    d. italics

## Short Answer

1. Which view displays worksheet data as it will appear when saved as HTML?

2. How can you easily store the formats from a cell or range?

3. Which format enhances cells or ranges using lines?

4. When you change the display of financial data to include a dollar sign, you are applying what kind of format?

5. Which formatting feature governs where data appears relative to the cell border?

6. Which format includes two places to the right of the decimal and a percent symbol?

7. Which menu should you use to add columns to a worksheet?

8. How do borders and shading differ?

9. How can you change font color?

10. How do you create a style?

## Fill in the Blank

1. A _____ surrounds a one or more cells to enhance appearance.

2. Currency format is one of many _____ formats.

3. You can save a series of formats as a _____.

4. Once you create a _____, the formats it contains can be applied to other worksheet ranges.

5. The _____ is a tool that allows you to copy formats from one location to another.

6. To insert rows into a worksheet, use the _____ menu.

7. Bold, italics, and alignment are examples of _____ formats.

8. The _____ displays worksheet data exactly as it will appear in a Web browser when saved as HTML.

9. Right is an example of _____.

10. When you add color to the background of a range, you are applying cell _____.

## For Discussion

1. What is a style? Why are styles useful?

2. List three font formats you can apply to a selection.

3. How does inserting columns into a worksheet differ from inserting worksheets into a workbook?

4. What is Web Page Preview? How does a Web Page Preview differ from a Print Preview?

5. List three common number formats.

# Hands-On Exercises

## 1. Indenting and Rotating Text

Excel supports indenting and rotating text as a method for formatting worksheet data to make it more visually appealing. In this exercise you will indent and rotate text in the Java Sales workbook.

1. Open the *Java Sales—4.xls* workbook.

2. Click the First Qtr worksheet tab to make it the active sheet.

3. Select cells B4:D4.

4. Select Cells from the Format menu.

5. Click the Alignment tab.

6. Change the Horizontal alignment to Center, and click the polygon next to 90 Degrees, as shown in Figure 3.32.

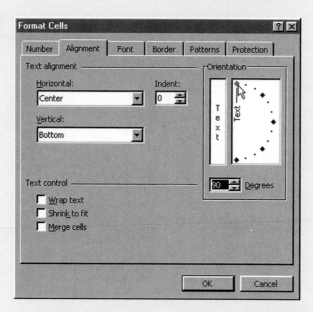

FIGURE 3.32

7. Click OK. Change the font format to bold for the selection.

8. Select cells A5:A8 and click the Increase Indent button on the Formatting toolbar, as shown in Figure 3.33.

FIGURE 3.33

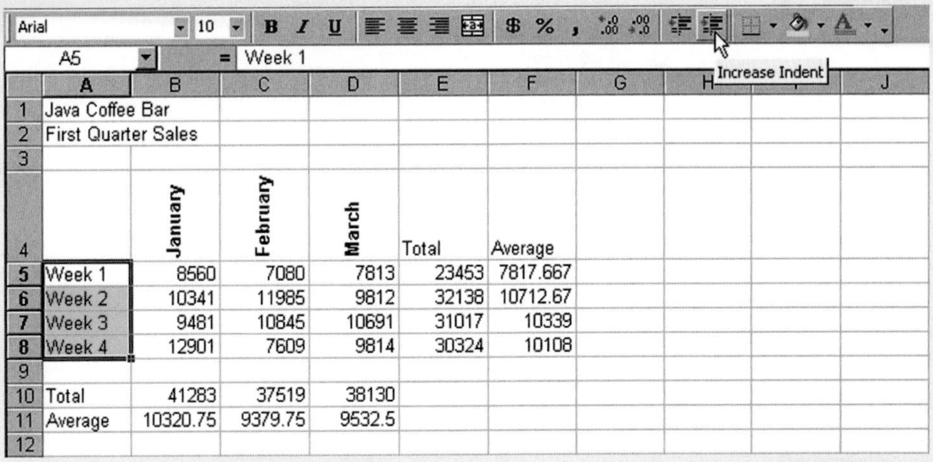

| | A | B | C | D | E | F |
|---|---|---|---|---|---|---|
| 1 | Java Coffee Bar | | | | | |
| 2 | First Quarter Sales | | | | | |
| 3 | | | | | | |
| 4 | | January | February | March | Total | Average |
| 5 | Week 1 | 8560 | 7080 | 7813 | 23453 | 7817.667 |
| 6 | Week 2 | 10341 | 11985 | 9812 | 32138 | 10712.67 |
| 7 | Week 3 | 9481 | 10845 | 10691 | 31017 | 10339 |
| 8 | Week 4 | 12901 | 7609 | 9814 | 30324 | 10108 |
| 9 | | | | | | |
| 10 | Total | 41283 | 37519 | 38130 | | |
| 11 | Average | 10320.75 | 9379.75 | 9532.5 | | |
| 12 | | | | | | |



9. Format all cells with numbers to currency style, and adjust column widths as necessary.
10. Add the borders and additional font formats shown in Figure 3.34.

FIGURE 3.34

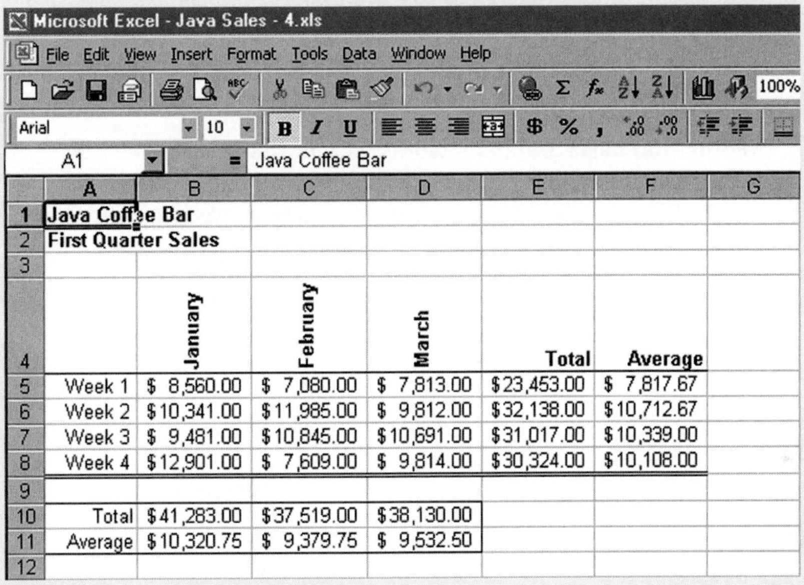

| | A | B | C | D | E | F |
|---|---|---|---|---|---|---|
| 1 | **Java Coffee Bar** | | | | | |
| 2 | **First Quarter Sales** | | | | | |
| 3 | | | | | | |
| 4 | | **January** | **February** | **March** | **Total** | **Average** |
| 5 | Week 1 | $ 8,560.00 | $ 7,080.00 | $ 7,813.00 | $23,453.00 | $ 7,817.67 |
| 6 | Week 2 | $10,341.00 | $11,985.00 | $ 9,812.00 | $32,138.00 | $10,712.67 |
| 7 | Week 3 | $ 9,481.00 | $10,845.00 | $10,691.00 | $31,017.00 | $10,339.00 |
| 8 | Week 4 | $12,901.00 | $ 7,609.00 | $ 9,814.00 | $30,324.00 | $10,108.00 |
| 9 | | | | | | |
| 10 | Total | $41,283.00 | $37,519.00 | $38,130.00 | | |
| 11 | Average | $10,320.75 | $ 9,379.75 | $ 9,532.50 | | |
| 12 | | | | | | |



11. Copy these formats to the Second Qtr sheet.
12. Save the workbook as *Java Sales—5.xls.*

## 2. Merging Worksheet Cells

There are times when you will want to center cell information across columns, and have the information remain centered regardless of the column width. To do this, you can use the ***Merge Cells*** feature.

1. Open the *Java Sales—5.xls* workbook if it is not currently open.
2. Click the Sales Summary tab to make it the active sheet.
3. Select the range A1:I1.
4. Click the Merge and Center button on the Formatting toolbar, as shown in Figure 3.35.

**FIGURE 3.35**

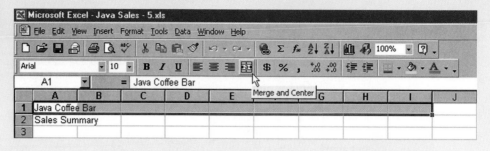

5. Use the Format Painter to apply this format to the range A2:I2.

6. Apply formats to the Sales Summary worksheet so that your worksheet appears like the one shown in Figure 3.36.

**FIGURE 3.36**

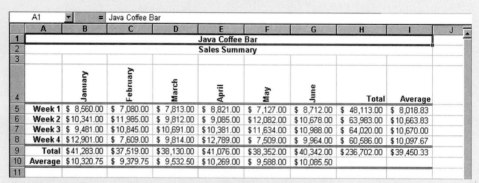

**Formatted Sales Summary worksheet for the Java Coffee Bar**

7. Select cells I4:I10, choose Delete from the Edit menu, and select the option to shift the cells left. This will delete the cells.

8. Save your workbook as *Java Sales—6.xls.*

9. Close the workbook.

# On Your Own Exercises

 **Web Tip**

If you cannot obtain a copy of these files from your instructor, visit the SELECT Web site to download the necessary files: http://www.prenhall/select

## 1. Formatting the Web Sites Workbook

Open the *Financial Sites 2.xls* workbook you modified in Project 1. Edit the workbook so it contains borders and shading to accentuate the sites. Save your workbook to the Investments folder with the name *Financial Sites 3.xls.*

## 2. Formatting Your Class Schedule

Open the *Class Schedule—By Day.xls* workbook you modified in Project 2. Apply any formats you deem appropriate to each worksheet in the workbook. Save the workbook as *Class Schedule—By Day 2.xls*.

## 3. Formatting Time Cards

Open the *Time Cards—Weekly Summary.xls* workbook file. Make sure all numeric data has appropriate number formats. Add borders and shading to make the workbook easier to read. Save the updated workbook as *Time Cards—Weekly Summary 2.xls*.

## 4. Formatting an Excel Address List

Open the *Updated Address.xls* workbook. Format each worksheet in the workbook with text formats appropriate to the data. Save the workbook as *Updated Addresses—2.xls*.

## 5. Formatting the January Sales Workbook

Ask your instructor or lab assistant where the file named *January—Update 2.xls* is located if you did not complete Exercise 1 of Project 2.

Modify the worksheet so that all numeric values are in currency format, and that all summary data has a border above the totals. Save the updated workbook as *January—Update 3.xls*.

## 6. Formatting the Utility Costs Workbook

Open the workbook named *Summary of Updated Utility Costs.xls* from your network or disk. Modify the worksheet by applying formats appropriate to the worksheet. Save your updated workbook to your Personal folder as *Formatted Summary of Updated Utility Costs.xls*.

# Creating More Complex Workbooks

**N**ow that you have mastered the basics of designing workbooks with multiple worksheets, you are ready to construct more complex workbook solutions for the Selections, Inc. department stores. In this project you will learn how to create and name ranges that can be used in formulas. In addition, you will learn how to prepare workbooks for printing by modifying the page setup, adding headers and footers, and defining print ranges.

## Objectives

After completing this project, you will be able to:

➤ Create range names

➤ Use ranges to select data

➤ Use ranges in formulas using the MIN, MAX, and AVERAGE functions

➤ Use logical functions

➤ Modify the page setup

➤ Set print areas

➤ Set and use print options

## Running Case

Mr. Traylor is very pleased with the work you have completed so far on the Selections, Inc. Sales Summary workbook. Now he wants you to roll up your sleeves and really get productive! As he reviewed the workbook structure, he told you he wants to be able to easily compare the sales summary data from quarter to quarter. When you finish making these changes, you will be ready to print copies of the workbook for Mr. Traylor.

# PROJECT 4

## The Challenge

Mr. Traylor would like you to add a text description indicating whether each quarter's sales figures are an increase or decrease from the previous quarter. Finally, he wants you to prepare the workbook for printing by including headers and footers and making any other necessary changes.

## The Strategy

Before enhancing this workbook, you can simplify many of the tasks Mr. Traylor requests by creating and naming ranges. Range names can be used in formulas and will also assist you when sorting the worksheet data. Adding summary data to each worksheet is an easy task, since Excel supports the MIN, MAX, and AVERAGE functions. By adding a lookup function you can reduce multiple instances of the department names, and the IF function will return a text label indicating whether the quarterly sales figures have increased or decreased from the previous quarter. You can add headers and footers to the workbook by modifying the current page setup, and change the orientation to landscape for better viewing. Finally, you can ensure that the worksheets will always print correctly by defining print areas. Figures 4.1 and 4.2 display how the Sales Summary and North worksheets will appear when printed.

**FIGURE 4.1**

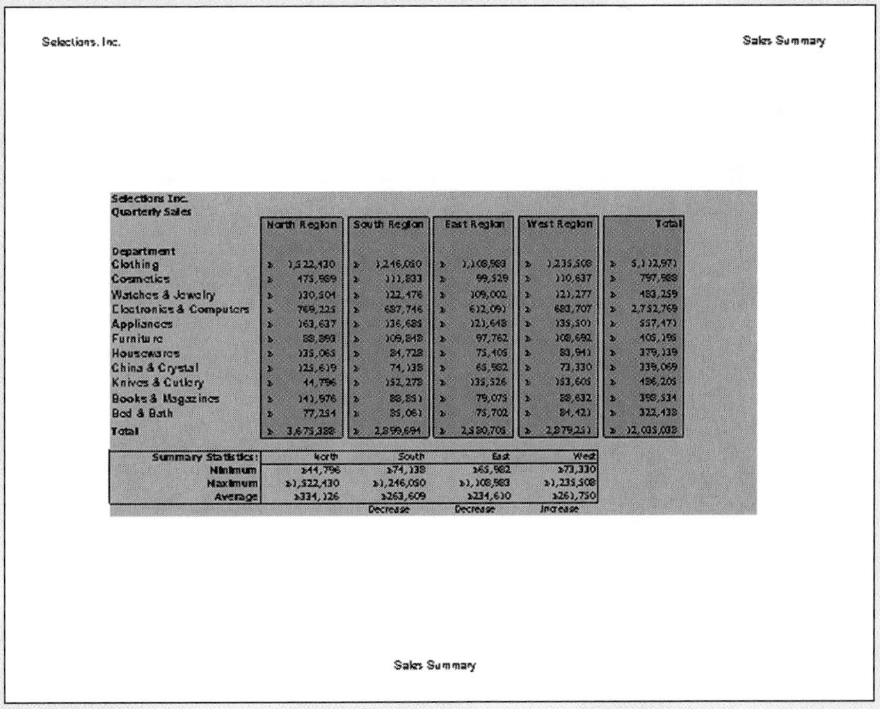

Selections, Inc. — Sales Summary

Selections Inc.
Quarterly Sales

| Department | North Region | South Region | East Region | West Region | Total |
|---|---|---|---|---|---|
| Clothing | $ 1,522,430 | $ 1,246,060 | $ 1,108,983 | $ 1,235,508 | $ 5,112,971 |
| Cosmetics | $ 475,989 | $ 111,833 | $ 99,529 | $ 110,637 | $ 797,988 |
| Watches & Jewelry | $ 130,504 | $ 122,476 | $ 109,002 | $ 121,277 | $ 483,259 |
| Electronics & Computers | $ 769,225 | $ 687,746 | $ 612,091 | $ 683,707 | $ 2,752,769 |
| Appliances | $ 163,637 | $ 136,686 | $ 121,648 | $ 135,501 | $ 557,471 |
| Furniture | $ 88,889 | $ 109,848 | $ 97,762 | $ 108,692 | $ 405,196 |
| Housewares | $ 135,065 | $ 84,728 | $ 75,405 | $ 83,941 | $ 379,139 |
| China & Crystal | $ 125,619 | $ 74,138 | $ 65,982 | $ 73,330 | $ 339,069 |
| Knives & Cutlery | $ 44,796 | $ 152,278 | $ 135,526 | $ 153,606 | $ 486,206 |
| Books & Magazines | $ 141,976 | $ 88,851 | $ 79,075 | $ 88,632 | $ 398,534 |
| Bed & Bath | $ 77,254 | $ 85,061 | $ 75,702 | $ 84,421 | $ 322,438 |
| Total | $ 3,675,388 | $ 2,899,694 | $ 2,580,706 | $ 2,879,251 | $ 12,035,038 |

| Summary Statistics: | North | South | East | West |
|---|---|---|---|---|
| Minimum | $44,796 | $74,138 | $65,982 | $73,330 |
| Maximum | $1,522,430 | $1,246,060 | $1,108,983 | $1,235,508 |
| Average | $334,126 | $263,609 | $234,610 | $261,750 |
| | | Decrease | Decrease | Increase |

Sales Summary

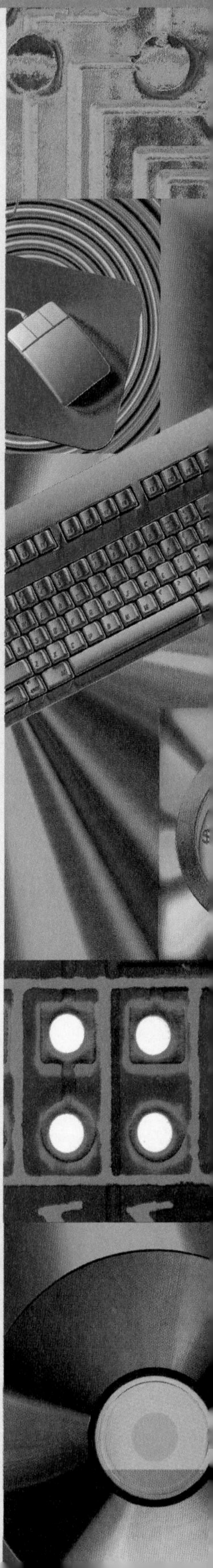

**FIGURE 4.2**

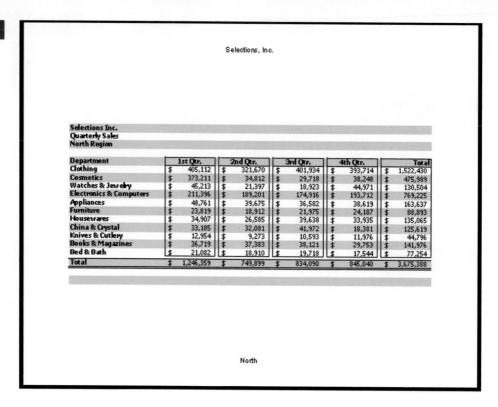

# The Setup

Launch Microsoft Excel and select the Excel settings listed in Table 4.1. This will ensure that your screen matches the illustrations and that the tasks in this project function as described.

**Table 4.1**

| Location | Make these settings: |
|---|---|
| **Office Assistant** | Hide the Office Assistant. |
| **Tools, Customize** | Click the Options tab and deselect the option to show recently used menu commands first. |
| **Tools, Customize** | Click the Options tab and deselect the option to display the Standard and Formatting toolbars on one row. |
| **View, Formula Bar** | Display the formula bar. |
| **View, Status Bar** | Display the status bar. |
| **View, Normal** | View the workbook in Normal view. |
| **Maximize** | Maximize the application and workbook windows. |
| **File, Open** | Open the *Selections.xls* workbook. |

# Naming Ranges

Many workbook tasks are simpler if you name and use ranges. A **name** is a text description that you give to an individual cell, adjacent range, or non-adjacent selection. You can refer to cells and ranges by name for inclusion in formulas, or to jump to a specific selection.

## TASK 1:   To Name Ranges

**1**  Highlight cells B6:B16 in the Sales Summary worksheet.

**2**  Click inside the Name box on the formula bar. The active cell is highlighted, as shown in Figure 4.3. In this case, the active cell is the uppermost left cell of the selection.

**FIGURE 4.3**

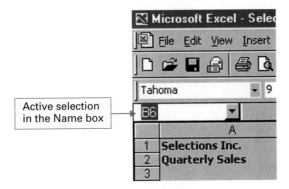

Active selection in the Name box

**3**  Type **NorthSummary** as the name for the range, and press (ENTER). The name now appears in the Name box.

**4**  Using the same procedure, name the ranges listed in Table 4.2.

**Table 4.2**

| Range | Name |
| --- | --- |
| D6:D16 | SouthSummary |
| F6:F16 | EastSummary |
| H6:H16 | WestSummary |

> **TIP**  Make sure you press (ENTER) after naming each range.

**5**  Select the range A5:J16.

**6**  Click the Name box and type **SummaryByRegion** as the name for this range, and press (ENTER).

**7**  Save the workbook.

## Using Ranges to Select Data

Once you have named a range, you can use the name to select the data, regardless of where the range is located in the current workbook. This feature is useful when you need to select a range to complete a task, such as applying formats or sorting data.

**TASK 2:** <u>To Select Data Using a Range Name</u>

**1** Click the North worksheet tab to make it the active sheet.

**2** Click the drop-down list arrow next to the Name box. Select WestSummary from the list, as shown in Figure 4.4.

**FIGURE 4.4**

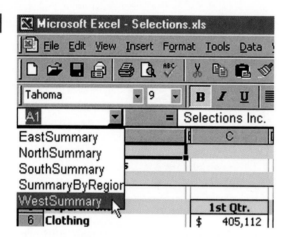

The focus switches to the Sales Summary sheet and the range H6:H16 is selected, as shown in Figure 4.5.

FIGURE 4.5

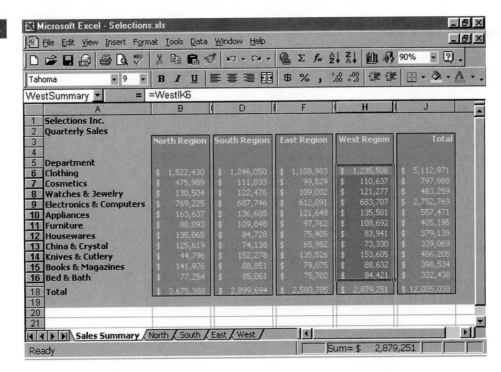

 **3** Select EastSales from the Name list. The selection changes so that cells F6:F16 are highlighted.

## Web Tip

Ranges are a powerful feature in Microsoft Excel. The macro language for Office, Visual Basic, includes additional capabilities for ranges. To see an example of what you can do with ranges in Excel using Visual Basic, visit http://www.microsoft.com/exceldev/tips/rngtot.htm.

## Using Range Names in Formulas

Another beneficial use for range names is that they can be used instead of cell references in formulas. Since Mr. Traylor wants to include a listing of the minimum, maximum, and average sales figures across all regions, you can use the range names you have created in the additional formulas that the Sales Summary worksheet requires.

> **TIP** If you insert columns or rows inside a named range, the range corresponding to the name increases accordingly. The same is true if you delete columns or rows inside the named range. You can always edit the range of cells corresponding to a name by selecting Name from the Insert menu, and then selecting Define.

**TASK 3:** <u>To Use Range Names in Formulas</u>

**1** In the Sales Summary worksheet, type **Summary Statistics:** in cell A20, **Minimum** in cell A21, **Maximum** in cell A22, and **Average** in cell A23.

**2** Select cells A20:A23 and change the alignment to right aligned and the font style to bold.

**3** Place the insertion point in cell B21.

**4** Click the Function *fx* button.

**5** In the Paste Function dialog box, choose Statistical in the Function category and MIN as the Function name, as shown in Figure 4.6.

| FIGURE 4.6 |

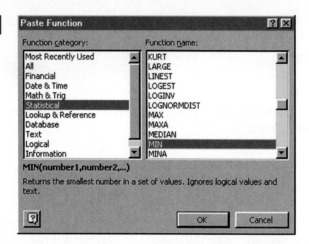

**6** Click OK. The formula palette will display the range B6:B20 as the first parameter for the function.

**7** Choose Name, Paste from the Insert menu, as shown in Figure 4.7.

**FIGURE 4.7**

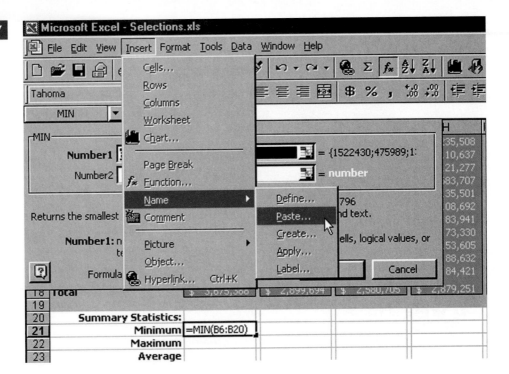

**8** Select NorthSummary in the Paste Name dialog box and click OK, as shown in Figure 4.8.

**FIGURE 4.8**

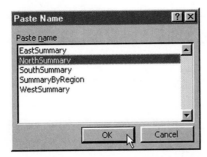

**9** The range name now appears in the formula palette. Click OK.

**10** The minimum value in the range is displayed in cell B21, as shown in Figure 4.9. Note the syntax for the formula.

FIGURE 4.9

| | A | B | D | |
|---|---|---|---|---|
| | | B21 ▼ | = =MIN(NorthSummary) ◄ | |
| 6 | Clothing | $ 1,522,430 | $ 1,246,050 | |
| 7 | Cosmetics | $ 475,989 | $ 111,833 | |
| 8 | Watches & Jewelry | $ 130,504 | $ 122,476 | |
| 9 | Electronics & Computers | $ 769,225 | $ 687,746 | |
| 10 | Appliances | $ 163,637 | $ 136,685 | |
| 11 | Furniture | $ 88,893 | $ 109,848 | |
| 12 | Housewares | $ 135,065 | $ 84,728 | |
| 13 | China & Crystal | $ 125,619 | $ 74,138 | |
| 14 | Knives & Cutlery | $ 44,796 | $ 152,278 | |
| 15 | Books & Magazines | $ 141,976 | $ 88,851 | |
| 16 | Bed & Bath | $ 77,254 | $ 85,061 | |
| 18 | Total | $ 3,675,388 | $ 2,899,694 | |
| 19 | | | | |
| 20 | Summary Statistics: | | | |
| 21 | Minimum | 44796 | | |
| 22 | Maximum | | | |
| 23 | Average | | | |
| 24 | | | | |

Formula containing a range name as a parameter

## Check Point

How else could you have created this formula? You could also create this formula by typing it directly into the cell or the formula bar.

**11** Type **=max(NorthSummary)** in cell B22 and press (ENTER).

**12** Type **=average(NorthSummary)** in cell B23 and press (ENTER).

**13** Select the range B21:B23 and change the number format to currency, 0 decimal places.

**14** Select cell B23. Your workbook appears as shown in Figure 4.10.

FIGURE 4.10

| | A | B | D | F | H | J | |
|---|---|---|---|---|---|---|---|
| | | B23 ▼ | = =AVERAGE(NorthSummary) | | | | |
| 5 | Department | | | | | | |
| 6 | Clothing | $ 1,522,430 | $ 1,246,050 | $ 1,108,983 | $ 1,235,508 | $ 5,112,971 | |
| 7 | Cosmetics | $ 475,989 | $ 111,833 | $ 99,529 | $ 110,637 | $ 797,988 | |
| 8 | Watches & Jewelry | $ 130,504 | $ 122,476 | $ 109,002 | $ 121,277 | $ 483,259 | |
| 9 | Electronics & Computers | $ 769,225 | $ 687,746 | $ 612,091 | $ 683,707 | $ 2,752,769 | |
| 10 | Appliances | $ 163,637 | $ 136,685 | $ 121,648 | $ 135,501 | $ 557,471 | |
| 11 | Furniture | $ 88,893 | $ 109,848 | $ 97,762 | $ 108,692 | $ 405,195 | |
| 12 | Housewares | $ 135,065 | $ 84,728 | $ 75,405 | $ 83,941 | $ 379,139 | |
| 13 | China & Crystal | $ 125,619 | $ 74,138 | $ 65,982 | $ 73,330 | $ 339,069 | |
| 14 | Knives & Cutlery | $ 44,796 | $ 152,278 | $ 135,526 | $ 153,605 | $ 486,205 | |
| 15 | Books & Magazines | $ 141,976 | $ 88,851 | $ 79,075 | $ 88,632 | $ 398,534 | |
| 16 | Bed & Bath | $ 77,254 | $ 85,061 | $ 75,702 | $ 84,421 | $ 322,438 | |
| 18 | Total | $ 3,675,388 | $ 2,899,694 | $ 2,580,705 | $ 2,879,251 | $ 12,035,038 | |
| 19 | | | | | | | |
| 20 | Summary Statistics: | | | | | | |
| 21 | Minimum | $44,796 | | | | | |
| 22 | Maximum | $1,522,430 | | | | | |
| 23 | Average | $334,126 | | | | | |
| 24 | | | | | | | |
| 25 | | | | | | | |

Sales Summary / North / South / East / West /

**15** Save your changes.

## TASK 4:   To Create Additional Formulas Using Range Names

**1** Using either procedure outlined in the previous task, enter the appropriate formulas in cells D21:D23, F21:F23, and H21:H23, respectively.

> **TIP**   Remember that you can copy formulas from one column to another. If you use this method in this case, you will need to change the name of each range in the formulas. When you are finished, make sure you check each additional formula for accuracy!

**2** Highlight cells A20:K24. Set the shading to Gray-25%.

**3** Enter an outside border around cells A20:H23, B20:H23, and B20:H20.

**4** Type **North** in cell B20, **South** in cell D20, **East** in cell F20, and **West** in cell H20.

> **TIP**   After you apply a border to one range, you can highlight the next range that will receive the border and select Repeat Borders from the Edit menu.

**5** Change the alignment of cells B20:H20 to right aligned. Your worksheet should now resemble the one shown in Figure 4.11.

**FIGURE 4.11**

| | A | B | D | F | H | J |
|---|---|---|---|---|---|---|
| | H20 | | = | West | | |
| 5 | Department | | | | | |
| 6 | Clothing | $ 1,522,430 | $ 1,246,050 | $ 1,108,983 | $ 1,235,508 | $ 5,112,971 |
| 7 | Cosmetics | $ 475,989 | $ 111,833 | $ 99,529 | $ 110,637 | $ 797,988 |
| 8 | Watches & Jewelry | $ 130,504 | $ 122,476 | $ 109,002 | $ 121,277 | $ 483,259 |
| 9 | Electronics & Computers | $ 769,225 | $ 687,746 | $ 612,091 | $ 683,707 | $ 2,752,769 |
| 10 | Appliances | $ 163,637 | $ 136,685 | $ 121,648 | $ 135,501 | $ 557,471 |
| 11 | Furniture | $ 88,893 | $ 109,848 | $ 97,762 | $ 108,692 | $ 405,195 |
| 12 | Housewares | $ 135,065 | $ 84,728 | $ 75,405 | $ 83,941 | $ 379,139 |
| 13 | China & Crystal | $ 125,619 | $ 74,138 | $ 65,982 | $ 73,330 | $ 339,069 |
| 14 | Knives & Cutlery | $ 44,796 | $ 152,278 | $ 135,526 | $ 153,605 | $ 486,205 |
| 15 | Books & Magazines | $ 141,976 | $ 88,851 | $ 79,075 | $ 88,632 | $ 398,534 |
| 16 | Bed & Bath | $ 77,254 | $ 85,061 | $ 75,702 | $ 84,421 | $ 322,438 |
| 18 | Total | $ 3,675,388 | $ 2,899,694 | $ 2,580,705 | $ 2,879,251 | $ 12,035,038 |
| 19 | | | | | | |
| 20 | Summary Statistics: | North | South | East | West | |
| 21 | Minimum | $44,796 | $74,138 | $65,982 | $73,330 | |
| 22 | Maximum | $1,522,430 | $1,246,050 | $1,108,983 | $1,235,508 | |
| 23 | Average | $334,126 | $263,609 | $234,610 | $261,750 | |
| 24 | | | | | | |
| 25 | | | | | | |

Sales Summary / North / South / East / West /

**6** Save your changes.

# Using Logical Functions

Mr. Traylor specified that he wants a way of seeing the sales trends for each quarter at a glance, and to know how they compared with the figures from the previous quarter. You can use a logical function to accomplish this task. A *logical function* is a function that analyzes a value and, based upon a condition, returns a result. Excel's *IF function* compares the value in one cell with either a predefined condition or the value in another cell.

In the next task you will add a conditional function to compare each quarter's sales figures with the sales for the preceding quarter. If the value exceeds the average, the text *Increase* is returned. If the value decreases, the word *Decrease* is returned.

## TASK 5: To Add an IF Function to Test Conditions

**1** Place the insertion point in cell D24 of the Sales Summary worksheet.

**2** Type **=IF(D23>B23,"Increase","Decrease")** as the formula for this cell, and press (ENTER).

**3** Copy this formula to cells F24 and H24 respectively. Change the alignment of cells D24, F24, and H24 to centered. When you are finished, the Sales Summary returns the text shown in Figure 4.12.

**FIGURE 4.12**

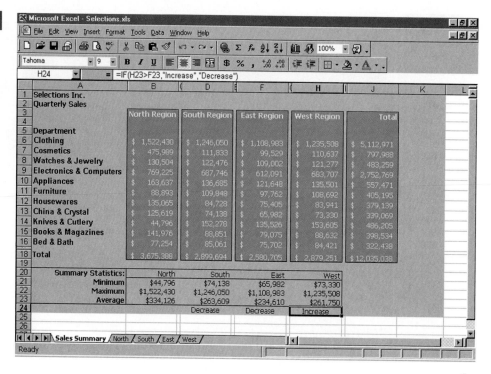

**4** Save your changes.

## Web Tip

Excel includes the IIF function, which returns multiple responses. See http://msdn.microsoft.com/library/officedev/off2000/refctiif.htm for more information.

## Break Point

If necessary, you can save your file, exit Excel, and continue this project later.

## Modifying the Page Setup of Worksheets

With more complex workbooks you often need to modify the page setup prior to printing. Changing the page setup includes the worksheet's **orientation**, or its layout on the page when printed. **Landscape orientation** aligns the paper so that it is wider than tall, **portrait orientation** so that it is taller than wide.

Excel's **Page Break Preview** allows you to determine whether you should change the orientation. Once the worksheet has the appropriate layout, you can add **headers** and **footers**, which is text that appears at the top and bottom of the printed page. Finally, you can define a **print area**, which prints a specific area of the worksheet.

TASK 6:   To Change Worksheet Orientation

① Open the *Selections.xls* workbook if necessary, and choose Page Break Preview from the View menu.

② Depending upon how your computer is configured, you may see the dialog box shown in Figure 4.13. If so, click OK.

FIGURE 4.13

**3**  Excel displays the current page breaks, with each page designated in gray text, as shown in Figure 4.14. The dashed blue line indicates the current page break.

**FIGURE 4.14**

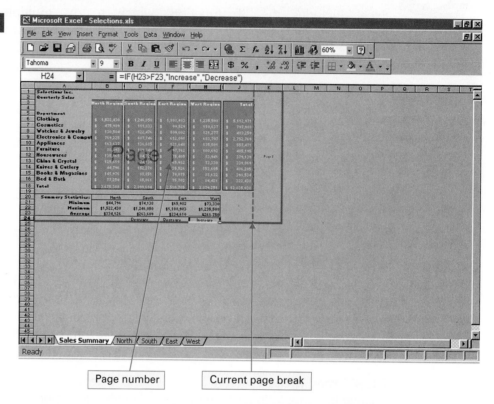

Page number

Current page break

**TROUBLESHOOTING**  The page numbers are difficult to see, as the background color for much of this worksheet is also gray.

**4**  Choose Page Setup from the File menu.

**5**  The Page Setup dialog box appears. Make sure the Page tab is active, change the orientation to Landscape, change the scaling to 95% of normal size, and click the Print Preview button, as shown in Figure 4.15.

**FIGURE 4.15**

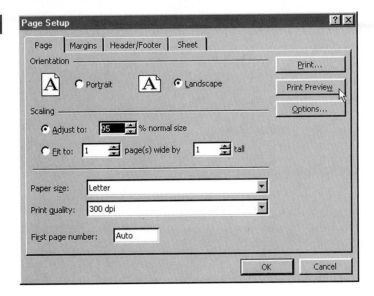

**6** The preview appears, as shown in Figure 4.16.

**FIGURE 4.16**

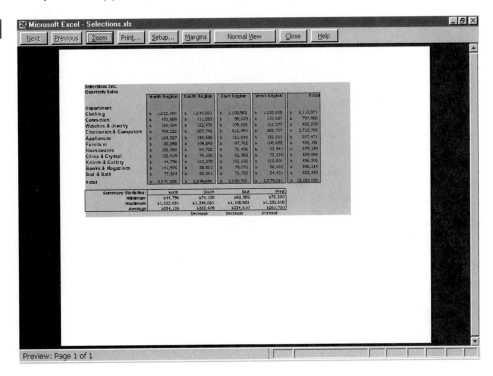

**TROUBLESHOOTING** Click the Zoom button in the Print Preview if necessary to display the entire worksheet.

You will notice that the worksheet data is not centered on the page. You can easily change this by centering the worksheet on the page.

**7** Click the Setup button at the top of the Preview window to return to the Page Setup dialog box.

**8** Click the Margins tab. Change the left and right margins to 1 inch.

> **TIP** You can either use the spin controls to increase the margins, or place the insertion point inside the text box that displays the current margin setting and type a new value.

**9** Click the checkboxes shown in Figure 4.17 to center the worksheet on the page.

**FIGURE 4.17**

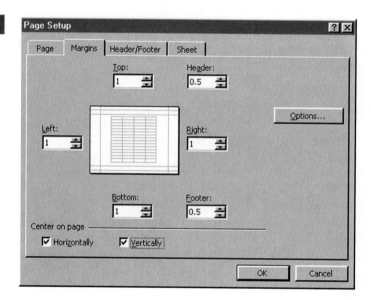

**10** Click OK.

**11** Click the Close [Close] button in the Preview window to close the Print preview.

**12** Select Normal from the View menu to switch to Normal view.

**13** Using the same procedure, change the page orientation, margins, and centering options of the North through West worksheets to the same settings.

**14** Save your changes.

## Check Point

Remember that you can apply changes to multiple worksheets by first selecting the range of worksheets.

> **TIP**  Consider checking spelling before printing worksheets. To check spelling, click the Spelling button on the Standard toolbar. To print multiple worksheets, select the worksheet tabs for the sheets you desire to print. Then, click the Print button on the Standard toolbar.

## Adding Headers and Footers to Worksheets

Headers and footers enhance the appearance of worksheets when they are printed. You can select predefined headers and footers, or create custom ones on your own.

### TASK 7:  To Add Headers and Footers to Worksheets

**1** Click the Sales Summary worksheet tab to make it the active sheet.

**2** Choose Page Setup from the File menu.

**3** Click the Header/Footer tab.

**4** The Header/Footer dialog box appears. You can select a header or footer from the list, or define a custom header and footer.

**5** Click the Custom Header button.

**6** In the Header dialog box, place the insertion point in the Left text box and type **Selections, Inc.**

**7** Place the insertion point in the Right text box and type **Sales Summary**. Click OK. The Header/Footer dialog box appears, as shown in Figure 4.18.

FIGURE 4.18

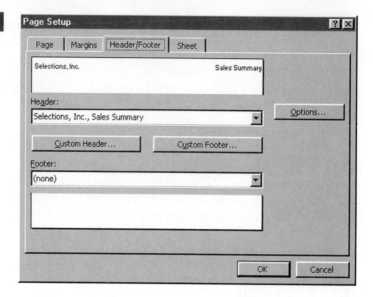

**TIP** You can add additional elements such as the current date, the time, or the page number to the header or footer using the buttons provided.

**8** Click OK to return to the Page Setup dialog box. Notice that the custom header is displayed in the preview pane.

**9** Click the Custom Footer button in the Page Setup dialog box.

**10** Place the insertion point in the Center section and click the Worksheet Name 🖵 button.

**11** Click OK to return to the Page Setup dialog box.

**12** The Header/Footer tab of the Page Setup dialog box appears, as shown in Figure 4.19.

**FIGURE 4.19**

Page Setup

| Page | Margins | Header/Footer | Sheet |

Selections, Inc.                                    Sales Summary

Header:
Selections, Inc., Sales Summary          ▼        Options...

Custom Header...          Custom Footer...

Footer:
Sales Summary          ▼

Sales Summary

OK          Cancel

**13** Click OK, and then click the Print Preview button. The header and footer appear, as shown in Figure 4.20.

FIGURE 4.20

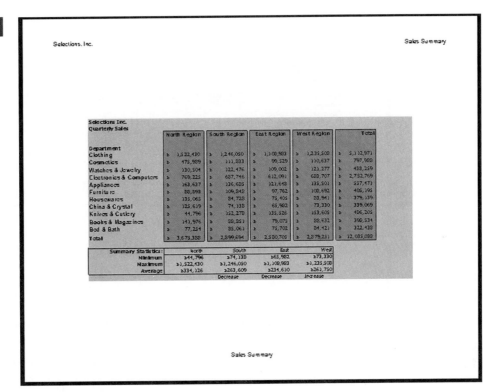

**14** Close the Preview.

**15** Using the same procedures, add a custom header to each of the regional worksheets with Selections, Inc. in the center pane of the header. Add the worksheet name to the center pane of the footer. Save your changes when you are finished. The North worksheet previews as shown in Figure 4.21.

FIGURE 4.21

Selections, Inc.

| Department | 1st Qtr. | 2nd Qtr. | 3rd Qtr. | 4th Qtr. | Total |
|---|---|---|---|---|---|
| Clothing | $ 405,112 | $ 321,670 | $ 401,934 | $ 393,714 | $ 1,522,430 |
| Cosmetics | $ 373,211 | $ 34,812 | $ 29,718 | $ 38,248 | $ 475,989 |
| Watches & Jewelry | $ 45,213 | $ 21,397 | $ 18,923 | $ 44,971 | $ 130,504 |
| Electronics & Computers | $ 211,396 | $ 189,201 | $ 174,916 | $ 193,712 | $ 769,225 |
| Appliances | $ 48,761 | $ 39,675 | $ 36,582 | $ 38,619 | $ 163,637 |
| Furniture | $ 23,819 | $ 18,912 | $ 21,975 | $ 24,187 | $ 88,893 |
| Housewares | $ 34,907 | $ 26,585 | $ 39,638 | $ 33,935 | $ 135,065 |
| China & Crystal | $ 33,185 | $ 32,081 | $ 41,972 | $ 18,381 | $ 125,619 |
| Knives & Cutlery | $ 12,954 | $ 9,273 | $ 10,593 | $ 11,976 | $ 44,796 |
| Books & Magazines | $ 36,719 | $ 37,383 | $ 38,121 | $ 29,753 | $ 141,976 |
| Bed & Bath | $ 21,082 | $ 18,910 | $ 19,718 | $ 17,544 | $ 77,254 |
| Total | $ 1,246,359 | $ 749,899 | $ 834,090 | $ 845,040 | $ 3,675,388 |

Selections Inc.
Quarterly Sales
North Region

North

**TIP** The worksheets you have created each print on a unique page, as you see from the Print Preview. If you ever need to add a page break to a worksheet, place the insertion point in the row below the location of the break, and select Page Break from the Insert menu.

## Setting and Clearing Print Areas

There are times when you want to print only a portion of a worksheet. By setting a print area, you can easily print an adjacent range or non-adjacent selection.

### TASK 8: To Set and Clear Print Areas

**1** Select Normal from the View menu to switch to Normal view, if necessary.

**2** Select the range A1:C19 of the Sales Summary worksheet.

**3** Choose Print Area, Set Print Area from the File menu, as shown in Figure 4.22.

FIGURE 4.22

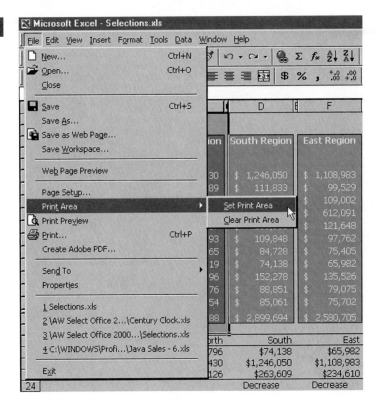

4  Click the Print Preview 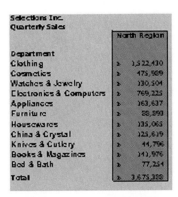 button on the Standard toolbar.

5  Click the Zoom button in the Print Preview window. A portion of the worksheet appears, as shown in Figure 4.23.

FIGURE 4.23

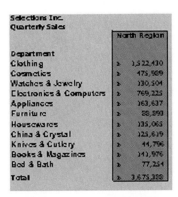

**TROUBLESHOOTING**  Depending upon your monitor and current display settings, you may need to use the scroll bars to reposition the preview.

6  Close the Print Preview window.

7  Choose Print Area, Clear Print Area from the File menu, as shown in Figure 4.24.

**FIGURE 4.24**

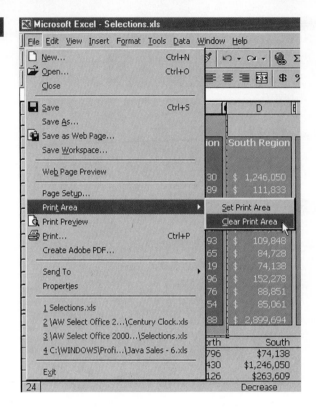

```
Microsoft Excel - Selections.xls
File  Edit  View  Insert  Format  Tools  Data  Window  Help
  New...                          Ctrl+N              ┊  ▼  ▼         Σ
  Open...                         Ctrl+O           ≡  ≡  ≡         $  %
  Close
  Save                            Ctrl+S                    D            E
  Save As...
  Save as Web Page...                          ion   South Region
  Save Workspace...
                                                30  $    1,246,050
  Web Page Preview                              89  $      111,833
  Page Setup...
  Print Area                            ►         Set Print Area
  Print Preview                                   Clear Print Area
  Print...                        Ctrl+P        93  $      109,848
  Create Adobe PDF...                           65  $       84,728
                                                19  $       74,138
  Send To                               ►       96  $      152,278
  Properties                                    76  $       88,851
                                                54  $       85,061
  1 Selections.xls                              88  $    2,899,694
  2 \AW Select Office 2...\Century Clock.xls
  3 \AW Select Office 2000...\Selections.xls    rth          South
  4 C:\WINDOWS\Profi...\Java Sales - 6.xls      796        $74,138
                                                430        $1,246,050
  Exit                                          126        $263,609
  24                                                       Decrease
```

**8** Click cell A1 and save your changes.

## Setting Other Print Options

There are additional options you can set in Excel before printing one or more worksheets in a workbook. This is useful when you want to further change Excel's default settings.

**TASK 9:** To Set Print Options

**1** Choose Page Setup from the File menu.

**2** Click the Sheet tab. The Page Setup dialog box appears, as shown in Figure 4.25.

FIGURE 4.25

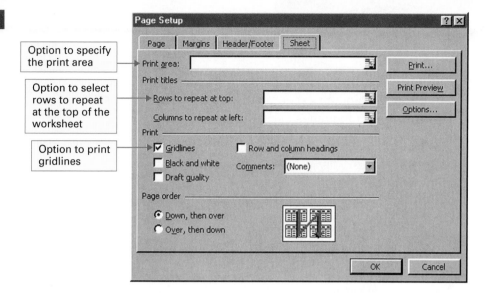

Option to specify the print area

Option to select rows to repeat at the top of the worksheet

Option to print gridlines

**3** Check the option for gridlines.

**4** Click OK.

**5** Select each worksheet in the workbook.

**6** Select Print from the File menu.

**7** Click OK to print a copy of each worksheet in the workbook.

**TROUBLESHOOTING** Make sure you select an active printer before printing!

**8** Close the Selections workbook.

## Summary and Exercises

### Summary

- After naming an Excel range, you can use the range name in formulas and can also select the range using the Name box.
- Logical functions compare data based upon the conditions you specify.
- You can modify a worksheet's Page Setup settings to enhance its appearance when printed.
- Headers and footers contain information that will print at the top and bottom of every page of a worksheet.
- Print areas define a range to be printed.

### Key Terms and Operations

#### Key Terms

| | |
|---|---|
| AutoFormat | name |
| footer | orientation |
| header | Page Break Preview |
| IF function | portrait orientation |
| landscape orientation | print area |
| logical function | |

#### Operations

| | |
|---|---|
| add custom headers and footers | set print areas |
| change worksheet orientation | use ranges in formulas |
| name ranges | use ranges to select data |
| | use the IF function |

### Study Questions

#### Multiple Choice

1. Which Excel feature allows you to simplify references to ranges in formulas?
   a. the IF function
   b. a range name
   c. a print area
   d. the Page Setup dialog box

2. Once you set a print area, how do you remove it?
   a. use an IF function
   b. use the Edit menu
   c. use the File menu
   d. use the Web Page Preview

3. Which menu do you use to change the orientation of a worksheet?
   a. File
   b. Edit
   c. View
   d. Insert

4. The MIN function is an example of a
   a. logical function.
   b. financial function.
   c. statistical function.
   d. lookup function.

5. The AVERAGE function does what?
   a. sums a range of cells
   b. calculates the maximum value in a range of cells
   c. calculates the future value for a range of cells
   d. calculates the mean value for a range of cells

6. How many conditions does the IF function support?
   a. 0
   b. 1
   c. 2
   d. 3

7. The formula =IF(A1>=0,"Acceptable") tests for which value in cell A1?
   a. a value equal to zero
   b. any value less than zero
   c. values greater than or equal to zero
   d. only the value zero

8. The IF function belongs to which category of function?
   a. logical
   b. lookup
   c. statistical
   d. financial

9. The IF function can be used to
   a. conduct a logical test.
   b. calculate a mean value.
   c. set a print area.
   d. minimize redundant data.

10. A formula contains the following function:
    =IF(A1>0,2,1)
    If cell A1 contains a negative number, what value is returned?
    a. 0
    b. 1
    c. 2
    d. −1

## Short Answer

1. Which function compares the values in two cells and returns data specific to the comparison?

2. How do you change the orientation of a worksheet?

3. What kind of function is IF?

4. What does the IF function do?

5. How do you set a print area?

6. What does the AVERAGE function do?

7. Once you define a print area, how do you print other portions of the workbook?

8. Which screen element do you use to name ranges?

9. How do you refer to a range by name in a formula?

10. AVERAGE belongs to what category of function?

## Fill in the Blank

1. The _____ function compares values and returns the appropriate text or value.

2. You can modify a worksheet's page setup using the _____ menu.

3. The _____ function conducts a logical test.

4. MIN and MAX are _____ functions.

5. The IF function is a _____ function.

6. You can use _____ to simplify range references in formulas.

7. If you want to add text at the top of every page of a worksheet, add a _____ to the sheet.

8. You use the _____ to name a range.

9. To set a print area, select _____ from the _____ menu.

10. Once you set a _____ , only a portion of a worksheet will be printed.

## For Discussion

1. Can you use range names in 3-D formulas? Explain.

2. Why should you consider setting print areas for worksheets?

3. When should you include MIN, MAX, and AVERAGE functions in a workbook?

4. State a case where an IF function is useful.

5. How do the MIN and MAX functions differ?

# Hands-On Exercises

## 1. Adding the MIN and MAX Functions to a Workbook

As you learned in this project, the MIN, MAX, and AVERAGE functions are useful for summarizing data. The workbook already includes the AVERAGE function; in this exercise you will modify the Java Sales worksheet to include the MIN and MAX functions. When you are finished, you will send the worksheet as an e-mail attachment to Mr. Traylor.

1. Open the *Java Sales—6.xls* workbook.

2. Select the 1st Qtr and 2nd Qtr worksheets.

3. Highlight cells F4:F8 and select Cells from the Insert menu, as shown in Figure 4.26.

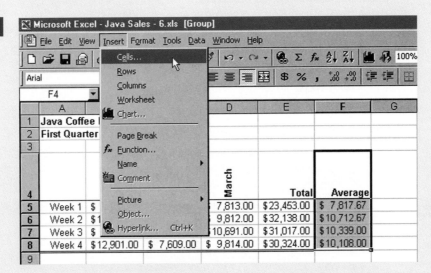

**FIGURE 4.26**

4. Choose the option in the Insert dialog box to shift the cells right and click OK, as shown in Figure 4.27.

**FIGURE 4.27**

5. Repeat this procedure to add two additional rows to the worksheet.

6. Type **Min** in cell F5 and **Max** in cell F6.

7. Add formulas to the appropriate cells to calculate the minimum and maximum values.

8. Press (CTRL) + G to open the Go To dialog box.

9. Type **A11** in the Reference: text box and click OK, as shown in Figure 4.28.

FIGURE 4.28

**Using the Go To dialog box to move to a specific cell**

10. Select A11:D12 and insert cells into the worksheet. Choose the option to shift cells down.

11. Type **Min** in cell A11 and **Max** in cell A12.

12. Add the appropriate formulas to the worksheet.

13. Adjust column widths and reapply formats as appropriate. Save the workbook as *Java Sales—7.xls.* When you are finished, the workbook will look similar to Figure 4.29.

FIGURE 4.29

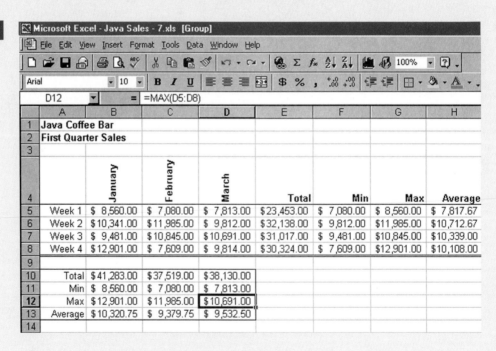

## 2. Preparing the Java Sales Summary Worksheet for Printing

Mr. Traylor wants to print the Java Sales worksheets after you make the following changes. First, you need to add a worksheet listing sales figures for the third quarter. Then you need to apply a different format to the worksheets using one of Excel's preset formats, called an ***AutoFormat***. Finally, he wants to print the quarterly worksheets without the minimum and maximum data. Complete this exercise as follows:

1. Open the *Java Sales—7.xls* workbook.

2. Click the 2nd Qtr worksheet tab and then select Move or Copy Sheet from the Edit menu.

3. Choose the options to create a copy at the end of the workbook, as shown in Figure 4.30. Click OK.

**FIGURE 4.30**

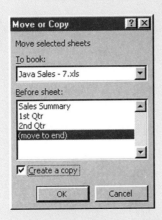

4. Rename the tab for this new worksheet as **3rd Qtr**, and change the text labels to reflect the correct months and sales quarter.

5. Highlight the range B5:E8 in this worksheet, select Clear from the Edit menu, and then select Contents, as shown in Figure 4.31. This clears the contents of these cells.

FIGURE 4.31

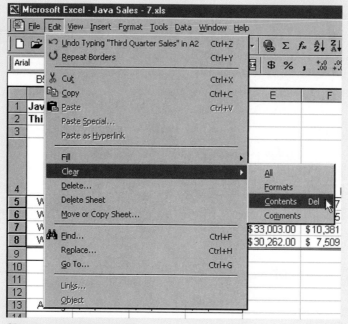

**Clearing a range of cells**

**TIP** Notice that you can also clear cell contents by highlighting a range and pressing the (DEL) key.

6. Enter the sales data shown in Figure 4.32 into cells B5:D8.

**FIGURE 4.32**

|   | A | B | C | D |
|---|---|---|---|---|
| 1 | Java Coffee Bar | | | |
| 2 | Third Quarter Sales | | | |
| 3 | | | | |
| 4 | | July | August | September |
| 5 | Week 1 | $ 9,125.34 | $ 8,099.45 | $ 7,095.23 |
| 6 | Week 2 | $10,789.33 | $12,986.34 | $13,908.45 |
| 7 | Week 3 | $11,673.12 | $11,034.81 | $12,855.12 |
| 8 | Week 4 | $ 9,087.12 | $12,344.09 | $11,094.98 |

7. Select the quarterly worksheets and highlight the range A4:H8. Click the Edit menu and choose Clear, Formats. Select Formats from the menu. This will clear the existing formats from the selection.

8. Select AutoFormat from the Format menu. Choose the Classic 3 AutoFormat by clicking it. When your screen matches Figure 4.33, click OK.

**FIGURE 4.33**

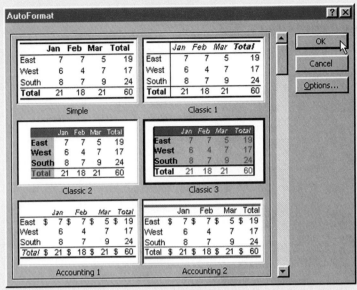

**Applying an AutoFormat to a range of cells**

9. Select the range A10:D13 and apply the same AutoFormat to this range.

10. Select columns F and G by clicking the heading for column F, pressing the (SHIFT) key, and clicking the heading for column G.

11. Select Column from the Format menu, and then select Hide, as shown in Figure 4.33. This will hide these columns for printing.

**FIGURE 4.34**

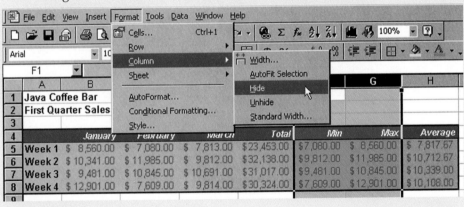

**Hiding columns**

12. Select rows 11 and 12 by clicking the row selector for row 11, pressing the (SHIFT) key, and clicking the row selector for row 12. Select Row from the Format menu and then select Hide. The workbook appears as shown in Figure 4.35. Notice the column and row headings.

FIGURE 4.35

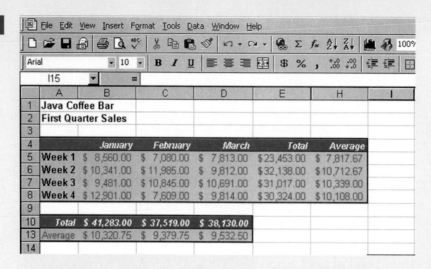

13. Print the selected worksheets.

14. Highlight columns E through H, select Column from the Format menu, and then select Unhide, as shown in Figure 4.36. This will display the hidden columns.

FIGURE 4.36

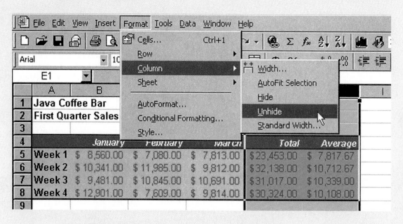

15. Repeat the same procedure to display rows 11 and 12, which are currently hidden.

16. Save the workbook as *Java Sales—8.xls*, and close the workbook.

## 3. Creating a Workbook from a Template and Sending the Workbook as an Electronic Mail Attachment

Mr. Traylor wants you to create an invoice workbook and send him an electronic copy for review. You can use one of Excel's templates, or preformatted workbooks, to create the invoice, and then use the File menu to send a copy to Mr. Traylor via e-mail.

1. Launch Excel if it is not currently running.

2. Select New from the File menu.

3. Click the Spreadsheet Solutions tab and highlight the Invoice template in the list. When your screen matches Figure 4.37, click OK.

**FIGURE 4.37**

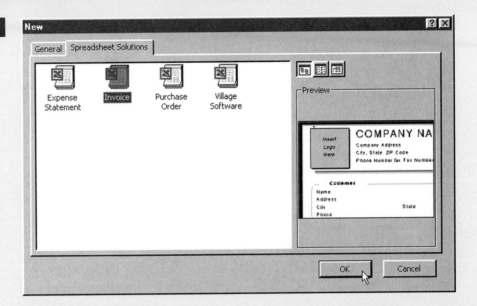

**TROUBLESHOOTING** Your icons may appear different from the ones shown here, depending on how your computer or network is configured and on the current view setting for the Spreadsheet Solutions dialog box.

4. When you see the dialog box indicating that this worksheet contains macros, click Enable Macros.

5. Save a copy of the workbook to your disk as *Selections Invoice.xls*.

6. Select Send To from the File menu, and select the option to send the workbook as an e-mail attachment, as shown in Figure 4.38.

**FIGURE 4.38**

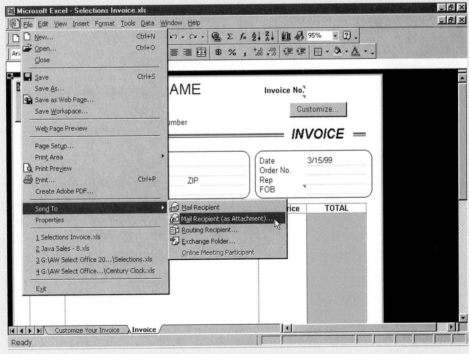

**Sending a workbook to a mail recipient as an attachment**

TIP To send a workbook as a mail attachment, you need to have a valid e-mail account and the appropriate mail server on your computer or network.

7. If Exchange Server launches, choose Cancel.

8. Close the workbook.

# On Your Own Exercises

 **Web Tip**

If you cannot obtain a copy of these files from your instructor, visit the SELECT Web site at http://www.prenhall.com/select to download the necessary files.

## 1. Modifying Page Setup for the Web Sites Workbook

Open the *Financial Sites 3.xls* workbook you modified in Project 3. Edit the workbook so it contains headers and footers and prints in landscape orientation. Save the workbook to the Investments folder with the name *Financial Sites 4.xls*.

## 2. Adding an IF Function to the Class Schedule Workbook

Open the *Class Schedule—By Day 2.xls* workbook you modified in Project 3. Add an IF function to the class schedule by day summary that tests to see whether the total number of hours taken on a given day exceed 9. If so, return the text "Difficult Schedule." If not, return "Average Schedule." Save the updated workbook as *Class Schedule—By Day 3.xls*.

## 3. Preparing Time Cards for Printing

Open the *Time Cards—Weekly Summary 2.xls* workbook file. Create three named ranges and use the names in the workbook's formulas. Save the updated workbook as *Time Cards—Weekly Summary 3.xls*.

## 4. Modifying an Excel Address List

Open the *Updated Addresses—2.xls* workbook. Add a header and footer to the worksheet. Set the orientation to landscape, and create a print area for all addresses. Save the workbook as *Updated Addresses—3.xls*.

## 5. Modifying the January Sales Workbook

Open the *January—Update 3.xls* workbook. Add MIN and MAX functions to each worksheet. Save the updated workbook as *January—Update 4.xls*.

## 6. Formatting the Utility Costs Workbook

Open the workbook named *Formatted Summary of Updated Utility Costs.xls* from your network or disk. Modify the worksheet by adding formulas to calculate the minimum, maximum, and average utility costs for each period. Save the updated workbook to your Personal folder as *Formatted Summary of Updated Utility Costs 2.xls*.

> **TIP** When printing worksheet data, you can print either the entire worksheet, or only selected cells.

Select the range of cells listing the minimum, maximum, and average utility costs for each period. Click the File menu, and choose Print. In the Print dialog box, click the Selection option on the Print What section. Click OK to print only the selected cells.

# Analyzing and Distributing Worksheet Data

After completing this project, you will be able to:

➤ Describe four common Excel chart types

➤ Create charts

➤ Change chart properties

➤ Delete charts

➤ Preview charts

➤ Print charts

➤ Add graphics to workbooks

➤ Publish worksheets to the Web

➤ View worksheet data on the Web

## Running Case

As you will recall from the step for designing electronic workbooks presented in the introduction, summarizing and distributing data are common tasks. Graphs and charts convey information visually, making it easy to understand relationships between numbers. You can add charts to the existing Selections, Inc. workbook to emphasize sales trends. By adding graphics and drawing objects to the workbook before saving it to the Web, you can communicate this important information to other Selections personnel.

# The Challenge

Mr. Traylor has reviewed all the work you have done for him, and now wants you to finalize the Selections workbook so it can be distributed internally on the corporate Intranet. Before posting this data, however, he wants to easily communicate to middle and upper management the sales trends by department for each region, and also the percentage of total sales across all regions for each department.

# The Strategy

Fortunately Excel has powerful charting capabilities to visually represent worksheet data. You can summarize the sales trends by department and region using a column chart. To summarize the total sales by department across regions, you can create and edit pie charts.

Joy Quinn of the advertising department at Selections gave you an electronic image file of the company logo. By adding this and additional drawing objects to the workbook prior to printing and exporting to the Web, you can easily enhance the overall appearance of the information. Figure 5.1 displays the Sales Summary worksheet prior to printing. Figures 5.2 and 5.3 show the column and pie charts you will export to the intranet.

**FIGURE 5.1**

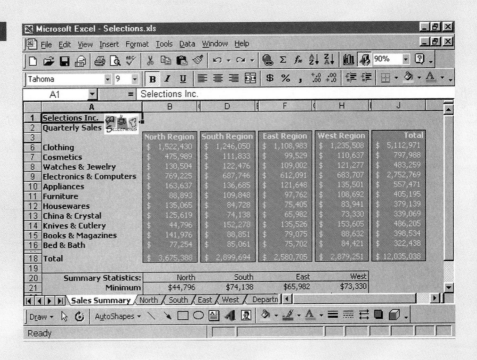

**FIGURE 5.2**

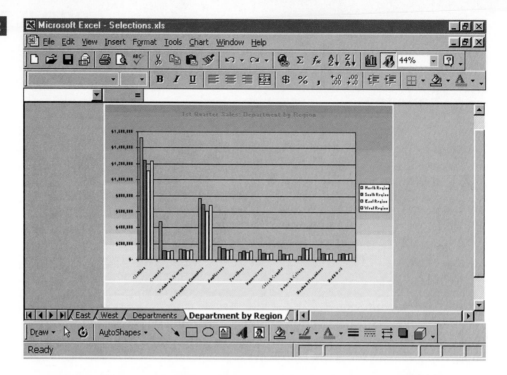

**FIGURE 5.3**

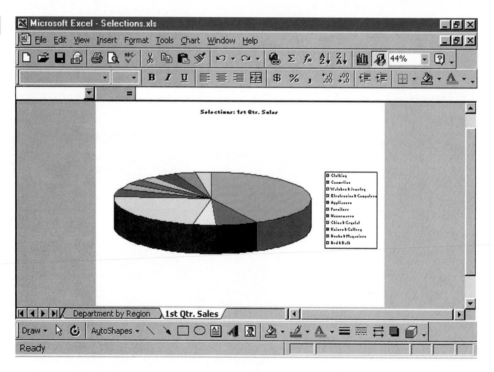

# The Setup

Launch Microsoft Excel and select the Excel settings listed in Table 5.1. This will ensure that your screen matches the illustrations and that the tasks in this project function as described.

**Table 5.1**

| Location | Make these settings: |
| --- | --- |
| **Office Assistant** | Hide the Office Assistant. |
| **Tools, Customize** | Click the Options tab and deselect the option to show recently used menu commands first. |
| **Tools, Customize** | Click the Options tab and deselect the option to display the Standard and Formatting toolbars on one row. |
| **View, Formula Bar** | Display the formula bar. |
| **View, Status Bar** | Display the status bar. |
| **View, Normal** | View the workbook in Normal view. |
| **View, Toolbars** | Display the Drawing toolbar. |
| **Maximize** | Maximize the application and workbook windows. |
| **File, Open** | Open the *Selections.xls* workbook. |

## Using Charts to Analyze and Summarize Worksheet Data

Charts make it easy for users to see comparisons, patterns, and trends in data. For instance, rather than having to analyze several columns of worksheet numbers, you can see at a glance whether sales are falling or rising over quarterly periods, or how department sales vary.

You can create a chart on its own sheet or as an embedded object on a worksheet. You can also publish a chart on a Web page. To create a chart, you must first enter the data for the chart on the worksheet. Then select that data and use the **Chart Wizard**, Excel's wizard that walks you through the steps of creating a chart. The Chart Wizard will step through the process of choosing the chart type and the various chart options.

You select the **chart type** depending upon the data you want to compare. For instance, when you want to show the parts of a whole, a **pie chart** is most appropriate. Trends over time are easily seen with a **line chart**. Both **column charts** and **bar charts** represent the same categories from different sources, such as the total gross national product from several countries. **X-Y scatter charts** compare pairs of values and often display correlations, such as the correlation between time in the computer lab and overall grade in a computer course.

Once you determine which kind of chart is most appropriate for your data, you can select a **chart sub-type**, which defines the look and feel of the specific chart, such as whether it is three-dimensional or contains summary data within the chart. Finally, you can easily change the **chart options**, such as whether a legend is displayed, the chart title, and any labels that accompany the chart's axes.

## Creating Charts

The easiest and most flexible way to create charts is by using the Chart Wizard. In the next task you will add a column chart comparing departmental sales by sales region to the Selections, Inc. workbook.

**TASK 1:** <u>To Insert a Column Chart into the Workbook</u>

**1** Highlight the row headings for rows 4 and 5, as shown in Figure 5.4.

**FIGURE 5.4**
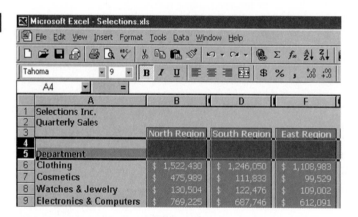

**2** Select Rows from the Insert menu, and then choose Hide, as shown in Figure 5.5. This hides the blank rows that separate the column headings from the worksheet data so you can select the headings and data as an adjacent selection.

FIGURE 5.5

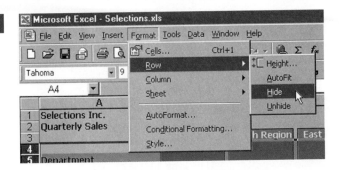

**3** Select the range A3:A16.

> **TROUBLESHOOTING** Make sure you do not accidentally select the dummy row 17, as it does not contain any data. If you select it, a blank data series will appear in your chart.

**4** While holding down the (CTRL) key, select the following ranges: B3:B16, D3:D16, F3:F16, H3:H16. The non-adjacent selection appears as shown in Figure 5.6.

FIGURE 5.6

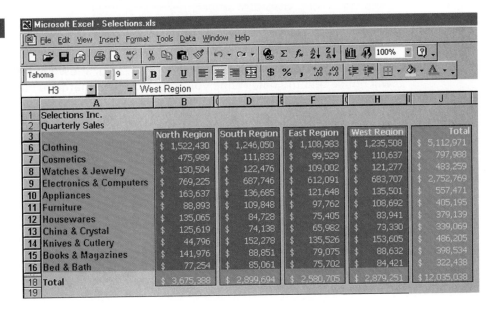

**5** Click the Chart Wizard button ⊞ on the Standard toolbar to start the Chart Wizard. The first step of the Chart Wizard is displayed.

> **TIP** Notice that only four steps are required to complete this chart!

**6** Accept the defaults displayed in Figure 5.7 and click the Next button.

**TROUBLESHOOTING** If these are not the default settings on your computer, select the options shown in Figure 5.7.

FIGURE 5.7

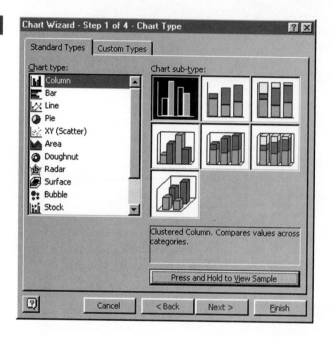

7 Accept the defaults in Step 2 of the Chart Wizard, shown in Figure 5.8. You will notice that the data range you selected has a marquee surrounding it.

FIGURE 5.8

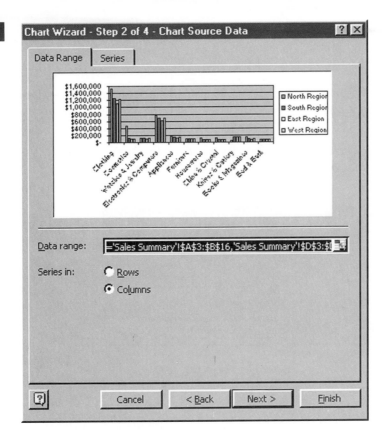

**8** Click Next. In Step 3 of the Chart Wizard, place the insertion point inside the Chart title: box and type **1st Quarter Sales: Department by Region** as the chart title.

**9** Press the TAB key once to move the insertion point into the next text box. The title appears in the preview pane, as shown in Figure 5.9.

FIGURE 5.9

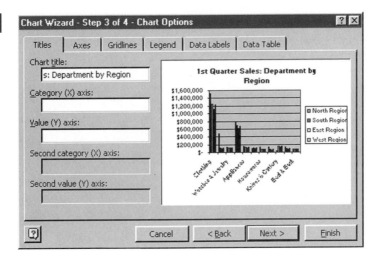

Since this chart contains so many categories, you will not add any additional labels.

**10** Click Next.

**11** The final step of the Chart Wizard asks about the location for this chart. Since it contains much data, the best option is to add it as a new worksheet. Select the As new sheet: button.

**12** Type **Department by Region** as the sheet name. When your screen matches Figure 5.10, click the Finish button.

FIGURE 5.10

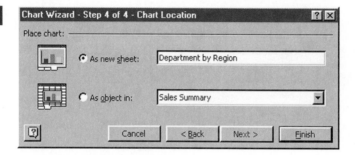

 Check Point

When you add a chart to a new worksheet, it becomes a graphic of the sheet, but is linked to the data series you used to create the chart. Thus, if the underlying data changes, the chart reconfigures to display the changes.

If you select the option to add the chart to an existing sheet it becomes a drawing object in that sheet. The chart is still dynamically linked to the data series.

**13** The chart is added to the workbook, as shown in Figure 5.11.

FIGURE 5.11

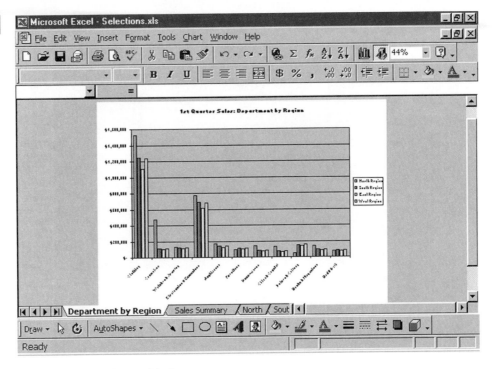

**Workbook with chart added**

**14** Change the position of the chart so it is the last worksheet in the workbook.

**15** Save your changes.

## TASK 2:    To Enter a Pie Chart into the Workbook

**1** Use the navigation buttons in the workbook window to display the Sales Summary worksheet tab.

**2** Click the Sales Summary tab to make it the active sheet.

**3** Select the range A6:A16, hold down the (CTRL) key, and select the range J6:J16, as shown in Figure 5.12.

**FIGURE 5.12**

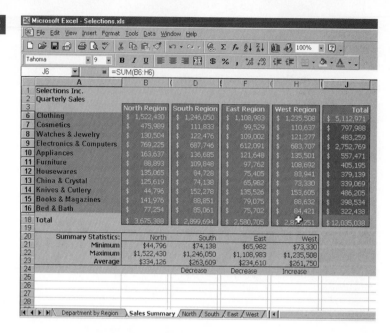

**4** Click the Chart Wizard button  on the Standard toolbar to start the Chart Wizard.

**5** Select Pie as the chart type, and Pie with a 3-D visual effect as the chart sub-type, as shown in Figure 5.13. Click Next.

**FIGURE 5.13**

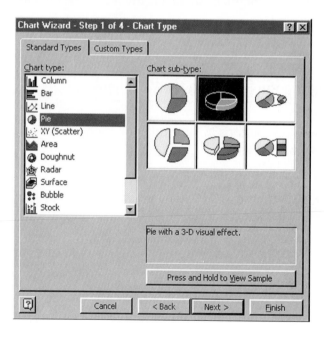

### ☑ Check Point

There is a marquee on the worksheet behind the Chart Wizard. What does this indicate? The marquee indicates the data range upon which the chart will be based. The data range can be either an adjacent or a non-adjacent selection.

**6**  Verify the default settings in Step 2 of the Chart Wizard, as shown in Figure 5.14, and click Next.

**FIGURE 5.14**

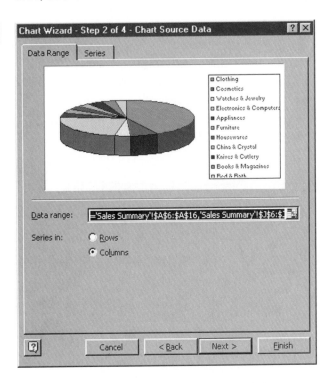

**7**  In Step 3 of the Chart Wizard, type **Selections: 1st Qtr. Sales** as the title for the chart. When your screen matches Figure 5.15, click Next.

**FIGURE 5.15**

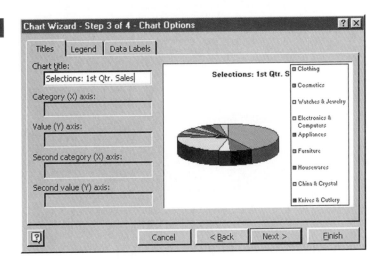

## Check Point

In Step 3 of the Chart Wizard shown in Figure 5.15, the text boxes for the axes are grayed out. Why is this the case? A pie chart is used to display parts of a whole, and depends upon only one data series. The chart title is sufficient to convey this information, so additional labels are not available.

**8** In the final step of the Chart Wizard, select the option to add the chart as a new sheet and type **1st Qtr. Sales** as the name for the worksheet, as shown in Figure 5.16. Click Finish.

**FIGURE 5.16**

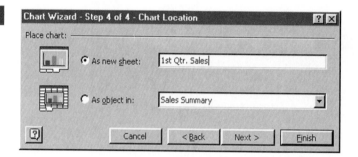

The chart shown in Figure 5.17 is added to the workbook.

**FIGURE 5.17**

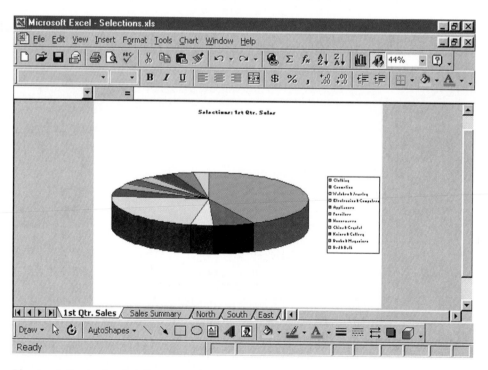

**Pie chart displaying 1st Quarter sales**

**9** Position the chart as the last worksheet in the workbook.

**10** Save your changes.

## Modifying Charts

Once you have created Excel charts, they can be easily modified. A chart is an **object**—something other than text, numbers, or formulas—that is added to a worksheet. A chart is a **linked object**, meaning that it is bound to the data in the series used to define it. If the underlying data changes, the chart is updated automatically.

When Excel creates a chart using the Chart Wizard, it adds elements to the chart that vary depending upon the chart type. Each element has **properties**, or settings that define how it appears. In the two tasks that follow, you will see how easily you can modify a chart's properties.

**TASK 3:** ## To Modify a Column Chart by Changing Its Properties

**1** Click the Department by Region worksheet tab to make the column chart you created the active sheet. Change the zoom to 44%.

**2** Click somewhere in the white area of the chart, as shown in Figure 5.18. Notice that the Name box and the comment next to the pointer both identify this chart element as the Chart Area.

> **TIP** If the Chart toolbar appears, close it.

**FIGURE 5.18**

Name box and comment identifying the chart element

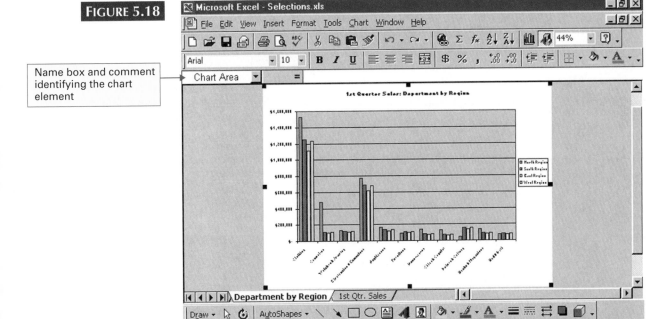

**3** Choose Selected Chart Area from the Format menu, as shown in Figure 5.19.

**FIGURE 5.19**

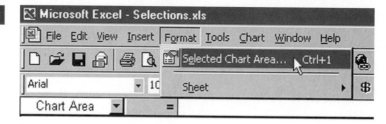

**4** Click the Fill Effects button in the Format Chart Area dialog box, as shown in Figure 5.20.

**FIGURE 5.20**

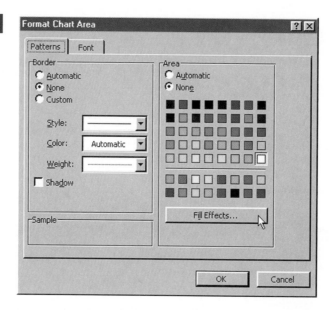

**5** The Fill Effects dialog box appears. Check the Preset color option, and select Daybreak from the Preset colors: drop-down list, as shown in Figure 5.21.

**FIGURE 5.21**

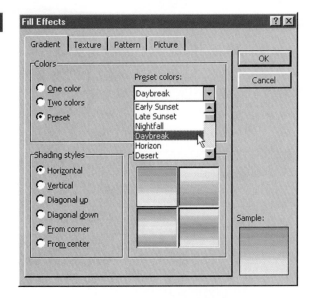

**6** Click OK to return to the Format Chart Area dialog box.

**7** Click OK. The chart is modified, as shown in Figure 5.22.

**FIGURE 5.22**

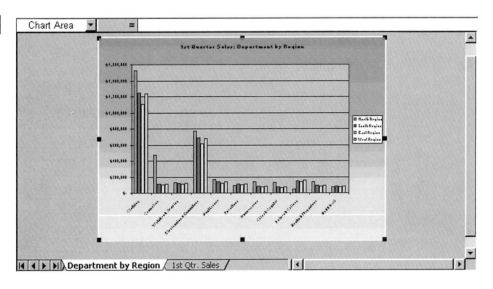

**8** Right-click the chart title and select Format Chart Title from the shortcut menu, as shown in Figure 5.23.

**FIGURE 5.23**

**9** Click the Font tab in the Format Chart title dialog box.

**10** Change the font size to 14 and the color to Red, as shown in Figure 5.24.

**FIGURE 5.24**

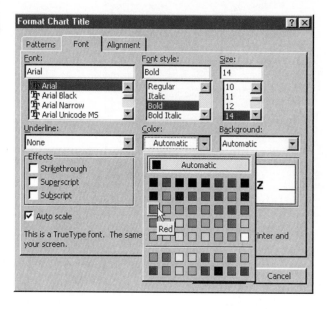

**11** Click OK. Your changes are displayed in the chart.

**12** Save your changes.

> **TIP** If you preview the chart, you may not see the colors you have selected, depending upon the current printer. To see color in a preview and have it print, you must have a color printer installed on your computer or network.

## Break Point

If necessary you can save your file, exit Excel, and continue this project later.

## Deleting Charts

As with any data or object in an Excel workbook, charts can be deleted. Because it is so easy to create charts using the Chart Wizard, you can design several charts, and then delete the ones you no longer need.

## TASK 4:  To Add a Chart to the Workbook and Then Delete It

**1** Click the North worksheet tab to make it the active sheet.

## Check Point

If the worksheet tab is not currently visible, how can you display it? To display worksheet tabs that currently are not visible, use the navigation controls in the lower-left corner of the worksheet window.

**2** Highlight the range A6:A16.

**3** Hold down the (CTRL) key and select the range K6:K16.

**4** Press the (F11) key.

> **TIP** The (F11) key is used to activate Excel's Create a chart in one step feature, which adds a worksheet to the current workbook based upon the default chart type.

**5** The chart named Chart3 shown in Figure 5.25 is added to the workbook.

**FIGURE 5.25**

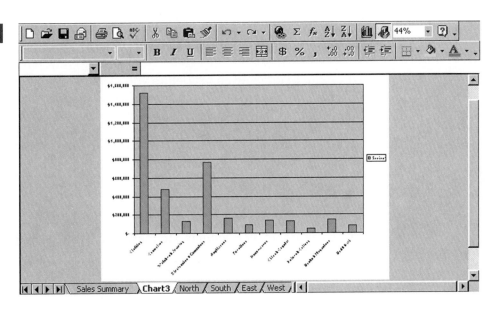

**6**  Select Delete Sheet from the Edit menu, as shown in Figure 5.26.

FIGURE 5.26

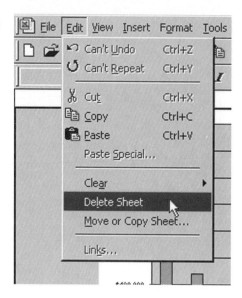

**7**  Verify that you want to delete the worksheet by clicking OK.

**8**  The chart is deleted from the workbook. Save your changes.

## Previewing Charts

It makes sense to preview charts before you actually print them. Since charts often contain multiple colors or shades of gray, they require more toner or ink when printed than worksheet data. Previewing charts also allows you to conduct a final check of the data before finalizing your reports.

TASK 5:  **To Preview Charts**

**1**  Click the Department by Region tab to make this chart the active sheet.

**2**  Click the Preview button ◻ on the Standard toolbar.

**3**  The print preview window displays the chart, as shown in Figure 5.27.

FIGURE 5.27

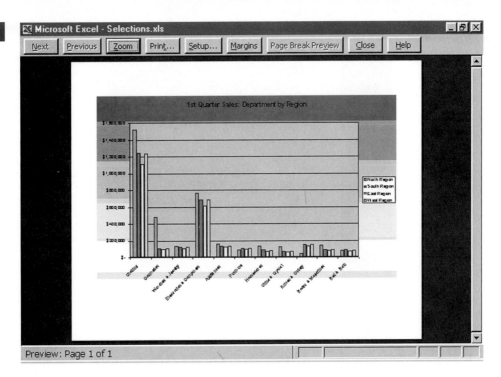

**TROUBLESHOOTING** Depending upon your current printer and settings, the preview may look different on your computer.

**4** Close the preview window.

**5** Click the 1st Qtr. Sales worksheet tab.

**6** Click the Print Preview button.

**7** The print preview window displays the chart, as shown in Figure 5.28.

FIGURE 5.28

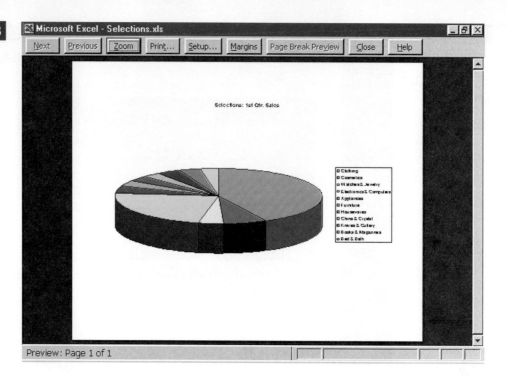

8 Close the preview window.

 **Web Tip**

As you may know, the Web has become an important medium for distributing information from almost every knowledge domain imaginable. Here is a Web site that emphasizes graphs and charts related to investing: http://www.investorlinks.com/quotes.html.

## Printing Charts

Once you have previewed your charts, you are ready to print them. You print charts as you print any Excel worksheet data: by using the File menu, or by using the Print button on the Standard toolbar.

 TASK 6: **To Print Charts**

1 Click the Department by Region worksheet tab.

2 Choose Print from the File menu.

**3** The Print dialog box for charts that you inserted as separate worksheets is identical to the Print dialog box for worksheets. As you can see from Figure 5.29, you can print more than one worksheet tab (if more than one is selected), and you can also set the number of copies to print.

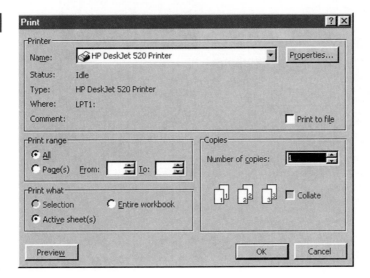

**FIGURE 5.29**

**The Print dialog box**

**4** Click OK to print one copy of the current chart.

**TROUBLESHOOTING** Your chart will print only if you have access to an active printer.

## Adding Graphics to Workbooks

In addition to chart objects, you can add a variety of graphics to Excel workbooks to enhance their appearance. Many organizations have company logos that are used for official correspondence. In this task you will add the Selections logo to the workbook.

**TASK 7:  To Add a Graphic to the Sales Summary Worksheet**

**1** Click the Sales Summary worksheet tab to make it the active sheet.

**2** Select cell A1.

**3** Select Picture from the Insert menu, and then select From File, as shown in Figure 5.30.

**FIGURE 5.30**

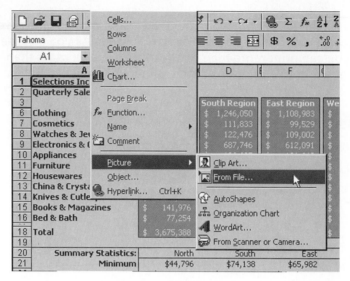

④ Locate the *Sm Selections Logo.gif* file on your floppy disk.

 **Web Tip**

If you do not have a copy of this file, you can download it from the SELECT Web site at http://www.prenhall.com/select.

⑤ Highlight the file name in the Insert Picture dialog box and click the Insert button, as shown in Figure 5.31.

**FIGURE 5.31**

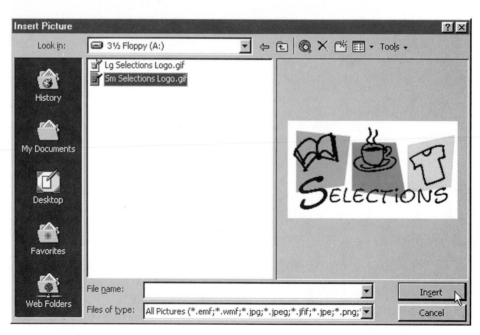

**6**    The image is inserted in the upper-left corner of the active sheet, as shown in Figure 5.32.

> **TIP** Depending on how your computer is configured, the Picture toolbar may appear on the screen.

**FIGURE 5.32**

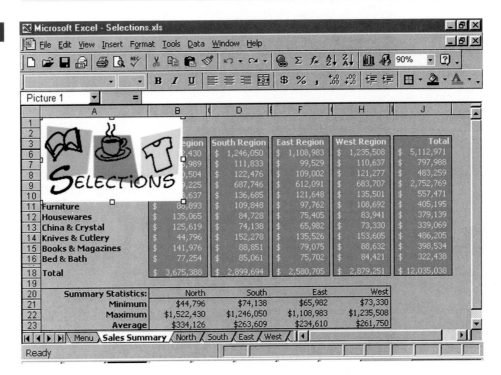

**7**    Since the image has just been added to the worksheet, it is currently selected. Move the mouse pointer to the lower-right selection handle and size the image smaller, as shown in Figure 5.33.

**FIGURE 5.33**

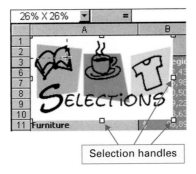

Selection handles

**8**    Position the mouse pointer immediately over the image, click the left mouse button, and drag the image to the location shown in Figure 5.34.

FIGURE 5.34

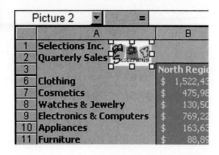

| | | A | B |
|---|---|---|---|
| 1 | | Selections Inc. | |
| 2 | | Quarterly Sales | |
| 3 | | | North Regio |
| 6 | | Clothing | $ 1,522,43 |
| 7 | | Cosmetics | $ 475,98 |
| 8 | | Watches & Jewelry | $ 130,50 |
| 9 | | Electronics & Computers | $ 769,22 |
| 10 | | Appliances | $ 163,63 |
| 11 | | Furniture | $ 88,89 |

**9** Save your changes.

## Publishing Workbooks to the Web

Your work is almost finished! Mr. Traylor wants you to publish a copy of the worksheet to the intranet so it can be reviewed internally. As you know from Project 2, by saving the workbook as a Web page it can be posted to a Web server.

**TASK 8: To Publish Workbooks to the Web**

**1** Select Save As Web Page from the File menu.

**2** Use the workspace in the Save As dialog box to create a new folder named *Selections Web*. Type **Selections Sales Summary.htm** in the File name text box of the Save As dialog box, as shown in Figure 5.35.

FIGURE 5.35

**3** Click the Publish button.

**4** The Publish as Web Page dialog box appears. You can use this dialog box to specify which components of your workbook you want to publish and whether you want users to interact with your worksheets through a Web browser. Since you are posting sales data, do not add interactivity. Accept the defaults as shown in Figure 5.36 and click the Publish button.

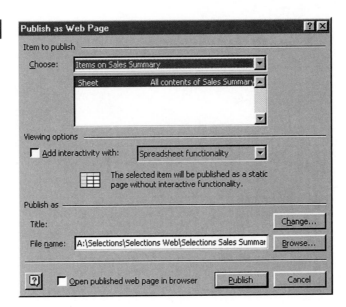

**FIGURE 5.36**

Your worksheet has successfully been published as an HTML file, which you can view with any browser.

**TROUBLESHOOTING** When developing Web resources you may want to consider omitting spaces from HTML filenames. Some browsers may return unpredictable results when opening files with spaces in the name.

**5** Save and close the workbook.

**TASK 9:** To View Excel Data on the Web

**1** Minimize Excel on the desktop and open your floppy disk using My Computer.

**2** Locate the *Selections Sales Summary.htm* document.

**3** Double-click the file to open it. If Microsoft Internet Explorer or a comparable Web browser is installed on your computer, your HTML file appears similar to Figure 5.37.

**FIGURE 5.37**

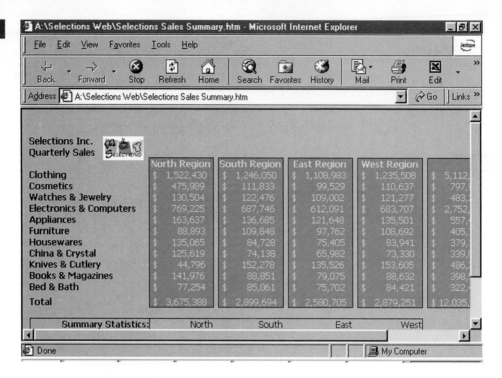

| Selections Inc. Quarterly Sales | North Region | South Region | East Region | West Region | |
|---|---|---|---|---|---|
| Clothing | $ 1,522,430 | $ 1,246,050 | $ 1,108,983 | $ 1,235,508 | $ 5,112, |
| Cosmetics | $ 475,989 | $ 111,833 | $ 99,529 | $ 110,637 | $ 797, |
| Watches & Jewelry | $ 130,504 | $ 122,476 | $ 109,002 | $ 121,277 | $ 483, |
| Electronics & Computers | $ 769,225 | $ 687,746 | $ 612,091 | $ 683,707 | $ 2,752, |
| Appliances | $ 163,637 | $ 136,685 | $ 121,648 | $ 135,501 | $ 557, |
| Furniture | $ 88,893 | $ 109,848 | $ 97,762 | $ 108,692 | $ 405, |
| Housewares | $ 135,065 | $ 84,728 | $ 75,405 | $ 83,941 | $ 379, |
| China & Crystal | $ 125,619 | $ 74,138 | $ 65,982 | $ 73,330 | $ 339, |
| Knives & Cutlery | $ 44,796 | $ 152,278 | $ 135,526 | $ 153,605 | $ 486, |
| Books & Magazines | $ 141,976 | $ 88,851 | $ 79,075 | $ 88,632 | $ 398, |
| Bed & Bath | $ 77,254 | $ 85,061 | $ 75,702 | $ 84,421 | $ 322, |
| Total | $ 3,675,388 | $ 2,899,694 | $ 2,580,705 | $ 2,879,251 | $ 12,035, |

Summary Statistics: North South East West

**4** Close the Web browser when you are finished viewing the HTML file.

**5** Close Excel.

 **Web Tip**

Did you know that the United States Department of the Treasury has graphical information available on the Web? Go to http://www.fms.treas.gov/bulletin/index.html and download the Adobe Acrobat versions of the reports you want to view.

# Summary and Exercises

## Summary

- Graphs and charts are often used to efficiently communicate numeric data.
- Excel supports many chart types that are appropriate for representing any data your workbook will contain.
- Once you create a chart, you can easily change its properties.
- Printing and previewing charts are common tasks.
- You can enhance the visual appeal of workbooks by adding graphics.
- You can publish Excel workbooks containing charts and other graphic elements to the Web.

## Key Terms and Operations

### Key Terms

| | |
|---|---|
| bar chart | line chart |
| chart options | linked object |
| chart sub-type | object |
| chart type | pie chart |
| Chart Wizard | properties |
| column chart | X-Y scatter chart |

### Operations

add graphics to workbooks
create a column chart
create a pie chart
delete charts
modify charts
preview charts
print charts
publish worksheets on the Web
view published worksheets on the Web

# Study Questions

## Multiple Choice

1. Which menu contains an option to publish worksheet data to the Web?
   a. File
   b. Edit
   c. View
   d. Insert

2. To add an existing graphic to a workbook, you first need to know the image's:
   a. file format.
   b. location.
   c. size.
   d. color.

3. Which chart type is best for representing the parts of a whole?
   a. column
   b. bar
   c. pie
   d. line

4. The bar chart is most similar to which other chart type?
   a. pie
   b. line
   c. column
   d. X-Y scatter

5. The _____ chart compares pairs of values.
   a. line
   b. pie
   c. bar
   d. X-Y scatter

6. Which chart type is best for showing trends over time?
   a. column
   b. bar
   c. pie
   d. line

7. Which menu do you use to preview a chart?
   a. File
   b. Edit
   c. View
   d. Insert

8. Which statement is false?
   a. A pie chart is best at representing the parts of a whole.
   b. Charts are visual representations of numeric data.
   c. A chart can never be deleted from a workbook.
   d. A column chart compares data from multiple data sources.

9. To delete a chart as a worksheet from a workbook, which menu do you use?
   a. File
   b. Edit
   c. Insert
   d. Help

10. What is the maximum percentage a pie chart will display?
    a. 10
    b. 25
    c. 75
    d. 100

## Short Answer

1. Which chart type is most like a column chart?

2. How many data series are represented in a pie chart?

3. Which chart type is used to represent correlations?

4. Which chart type is used to show trends over time?

5. What is a chart?

6. How can you delete a chart from a workbook?

7. How do you look at a chart before printing it?

8. How do you add graphics to a worksheet?

9. Which tool helps you create charts?

10. Which application do you use to view worksheet data that has been published to the Web?

## Fill in the Blank

1. A _____ chart represents parts of a whole.

2. To insert a chart on a separate worksheet, use the _____ option in the Step 4 of the Chart Wizard.

3. The data used to create a pie chart is called the _____.

4. A(n) _____ chart is never used to plot more than one data series.

5. A(n) _____chart shows the relationship between pairs.

6. A(n) _____ chart belongs to a particular worksheet.

7. You can add graphic files to workbooks using the _____ menu.

8. You can publish a worksheet to the Web using the _____ menu.

9. A(n) _____ chart is almost identical to a(n) _____ chart, the only difference being the orientation of the data series.

10. To allow multiple users to interact with a workbook, you can _____ it to the Web.

## For Discussion

1. Why are charts useful? What kind of information do they convey?

2. When should you consider using a pie chart? A line chart? A column chart? Describe a situation where each type of chart is useful.

3. How does inserting a chart as a separate worksheet differ from embedding a chart into an existing worksheet?

4. Why might you want to add graphics to a workbook?

5. When might you want to publish a worksheet to the Web that supports interactivity?

# Hands-On Exercises

### 1. Adding a Menu Worksheet to a Workbook

There may be times when a workbook has become so complex that you want to add an initial worksheet to the workbook that explains how to navigate within the book. In this exercise you will create a worksheet that will act as a menu to the various worksheets in the Selections workbook.

1. Launch Excel if it is not currently running, and open the Selections workbook.

2. Add a worksheet as the first sheet in the book. Rename the sheet *Menu*.

3. Insert the *Lg Selections Logo.gif* file into the worksheet.

4. Enter the text labels shown in Figure 5.38 into the worksheet.

**FIGURE 5.38**

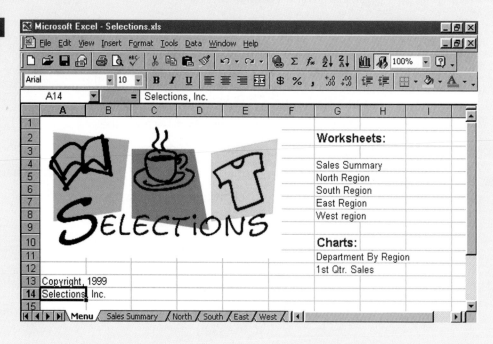

5. Save a copy of the workbook as *Selections—First Quarter.xls*.

6. Select Toolbars from the View menu, and display the Drawing toolbar.

7. Select Block Arrows from the AutoShapes menu on the Drawing toolbar. Select the Pentagon arrow, as shown in Figure 5.39.

**FIGURE 5.39**

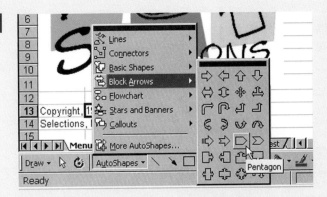

8. Draw a block arrow in the approximate position shown in Figure 5.40.

**FIGURE 5.40**

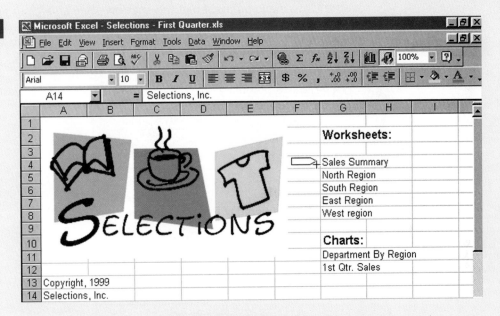

9. With the arrow selected, choose the Fill button on the drawing toolbar, and choose Indigo as the arrow's fill color, as shown in Figure 5.41.

**FIGURE 5.41**

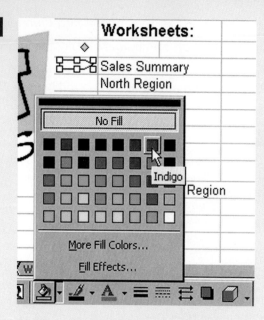

10. With the draw object still highlighted, click the Shadow button on the Drawing toolbar. Select the shadow style shown in Figure 5.42.

**FIGURE 5.42**

11. Select Shadow Settings from the Shadow button. Using the tools on the Shadow Settings toolbar, nudge the shadow so it looks similar to Figure 5.43.

**FIGURE 5.43**

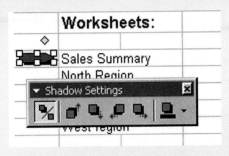

12. Using the Copy and Paste buttons, select the current arrow and create additional arrows for each of the text entries.

13. Close the Shadow Setting toolbar when you are finished using it.

14. Select the buttons to the left of the two chart names, and change the fill color to Dark Red. When you are finished, the worksheet should look similar to the one shown in Figure 5.44.

**FIGURE 5.44**

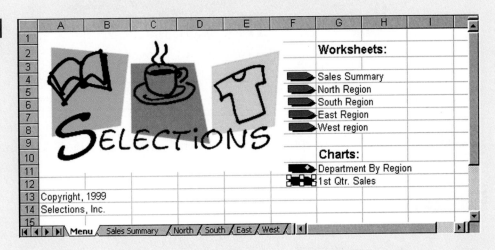

15. Save your changes. Close the workbook if you do not intend to finish the next exercise at this time.

## 2. Adding Hyperlinks to a Worksheet

In this exercise you will add hyperlinks to the worksheet you created in the previous exercise.

1. Open the *Selections—First Quarter.xls* workbook if it is not currently open.

## Web Tip

You may obtain a copy of this file from the SELECT Web site at http://www.prenhall.com/select if you do not have it.

2. Click the Menu tab if it is not currently the active sheet.

3. Select Options from the Tools menu.

4. Click the View tab and deselect the Gridlines option. When your screen matches Figure 5.45, click OK.

**FIGURE 5.45**

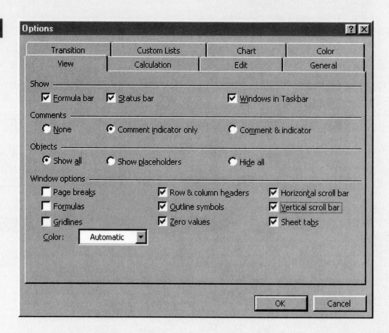

5. Select cell G4 and right-click. Choose Hyperlink from the shortcut menu, as shown in Figure 5.46.

**FIGURE 5.46**

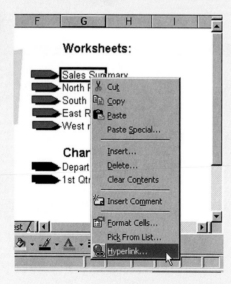

The Insert Hyperlink dialog box appears. Click the Place in This Document button in the bar to the left, as shown in Figure 5.47.

**FIGURE 5.47**

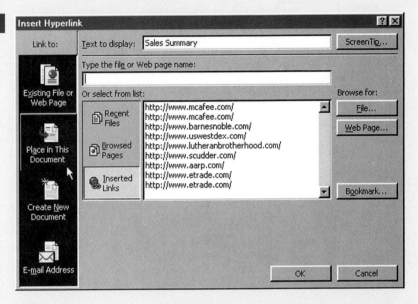

6. Click the plus sign (+) next to Cell Reference to open the list, and select Sales Summary, as shown in Figure 5.48.

**FIGURE 5.48**

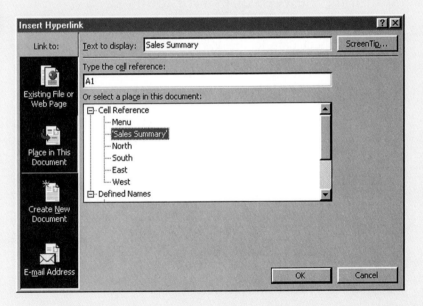

7. Click OK. The text label is changed to a hyperlink, as shown in Figure 5.49. Now that the label is a hyperlink, you can click it to go the cell A1 of the Sales Summary sheet.

FIGURE 5.49

**Worksheets:**

Sales Summary
North Region
South Region
East Region
West region

8. Add hyperlinks to the remaining text labels so that each links to the appropriate worksheet tab.

TIP You cannot add hyperlinks to the chart sheets.

9. Select a cell in each of the existing worksheets and type Menu as the text label. Add a hyperlink from each sheet back to the menu.
10. Save your changes and close the workbook.

# On Your Own Exercises

## 1. Publishing the Web Sites Workbook

Open the *Financial Sites 4.xls* workbook you modified in Project 3. Publish all worksheet data to the Web. Open the HTML version using your Web browser. Close both files when you are finished.

## 2. Printing Your Class Schedule to the Web

Open the *Class Schedule—By Day 3.xls* workbook you modified in Project 3. Print the sheet containing course information to the Web. Close the workbook when you are finished.

## 3. Adding a Graphic to the Time Cards Workbook

Open the *Time Cards—Weekly Summary 3.xls* workbook file. Insert a ClipArt image of your choosing to the workbook. Save the updated workbook as *Time Cards—Weekly Summary 4.xls*.

## 4. Publishing Addresses to the Web

Open the *Updated Addresses—3.xls* workbook. Publish your address list to the Web. Close the workbook when you are finished.

## 5. Charting January Sales

Open the *January—Update 4.xls* workbook. Create a column chart comparing all sales by category. Publish the chart to the Web. Save the updated workbook as *January—Update 5.xls*.

## 6. Creating a Chart to Show Utility Costs

Open the workbook named *Formatted Summary of Updated Utility Costs 2.xls* from your network or floppy disk. Add a line chart showing the changes in utility costs over time. Save the updated workbook to your Personal folder as *Formatted Summary of Updated Utility Costs 3.xls*.

# Using Financial Functions

**B**y using Excel's financial functions, you can quickly and easily run the numbers for a loan of any magnitude.

## Running Case

Even businesses need to borrow money at times! The regional accounting office for Selections has allocated money for many of its stores to expand next year. To pay for this expansion, Mr. Traylor wants you to analyze a multitude of loan options to determine the best scenario for the Selections, Inc. department stores.

# PROJECT 6

## The Challenge

Mr. Traylor has asked you to construct an amortization schedule so he can compare different loan scenarios. After you complete the workbook, he will determine the optimum loan scenario on a store-by-store basis before contacting specific lending institutions for funding.

## The Solution

Excel has a number of financial functions that will make creating this workbook a simple task! By entering four numeric constants and using the PMT, PPMT, IPMT, and PV financial functions, you can create the workbook Mr. Traylor needs. Your completed amortization schedule will look like the one shown in Figure 6.1.

**FIGURE 6.1**

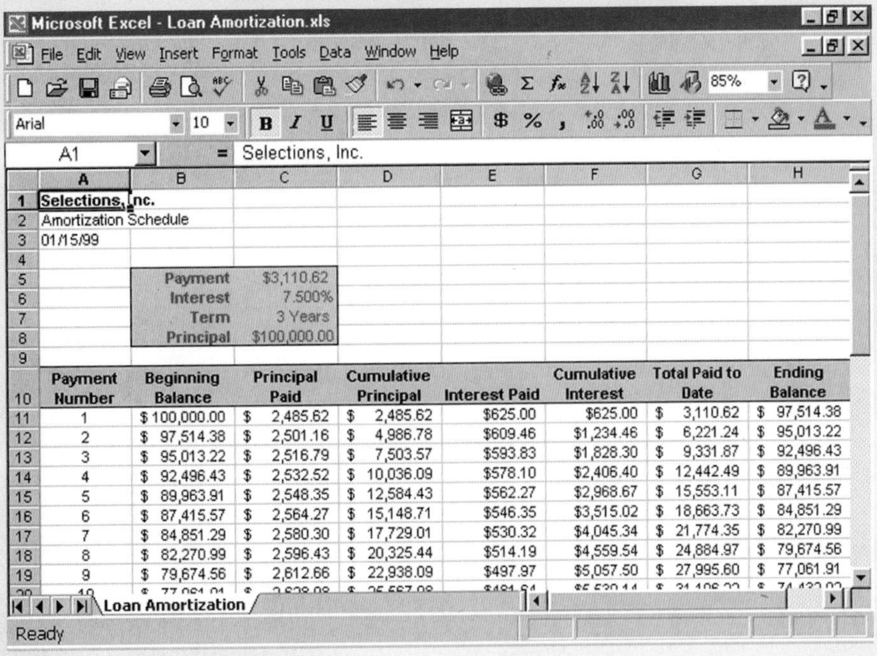


| | A | B | C | D | E | F | G | H |
|---|---|---|---|---|---|---|---|---|
| 1 | Selections, Inc. | | | | | | | |
| 2 | Amortization Schedule | | | | | | | |
| 3 | 01/15/99 | | | | | | | |
| 4 | | | | | | | | |
| 5 | | Payment | $3,110.62 | | | | | |
| 6 | | Interest | 7.500% | | | | | |
| 7 | | Term | 3 Years | | | | | |
| 8 | | Principal | $100,000.00 | | | | | |
| 9 | | | | | | | | |
| 10 | Payment Number | Beginning Balance | Principal Paid | Cumulative Principal | Interest Paid | Cumulative Interest | Total Paid to Date | Ending Balance |
| 11 | 1 | $ 100,000.00 | $ 2,485.62 | $ 2,485.62 | $625.00 | $625.00 | $ 3,110.62 | $ 97,514.38 |
| 12 | 2 | $ 97,514.38 | $ 2,501.16 | $ 4,986.78 | $609.46 | $1,234.46 | $ 6,221.24 | $ 95,013.22 |
| 13 | 3 | $ 95,013.22 | $ 2,516.79 | $ 7,503.57 | $593.83 | $1,828.30 | $ 9,331.87 | $ 92,496.43 |
| 14 | 4 | $ 92,496.43 | $ 2,532.52 | $ 10,036.09 | $578.10 | $2,406.40 | $ 12,442.49 | $ 89,963.91 |
| 15 | 5 | $ 89,963.91 | $ 2,548.35 | $ 12,584.43 | $562.27 | $2,968.67 | $ 15,553.11 | $ 87,415.57 |
| 16 | 6 | $ 87,415.57 | $ 2,564.27 | $ 15,148.71 | $546.35 | $3,515.02 | $ 18,663.73 | $ 84,851.29 |
| 17 | 7 | $ 84,851.29 | $ 2,580.30 | $ 17,729.01 | $530.32 | $4,045.34 | $ 21,774.35 | $ 82,270.99 |
| 18 | 8 | $ 82,270.99 | $ 2,596.43 | $ 20,325.44 | $514.19 | $4,559.54 | $ 24,884.97 | $ 79,674.56 |
| 19 | 9 | $ 79,674.56 | $ 2,612.66 | $ 22,938.09 | $497.97 | $5,057.50 | $ 27,995.60 | $ 77,061.91 |

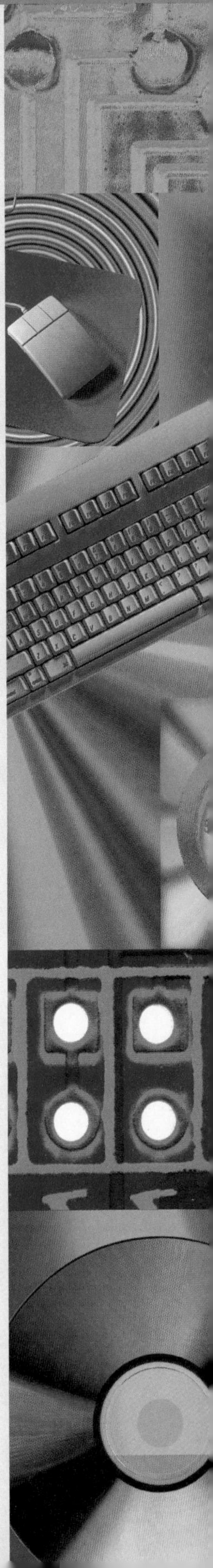

# The Setup

Launch Microsoft Excel and select the Excel settings listed in Table 6.1. This will ensure that your screen matches the illustrations and that the tasks in this project function as described.

**Table 6.1**

| Location | Make these settings: |
|---|---|
| **Office Assistant** | Hide the Office Assistant. |
| **Tools, Customize** | Click the Options tab and deselect the option to show recently used menu commands first. |
| **Tools, Customize** | Click the Options tab and deselect the option to display the Standard and Formatting toolbars on one row. |
| **View, Formula Bar** | Display the formula bar. |
| **View, Status Bar** | Display the status bar. |
| **View, Normal** | View the workbook in Normal view. |
| **Maximize** | Maximize the application and workbook windows. |
| **Worksheet Tab for Sheet1** | Double-click and rename this tab Loan Amortization, and delete the remaining worksheets. |

# Using Excel to Amortize a Loan

As you learned in the introduction, a great advantage of Excel and other electronic spreadsheets is their ability to perform "what-if" analyses. The computer can easily store and retrieve data and perform calculations, so Microsoft Excel can be used to develop sophisticated models to assist in decision making.

## Amortizing a Loan

One decision that individuals and managers often undertake involves assessing the terms under which they will borrow money. Loan payments are amortized; **amortization** is the process of distributing monthly payments over the life of a loan. The factors determining a loan's repayment include the amount of the loan, the percent interest charged by the bank or lending organization, and the length of time over which the loan will be repaid. Each of these factors has a technical name:

• The amount borrowed is the **principal**

- The percent interest is the **rate**
- The time period over which payments are made is the **term**

Depending on the values associated with each factor, varying portions of each loan payment apply to the principal and the interest payment. In general, borrowers aim to pay off the principal in as short an amount of time as financially possible.

## Understanding Loan Payments

An **amortization schedule** lists the outstanding balance, monthly payment, amount of each payment that applies to the principal, and the amount of each payment that applies to the outstanding principal for the life of a loan. In this project, you will learn to use financial functions to create an amortization schedule.

## The Power of Excel

In this project you will create a loan amortization worksheet by entering four numeric constants and hundreds of formulas. By carefully planning the structure of the worksheet, you can efficiently utilize **absolute cell references**, which are references in formulas preceded with a dollar sign ($) symbol before both the row and column reference. Absolute references always refer to the same cell when the formula is copied elsewhere in the worksheet; an important consideration, when the amount of the principal, the interest rate, and the term of the loan all impact the monthly payment. Other formulas you create will use **relative cell references**, which will change the row and column.

This worksheet will also contain **checks and balances**, to ensure that the calculations are accurate. The checks and balances you will use are specific calculations performed by more than one method, and compared with one another, to assure accuracy throughout the worksheet. Recall that checking the accuracy of a worksheet's data is an important step in designing electronic workbooks.

## Defining the Structure of the Amortization Schedule

The amortization schedule's structure is defined by entering text labels specifying where the payment, interest, term, and loan repayment data appears in the worksheet. Remember that Excel uses two categories of constants: **text constants** define the structure of the worksheet, and **numeric constants** comprise the data upon which the **loan scenario** is based.

When you enter the constants, you format them to enhance the appearance of the worksheet.

**TASK 1:** To Define the Structure of the Amortization Schedule

**1** Type **Selections, Inc.** in cell A1.

**2** Type **Amortization Schedule** in cell A2.

**3** Type **=NOW()** as a formula in cell A3 and click the Enter button on the formula bar.

> **TIP** The =NOW() function is a Date & Time function that displays the date and time according to the computer's system clock. This date is dynamic; as the system clock changes, the date is updated.

**4** Select Cells from the Format menu. Click the Number tab in the Format Cells dialog box, choose Date as the category, and choose the date type shown in Figure 6.2.

**FIGURE 6.2**

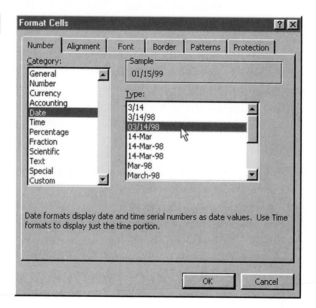

**5** Click the Alignment tab and set the horizontal alignment of the cell to Left.

**6** Click OK.

**7** Type **Payment** in cell B5, **Interest** in cell B6, **Term** in cell B7, and **Principal** in cell B8. Set the alignment of these cells to right aligned.

**8** Type **Payment Number** in cell A10, **Beginning Balance** in cell B10, **Principal Paid** in cell C10, **Cumulative Principal** in cell D10, **Interest Paid** in cell E10, **Cumulative Interest** in cell F10, **Total Paid to Date** in cell G10, and **Ending Balance** in cell H10.

## TASK 2: To Apply Additional Formats to the Text Constants

**1** Select the range A10:H10 and set the font style to bold. Using the Fill Color button ![fill color] on the Formatting Toolbar, set the fill color of the selection to Gray-25%. The worksheet appears as shown in Figure 6.3.

**FIGURE 6.3**

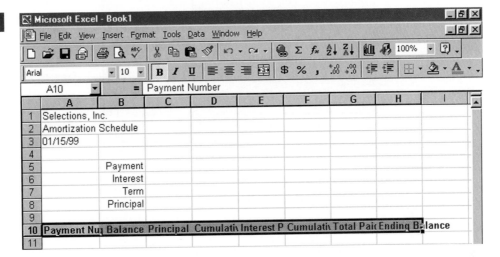

**2** Select the range B5:C8. Set the fill color of the selection to Gray-25%.

**3** Select the range B5:C5. Using the Font Color button on the Formatting toolbar, set the font color of this selection to Dark Red, as shown in Figure 6.4.

**FIGURE 6.4**

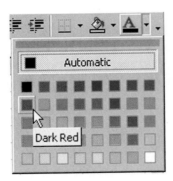

**4** Select the Borders button ![borders] on the Formatting toolbar. Insert a thin border around the selection.

**5** Set the font style of the selection to bold.

**6** Select the range A10:H10, and select Cells from the Format menu. Select the Alignment tab.

**7** Set the Horizontal text alignment to center, and check the option to wrap text, as shown in Figure 6.5. Click OK.

**FIGURE 6.5**

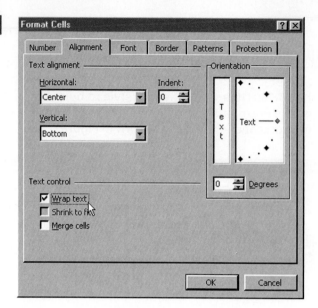

**8** Select the Borders tool 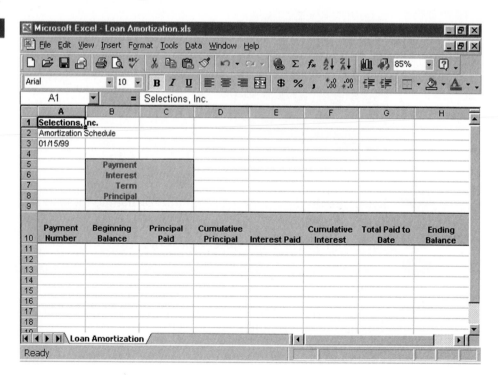 on the Formatting toolbar. Select the option to add a Top and Bottom Border to the selection.

**9** Use the column headings to select columns B through H.

**10** Set the width of the selected columns to 12.00. Save the workbook to your floppy disk in a folder titled *Loan*. Save the workbook as *Loan Amortization.xls*.

**11** Change the Zoom control on the Standard toolbar to 85%.

**12** Select cell A1 and change the font to bold. The workbook should look like the one shown in Figure 6.6.

**FIGURE 6.6**

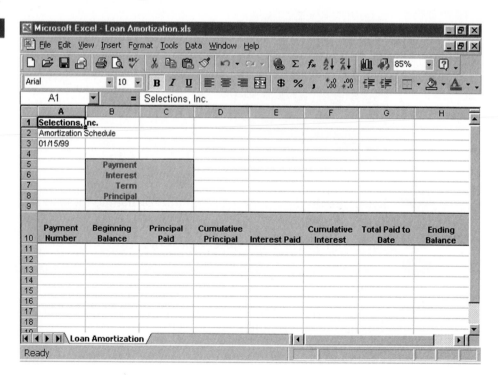

# Entering Numeric Constants

Excel will calculate a loan payment using three factors: the loan principal, the interest rate, and the term. You will enter these values in the range C6:C8 of your worksheet. All loan repayment data is calculated using these values.

## TASK 3:    To Enter and Format Numeric Constants

**1** Place the cell pointer in cell C6, type **.075**, and press (ENTER).

**2** Click cell C6 again to make it the active cell, select Cells from the Format Menu, and click the Number tab.

**3** Select Percentage as the category, and specify three decimal places, as shown in Figure 6.7. Click OK.

**FIGURE 6.7**

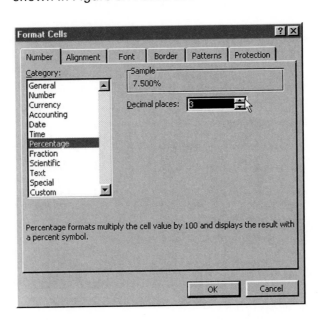

**4** Make cell C7 the active cell, type the value **3**, and press (ENTER).

**5** Place the cell pointer in cell C7, select Cells from the Format menu, and click the Number tab if necessary.

**6** Choose Custom as the category, and place the insertion point in the Type: text box.

**7** Enter **## "Years"** as the custom format, as shown in Figure 6.8. The Sample box shows how the current value will appear.

**FIGURE 6.8**

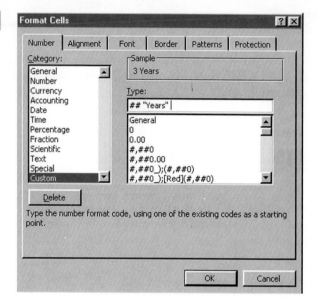

**8** Click OK. This places the text string *Years* after the numeric value in the cell.

**9** Place the cell pointer in cell C8, type **100000**, and press (ENTER).

**10** Make cell C8 the active cell and select Cells from the Format menu. Click the Number tab and select Currency as the category. Make sure two decimal places are specified.

**11** Click OK. After entering and formatting the three numeric constants, the worksheet should look like the one shown in Figure 6.9.

**FIGURE 6.9**

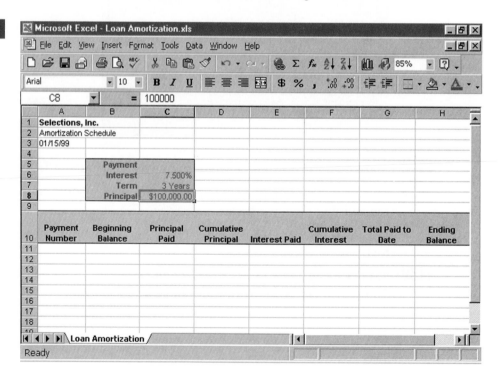

## Calculating the Loan Payment Using Excel's PMT Function

After you specify the rate, term, and principal in the Excel worksheet, you can calculate the loan payment. The PMT (payment) function is a financial function used to calculate the periodic payment of a loan, assuming a constant interest rate and constant payments over the life of the loan. You will recall that functions perform calculations by using specific values, called **arguments**, in a particular order, called the **syntax**. The PMT function uses five arguments, three of which are required. Each argument is separated from the others with a comma. The general syntax for the PMT function is:

=PMT(interest rate, number of payments, present value)

> **TIP** Search for PMT in the Help system for more information about the arguments accompanying this function.

**TASK 4:** To Calculate the Loan Payment Using the PMT Function

**1** Place the cell pointer in cell C5 to make it the active cell.

**2** Type **=PMT(C6/12,C7\*12,-C8)** as the formula for this cell and press (ENTER). The value shown in Figure 6.10 is displayed.

## Check Point

If you need help constructing this formula, what should you do? To get assistance using one of Excel's functions, use the formula palette to construct the formula.

| FIGURE 6.10 | C5 | ▼ | = | =PMT(C6/12,C7*12,-C8) | |
|---|---|---|---|---|---|

| | A | B | C | D | E |
|---|---|---|---|---|---|
| 1 | **Selections, Inc.** | | | | |
| 2 | Amortization Schedule | | | | |
| 3 | 01/15/99 | | | | |
| 4 | | | | | |
| 5 | | Payment | $3,110.62 | | |
| 6 | | Interest | 7.500% | | |
| 7 | | Term | 3 Years | | |
| 8 | | Principal | $100,000.00 | | |
| 9 | | | | | |

**3** Save your changes.

## Web Tip

Speaking of loans, do you need to finance your education? Visit http://www.finaid.org for information about student loans and other sources of funding.

## Calculating the Beginning Balance Using Excel's PV Function

Although the beginning balance of the loan that appears in cell B11 is the same as the principal displayed in cell C8, the PV function can be used to enter a "check" into the worksheet. By using the PV function in cell B12 rather than merely including a reference to cell C5, you verify the accuracy of the worksheet.

As with the PMT function, the PV (present value of an annuity) function requires three arguments: rate, term, and payment. The general syntax for the PV function is:

=PV(interest rate, number of payments, periodic payment)

**TASK 5:** To Calculate the Beginning Balance Using the PV Function

**1** Place the cell pointer in cell B11.

**2** Type **=PV(C6/12,C7*12,-C5)** and press (ENTER).

TIP   As with the PMT function, the annual interest rate must be divided by the number of annual periods (12) per year. You must multiply the term (in years) by the number of payments made each year (12). The payment must be preceded by a minus sign.

The value displayed in cell B11 should appear as shown in Figure 6.11.

**FIGURE 6.11**

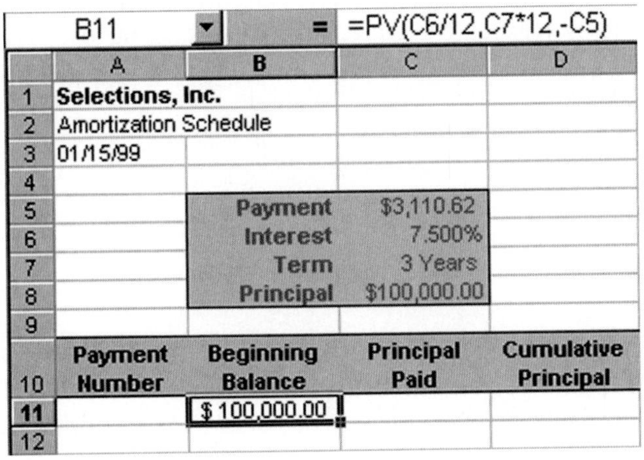

| B11 | ▼ | = | =PV(C6/12,C7*12,-C5) |
|---|---|---|---|

| | A | B | C | D |
|---|---|---|---|---|
| 1 | Selections, Inc. | | | |
| 2 | Amortization Schedule | | | |
| 3 | 01/15/99 | | | |
| 4 | | | | |
| 5 | | Payment | $3,110.62 | |
| 6 | | Interest | 7.500% | |
| 7 | | Term | 3 Years | |
| 8 | | Principal | $100,000.00 | |
| 9 | | | | |
| 10 | Payment Number | Beginning Balance | Principal Paid | Cumulative Principal |
| 11 | | $ 100,000.00 | | |
| 12 | | | | |

**3**   Save the workbook.

# Calculating the Principal Paid in Each Payment Using Excel's PPMT Function

The amount of each loan payment that applies to the loan principal (rather than the accrued interest) varies throughout the term of the loan. As with most annuity functions, the actual variance depends upon the loan's rate, term, and principal. The PPMT (periodic principal payment) returns the payment on the principal for a given period. The PPMT function requires four arguments: the rate, the specific period, the number of payments, and the present value of the annuity for the period. Practically speaking, this means that you pay more interest to the bank than you do toward your debt in the early loan payments. This is how the lending institution makes its money, and minimizes its risk if you default on the loan.

In this function, the ***present value*** refers to the total amount that a series of future payments is worth now—this is the loan principal. The general syntax is:

=PPMT(interest rate, payment period, number of payments, present value)

This function, which is copied to other cells in the amortization schedule, includes both absolute cell references and one mixed cell reference. A **mixed reference** means that the column reference remains constant, but the row reference varies. The function also will need to reference the specific payment (by payment number) within the period. This data is supplied to the function from column A of the amortization schedule.

> **TIP** The term *mixed reference* is a carryover from Lotus 1-2-3 and is not used in Microsoft Excel. Therefore, this term will not be found in the Help System. It is a useful term, however, because it conveys the idea that part of the reference is relative and part is absolute. In Excel, mixed references are also referred to as absolute references.

 ## Web Tip

Is all this financial-speak making your head spin? There is a wealth of information about finances and investing available on line. Visit the Motley Fool at http://www.fool.com for a variety of perspectives concerning finances and investing.

 **TASK 6:** ## To Calculate the Periodic Principal Payment Using the PPMT Function

**1** Click cell A11 to make it the active cell.

**2** Type **1** as a numeric constant representing the first periodic payment.

**3** Place the insertion point in cell C11, making it the active cell. Type **=-PPMT($C$6/12,$A11,$C$7\*12,$C$8)** and press (ENTER). The worksheet should display the value shown in Figure 6.12.

**FIGURE 6.12**

| C11 | | = =-PPMT($C$6/12,$A11,$C$7*12,$C$8) | | | |
|---|---|---|---|---|---|
| | A | B | C | D | E | F |

| | A | B | C | D | E | F |
|---|---|---|---|---|---|---|
| 1 | Selections, Inc. | | | | | |
| 2 | Amortization Schedule | | | | | |
| 3 | 01/15/99 | | | | | |
| 4 | | | | | | |
| 5 | | Payment | $3,110.62 | | | |
| 6 | | Interest | 7.500% | | | |
| 7 | | Term | 3 Years | | | |
| 8 | | Principal | $100,000.00 | | | |
| 9 | | | | | | |
| 10 | Payment Number | Beginning Balance | Principal Paid | Cumulative Principal | Interest Paid | Cumulative Interest |
| 11 | 1 | $ 100,000.00 | $ 2,485.62 | | | |
| 12 | | | | | | |

# Check Point

Let's analyze this formula. The entire payment is preceded by a minus sign, because annuity payments must be specified as a negative value. The references to the rate (cell C6), term (cell C7), and present value (cell C8) are absolute, because the formula must always reference the same cells, regardless of where the formula is copied in the worksheet. Cell C11 contains a mixed reference: The row reference must change to reflect the periodic payment as the formula is copied down the amortization schedule, but column A must be referenced when the formula is copied to cell E11 to construct the IPMT function. It is not mandatory that cells C6, C7, and C8 contain absolute references. Technically, these could contain mixed references to specify which part of the reference should remain constant (C$6, for example); only the row designation must remain constant as the formulas are copied. The worksheet also uses the IPMT function, which shares the same arguments as the PPMT function, so absolute references are used to assist in creating these formulas. In general, it is a good practice to use absolute references unless the column reference must change if the formula is copied to another column in the worksheet.

## Calculating the Interest Paid in Each Payment Using the IPMT Function

The method for calculating the portion of a loan payment that applies to the interest payment is almost identical to the method for calculating a periodic principal payment. The only difference is that the IPMT (periodic interest payment) function is used. The general syntax for the IPMT function is:

=IPMT(interest rate, payment period, number of payments, present value)

**TASK 7:    To Calculate the Periodic Interest Payment**

**1** Select cell C11.

**2** Copy the contents of the cell.

**3** Place the insertion point in cell E11.

**4** Select Paste using either the Edit menu or the Standard toolbar.

**5** Edit the formula in the formula bar by changing the function from PPMT to IPMT. The worksheet should now look like the one shown in Figure 6.13.

**FIGURE 6.13**

| E11 | ▼ | = | =-IPMT($C$6/12,$A11,$C$7*12,$C$8) | | |
|---|---|---|---|---|---|
| | A | B | C | D | E | F |

| | A | B | C | D | E | F |
|---|---|---|---|---|---|---|
| 1 | Selections, Inc. | | | | | |
| 2 | Amortization Schedule | | | | | |
| 3 | 01/15/99 | | | | | |
| 4 | | | | | | |
| 5 | | Payment | $3,110.62 | | | |
| 6 | | Interest | 7.500% | | | |
| 7 | | Term | 3 Years | | | |
| 8 | | Principal | $100,000.00 | | | |
| 9 | | | | | | |
| 10 | Payment Number | Beginning Balance | Principal Paid | Cumulative Principal | Interest Paid | Cumulative Interest |
| 11 | 1 | $100,000.00 | $ 2,485.62 | | $625.00 | |
| 12 | | | | | | |

**6** Save the workbook.

# Constructing Formulas to Calculate the Cumulative Principal, Cumulative Interest, Total Payments, and Ending Balance

When building an amortization schedule in Excel, it is helpful to display not only the current principal and interest payments, but the cumulative payments as well. For the first payment, the periodic principal and interest payment equal the cumulative payments. In subsequent rows, however, the cumulative payment figures increase. The total payments to date can be calculated by adding the cumulative principal and the cumulative interest payments.

## Break Point

If necessary, you can save the workbook, exit Excel, and continue this project later.

**TASK 8:** To Construct Formulas to Determine the Cumulative Interest, Cumulative Principal, Total Payments, and Ending Balance

**1** Select cell D11 as the active cell.

**2** Type **=C11**.

**3** Place the insertion point in cell F11 and type **=E11**.

**4** Place the insertion point in cell G11 and type **=D11+F11**.

## Check Point

The value displayed in cell G11 should be identical to the value in cell C5. This provides another "check" to verify the accuracy of your worksheet.

**5** Place the insertion point in cell H11.

**6** Type **=B11-C11**. The ending balance is the principal that must be paid to fulfill the repayment obligation. This is equal to the beginning balance minus the principal payment. The worksheet should appear similar to the one shown in Figure 6.14.

**FIGURE 6.14**

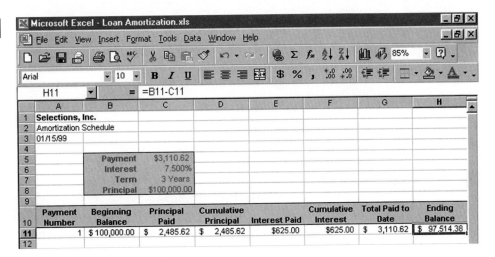

**7** Save the worksheet.

## Using the Fill Handle to Complete the Amortization Schedule

After you enter formulas in row 12 of the amortization schedule, you can use the fill handle to copy the formula to other portions of the worksheet. The default amortization schedule covers a loan with a term of three years, a principal of $12,000, and an annual interest rate of 7.50%.

> **TIP** Here is where you will finally see the power of Excel to replicate formulas!

### TASK 9: To Use the Fill Handle to Complete the Amortization Schedule

**1** Place the insertion point in cell A12 to make it the active cell.

**2** Type **=A11+1**.

**3** Type **=H11** in cell B12. The beginning balance for this payment equals the ending balance after the last payment was made.

**4** Highlight the range C11:H11. Using the fill handle, copy the range down to row 12, as shown in Figure 6.15.

**FIGURE 6.15**

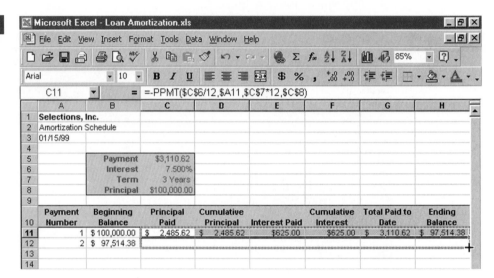

**5** Highlight cell D12, change the formula to **=D11+C12**, and click the Enter button on the formula bar to update the formula. The result shown in Figure 6.16 is returned.

**FIGURE 6.16**

| | B | C | D | E |
|---|---|---|---|---|
| | D12 ▼ = =D11+C12 | | | |
| 1 | Inc. | | | |
| 2 | Schedule | | | |
| 3 | | | | |
| 4 | | | | |
| 5 | Payment | $3,110.62 | | |
| 6 | Interest | 7.500% | | |
| 7 | Term | 3 Years | | |
| 8 | Principal | $100,000.00 | | |
| 9 | | | | |
| 10 | Beginning Balance | Principal Paid | Cumulative Principal | Interest Paid |
| 11 | $ 100,000.00 | $ 2,485.62 | $ 2,485.62 | $625.00 |
| 12 | $ 97,514.38 | $ 2,501.16 | $ 4,986.78 | $609.46 |
| 13 | | | | |
| 14 | | | | |

**6**  Highlight cell F12 and change the formula to **=F11+E12**, and then highlight cell G12 and change the formula to **=D12+F12** (Figure 6.17).

**FIGURE 6.17**

| | G12 | ▼ | = | =D12+F12 | | | | |
|---|---|---|---|---|---|---|---|---|
| | A | B | C | D | E | F | G | H |
| 1 | Selections, Inc. | | | | | | | |
| 2 | Amortization Schedule | | | | | | | |
| 3 | 01/15/99 | | | | | | | |
| 4 | | | | | | | | |
| 5 | | Payment | $3,110.62 | | | | | |
| 6 | | Interest | 7.500% | | | | | |
| 7 | | Term | 3 Years | | | | | |
| 8 | | Principal | $100,000.00 | | | | | |
| 9 | | | | | | | | |
| 10 | Payment Number | Beginning Balance | Principal Paid | Cumulative Principal | Interest Paid | Cumulative Interest | Total Paid to Date | Ending Balance |
| 11 | 1 | $ 100,000.00 | $ 2,485.62 | $ 2,485.62 | $625.00 | $625.00 | $ 3,110.62 | $ 97,514.38 |
| 12 | 2 | $ 97,514.38 | $ 2,501.16 | $ 4,986.78 | $609.46 | $1,234.46 | $ 6,221.24 | $ 95,013.22 |
| 13 | | | | | | | | |

**7**  Highlight the range A12:H12. Using the fill handle, use AutoReplication to copy this row of formulas through row 46, and release the mouse button. The values should calculate as shown in Figure 6.18.

**FIGURE 6.18**

| | A12 | ▼ | = | =A11+1 | | | | |
|---|---|---|---|---|---|---|---|---|
| | A | B | C | D | E | F | G | H |
| 29 | 19 | $ 52,800.81 | $ 2,780.62 | $ 49,979.80 | $330.01 | $9,122.01 | $ 59,101.81 | $ 50,020.20 |
| 30 | 20 | $ 50,020.20 | $ 2,798.00 | $ 52,777.80 | $312.63 | $9,434.64 | $ 62,212.44 | $ 47,222.20 |
| 31 | 21 | $ 47,222.20 | $ 2,815.48 | $ 55,593.28 | $295.14 | $9,729.78 | $ 65,323.06 | $ 44,406.72 |
| 32 | 22 | $ 44,406.72 | $ 2,833.08 | $ 58,426.36 | $277.54 | $10,007.32 | $ 68,433.68 | $ 41,573.64 |
| 33 | 23 | $ 41,573.64 | $ 2,850.79 | $ 61,277.15 | $259.84 | $10,267.15 | $ 71,544.30 | $ 38,722.85 |
| 34 | 24 | $ 38,722.85 | $ 2,868.60 | $ 64,145.75 | $242.02 | $10,509.17 | $ 74,654.92 | $ 35,854.25 |
| 35 | 25 | $ 35,854.25 | $ 2,886.53 | $ 67,032.29 | $224.09 | $10,733.26 | $ 77,765.55 | $ 32,967.71 |
| 36 | 26 | $ 32,967.71 | $ 2,904.57 | $ 69,936.86 | $206.05 | $10,939.31 | $ 80,876.17 | $ 30,063.14 |
| 37 | 27 | $ 30,063.14 | $ 2,922.73 | $ 72,859.59 | $187.89 | $11,127.20 | $ 83,986.79 | $ 27,140.41 |
| 38 | 28 | $ 27,140.41 | $ 2,940.99 | $ 75,800.58 | $169.63 | $11,296.83 | $ 87,097.41 | $ 24,199.42 |
| 39 | 29 | $ 24,199.42 | $ 2,959.38 | $ 78,759.96 | $151.25 | $11,448.08 | $ 90,208.03 | $ 21,240.04 |
| 40 | 30 | $ 21,240.04 | $ 2,977.87 | $ 81,737.83 | $132.75 | $11,580.83 | $ 93,318.65 | $ 18,262.17 |
| 41 | 31 | $ 18,262.17 | $ 2,996.48 | $ 84,734.31 | $114.14 | $11,694.96 | $ 96,429.28 | $ 15,265.69 |
| 42 | 32 | $ 15,265.69 | $ 3,015.21 | $ 87,749.52 | $95.41 | $11,790.38 | $ 99,539.90 | $ 12,250.48 |
| 43 | 33 | $ 12,250.48 | $ 3,034.06 | $ 90,783.58 | $76.57 | $11,866.94 | $102,650.52 | $ 9,216.42 |
| 44 | 34 | $ 9,216.42 | $ 3,053.02 | $ 93,836.60 | $57.60 | $11,924.54 | $105,761.14 | $ 6,163.40 |
| 45 | 35 | $ 6,163.40 | $ 3,072.10 | $ 96,908.70 | $38.52 | $11,963.06 | $108,871.76 | $ 3,091.30 |
| 46 | 36 | $ 3,091.30 | $ 3,091.30 | $100,000.00 | $19.32 | $11,982.39 | $111,982.39 | $ 0.00 |
| 47 | | | | | | | | |

**TIP**  Notice that the Ending Balance equals zero at payment 36. This verifies that the amortization schedule is calculating the loan repayment figures correctly.

**8**  Scroll to the top of the worksheet, highlight Column A, and set the alignment of the selection to Center, as shown in Figure 6.19.

FIGURE 6.19

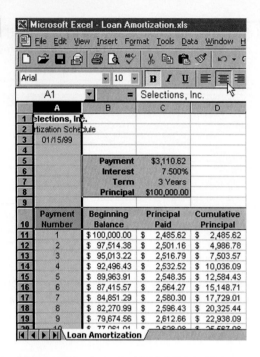

**9** Highlight the range A1:A3. Set the alignment to Left (Figure 6.20).

**FIGURE 6.20**

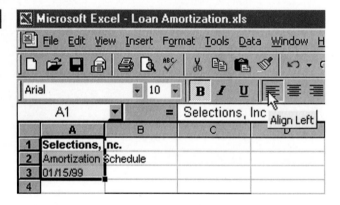

**10** Highlight cell A1 and save your changes. The workbook should now look like the one shown in Figure 6.21.

**FIGURE 6.21**

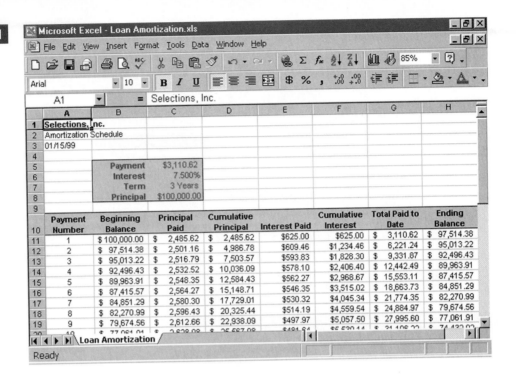

## Freezing Worksheet Panes to Assist in Viewing Large Worksheets

Your amortization schedule is now fully functional. Take a moment to note the power of Microsoft Excel: By using financial functions and copying these formulas down the worksheet, the entire loan repayment table is based upon four numeric constants—even though your worksheet presently contains almost three hundred formulas.

Viewing large worksheets can be problematic because the heading rows scroll out of view as you move down the worksheet. To alleviate this problem, certain rows can be *frozen* so they always appear on the screen. In the next task, you will freeze the worksheet headings so the entire amortization schedule can be viewed with the headings visible on the screen.

### TASK 10: To Freeze Worksheet Panes to Assist Viewing

**1** Place the insertion point in cell A11.

**2** Select Freeze Panes from the Window menu, as shown in Figure 6.22.

**FIGURE 6.22**

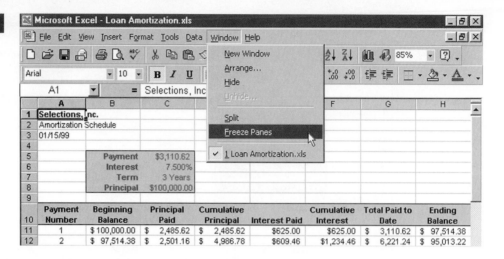

3. Select Go To from the Edit menu, as shown in Figure 6.23.

**FIGURE 6.23**

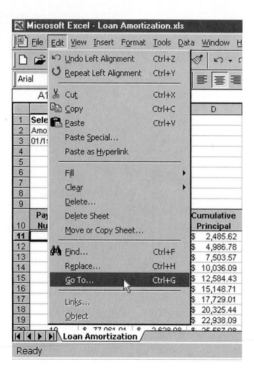

4. The Go To dialog box appears. Type **A46** in the Reference: text box and click OK, as shown in Figure 6.24.

**FIGURE 6.24**

**5** Cell A46 becomes the active cell, and rows 1 through 10 and additional rows up to row 46 become visible, as shown in Figure 6.25.

**FIGURE 6.25**

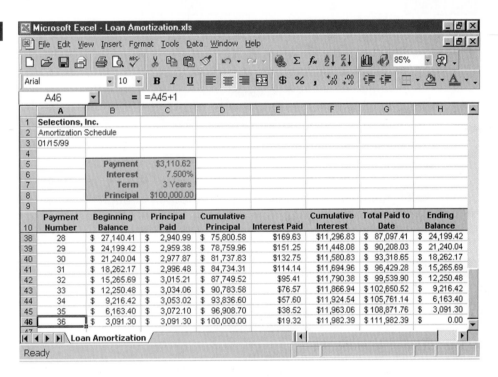

As you scroll through the worksheet, rows 1 through 10 always remain visible.

**TIP**   To unfreeze the panes, select Unfreeze Panes from the Window menu.

# Changing the Loan Scenario

Using this workbook, Mr. Traylor can easily compare alternative loan scenarios. To see how easy it is to view another loan scenario, simply change the principal and term values, and then add additional rows to the worksheet.

TASK 11: To Change the Loan Scenario

**1** Enter **4** in cell C7 and press (ENTER).

**2** Type **250000** in cell C8 and press (ENTER). Notice that the monthly payment changes to $6,044.73, as shown in Figure 6.26.

**FIGURE 6.26**

|  | A | B | C |
|---|---|---|---|
| 1 | Selections, Inc. | | |
| 2 | Amortization Schedule | | |
| 3 | 01/15/99 | | |
| 4 | | | |
| 5 | | Payment | $6,044.73 |
| 6 | | Interest | 7.500% |
| 7 | | Term | 4 Years |
| 8 | | Principal | $250,000.00 |
| 9 | | | |

**3** Scroll to the bottom of the worksheet and highlight the range A46:H46.

**4** Using the fill handle, drag the selection through row 58 and release the left mouse button. Your amortization schedule should now resemble the one shown in Figure 6.27.

**FIGURE 6.27**

| | A | B | C | D | E | F | G | H |
|---|---|---|---|---|---|---|---|---|
| 1 | Selections, Inc. | | | | | | | |
| 2 | Amortization Schedule | | | | | | | |
| 3 | 01/15/99 | | | | | | | |
| 4 | | | | | | | | |
| 5 | | Payment | $6,044.73 | | | | | |
| 6 | | Interest | 7.500% | | | | | |
| 7 | | Term | 4 Years | | | | | |
| 8 | | Principal | $250,000.00 | | | | | |
| 9 | | | | | | | | |
| 10 | Payment Number | Beginning Balance | Principal Paid | Cumulative Principal | Interest Paid | Cumulative Interest | Total Paid to Date | Ending Balance |
| 50 | 40 | $ 52,740.69 | $ 5,715.10 | $ 202,974.40 | $329.63 | $38,814.61 | $ 241,789.02 | $ 47,025.60 |
| 51 | 41 | $ 47,025.60 | $ 5,750.82 | $ 208,725.22 | $293.91 | $39,108.52 | $ 247,833.74 | $ 41,274.78 |
| 52 | 42 | $ 41,274.78 | $ 5,786.76 | $ 214,511.98 | $257.97 | $39,366.49 | $ 253,878.47 | $ 35,488.02 |
| 53 | 43 | $ 35,488.02 | $ 5,822.93 | $ 220,334.90 | $221.80 | $39,588.29 | $ 259,923.20 | $ 29,665.10 |
| 54 | 44 | $ 29,665.10 | $ 5,859.32 | $ 226,194.22 | $185.41 | $39,773.70 | $ 265,967.92 | $ 23,805.78 |
| 55 | 45 | $ 23,805.78 | $ 5,895.94 | $ 232,090.16 | $148.79 | $39,922.49 | $ 272,012.65 | $ 17,909.84 |
| 56 | 46 | $ 17,909.84 | $ 5,932.79 | $ 238,022.95 | $111.94 | $40,034.42 | $ 278,057.37 | $ 11,977.05 |
| 57 | 47 | $ 11,977.05 | $ 5,969.87 | $ 243,992.82 | $74.86 | $40,109.28 | $ 284,102.10 | $ 6,007.18 |
| 58 | 48 | $ 6,007.18 | $ 6,007.18 | $ 250,000.00 | $37.54 | $40,146.82 | $ 290,146.82 | $ 0.00 |

|◄ ◄ ► ►| \ Loan Amortization /

Ready        Sum=7671321.58

**5** Using the vertical scroll bar, move to the top of the worksheet and make cell A1 the active cell.

**6** Save and close the workbook.

# Summary and Exercises

## Summary

- Excel contains many financial functions for comparing scenarios involving investments or payments.
- Three numeric values—principal, interest, and term—are required to determine a loan payment.
- The PMT function is used to calculate a loan payment.
- The PV function is used to calculate the present value of an annuity.
- The PPMT function is used to calculate the portion of a loan payment that applies to the outstanding principal.
- The IPMT function is used to calculate the portion of a loan payment that applies to interest.
- A complex workbook such as an amortization schedule will contain hundreds of formulas.
- You can freeze worksheet panes to assist viewing large worksheets.

## Key Terms and Operations

### Key Terms

| | |
|---|---|
| absolute reference | present value |
| amortization | principal |
| amortization schedule | rate |
| annuity functions | relative reference |
| argument | syntax |
| macro | term |
| mixed reference | text constants |
| loan scenario | Visual Basic |
| numeric constants | |

### Operations

construct a formula using the IPMT (interest payment) function
construct a formula using the PMT (payment) function
construct a formula using the PPMT (periodic payment) function
construct a formula using the PV (present value of an annuity) function
create an amortization schedule
create formulas to calculate the cumulative interest and cumulative principal
determine the ending balance
freeze worksheet panes
use AutoFill to copy formulas

# Study Questions

## Multiple Choice

1. A worksheet is being constructed to determine the monthly payment required to return $250,000 in the year 2025. Which financial function should be used to perform this calculation?
   a. PMT
   b. IPMT
   c. PV
   d. FV

2. A worksheet includes a formula for calculating the payment on a loan. To see the amount of the monthly payment that applies to the interest payment, you will use which function?
   a. PMT
   b. IPMT
   c. NOW()
   d. PPMT

3. Which statement concerning the use of the PV annuity function is false?
   a. An annuity payment should be entered as a negative value.
   b. The present value of the investment is required.
   c. The total number of payment periods in the annuity is required.
   d. The interest rate can fluctuate over the life of the annuity.

4. Which of the following most likely refers to the principal of a loan in a financial function?
   a. H6/12
   b. I7*12
   c. –J7
   d. $g$3/12

5. Which of the following formulas includes an absolute reference to an annuity payment?
   a. =PMT($a$1/12,c7*12, d7)
   b. =PPMT($a$1/12,c7*12, e7)
   c. =PMT(h6/12,I$7*12,–j7)
   d. =IPMT($a$1/12,c7*12, –e7)
   e. =PMT(a1/12,$b7*12,–$r$5)

6. A relative reference will never contain
   a. a dollar sign before the row reference.
   b. a dollar sign before the column reference.
   c. a dollar sign before both the row and the column reference.
   d. all of the above.

7. The principal payment (PPMT) function is most similar to which function?
   a. PMT
   b. PV
   c. IPMT
   d. PPMT

8. Which function calculates the portion of a loan payment applied toward the principal?
    a. PMT
    b. PV
    c. IPMT
    d. PPMT

9. You can freeze worksheet panes using which menu?
    a. Format
    b. Edit
    c. Data
    d. View
    e. Window

10. The =NOW() function is in which category of functions?
    a. Financial
    b. Statistical
    c. Date/Time
    d. Logical

## Short Answer

1. Examine the function =PMT(H6/12,I7*12,–J7). Which element refers to the present value of the loan?

2. Explain how the term of a loan affects the total amount paid.

3. What does the PPMT function calculate?

4. What is a mixed reference?

5. Why should the formulas in an amortization schedule contain absolute references?

6. What is the maximum number of arguments that can be included with the PMT function?

7. What value does the PPMT function return?

8. If you are having difficulty viewing the headings in a large worksheet, what should you do?

9. What character precedes a mixed reference?

10. How should annuity payments be entered in a formula?

## Fill in the Blank

1. The _____ function is very similar to the PPMT function.

2. A(n) _____ payment is usually preceded by a minus (–) sign.

3. A(n) _____ reference contains a dollar sign symbol before both the row and column reference.

4. The PPMT function requires _____ arguments.

5. A table listing loan payments shows how the repayment is _____ over time.

6. The PV function calculates the _____ of an annuity.

7. The IPMT function is used to determine the portion of a loan payment that applies to the _____.

8. You can _____ worksheet panes if viewing a large worksheet becomes cumbersome.

9. The time period over which a loan is repaid is the _____.

10. The FV function is similar to the _____ function.

## For Discussion

1. What is the FV function? How does the data it returns differ from data returned by the PV function?

2. What is a macro? How is a macro recorded and applied?

3. How can worksheets, such as the amortization schedule you created in this project, be protected from changes?

4. What arguments are required by the PMT function? Is the order in which these appear in a formula significant?

# Hands-On Exercises

## 1. Protecting Cells in a Workbook

In many settings, portions of a worksheet should be protected to prohibit users from inadvertently making destructive changes to the workbook. By unlocking the cells to which users need access and protecting the worksheet, you can easily achieve this objective! Open the *Java Bar Loan Amortization* workbook and do the following:

1. Select the nonadjacent ranges C6:C8 and A13:H46.

2. Select Cells from the Format menu.

3. Click the Protection tab.

4. Deselect the Locked checkbox in the Format Cells dialog box.

5. Click OK.

6. Select Protection from the Tools menu.

7. Select Protect Sheet.

8. Do not enter a protection password in the Protect Sheet dialog box.

9. Click OK.

10. Save the updated workbook as *Protected Loan Analysis.xls*.

## 2. Creating Excel Macros

When using Excel you often may need to complete a series of tasks more than once. By recording a macro, you can easily apply these procedures again by simply playing the macro. A *macro* is a series of commands and functions stored in a Visual Basic module that can be run whenever you need to perform the task again. (*Visual Basic* is the programming language used throughout the Office environment for recording macros. If you know Visual Basic, you can easily edit a macro you have created.)

It would be nice if your amortization worksheet could easily be returned to a predictable state after the loan's term is modified, since the worksheet will either display errors or not display the entire repayment schedule. You can create a macro to set the default values and create the appropriate number of loan repayment formulas.

Complete the following:

1. Launch Excel if it is not already running.
2. Open the *Loan Amortization.xls* workbook.
3. Save a copy of the workbook as *Loan Defaults.xls*.
4. Select Macro from the Tools menu, and choose Record New Macro.
5. Type **SetDefaults** as the name of the macro, and make sure the macro is stored in the current workbook, as shown in Figure 6.28. Click OK.

**FIGURE 6.28**

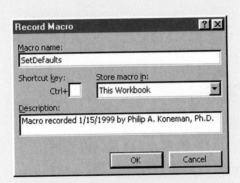

**TIP**  Every procedure you now apply will become a part of the macro. You will also notice that the Stop Recording toolbar is now visible on the screen.

6. Click cell A13 to make it the active cell.
7. While simultaneously holding down the (SHIFT) and (CTRL) keys, press the (END) key. The range A13:H58 is now selected, as shown in Figure 6.29.

FIGURE 6.29

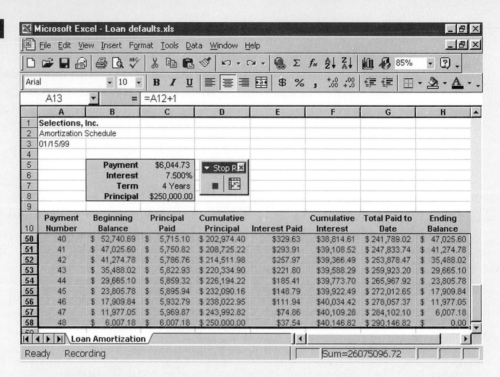

8. Press the (DEL) key to delete the selected portion of the amortization schedule.

9. Type **.075** in cell C6 as the rate, **3** in cell C7 as the term, and **100000** in cell C8 as the principal.

10. Select the range A12:H12 and use the fill handle to copy the formulas through row 46.

11. Scroll to the top of the worksheet and make cell A1 the active cell.

12. Click the Stop Recording button, as shown in Figure 6.30.

FIGURE 6.30

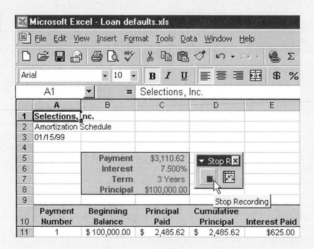

13. You have now successfully recorded a macro. Any time you change the worksheet scenario and then want to restore it to a predictable state, select Macros from the Tools menu and run the macro.

14. Save the workbook.

## 3. Calculating the Future Value of an Investment

The future value of an annuity (FV) function is one of Excel's financial functions that will calculate the future value of an investment. In this example the FV function requires four arguments: the interest rate, the number of contribution periods, the contribution made each period, and the initial value of the investment. In this exercise you will compare three investment scenarios using the FV function. The completed worksheet is shown in Figure 6.31.

**FIGURE 6.31**

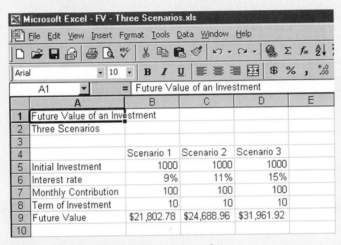

Comparing three investment scenarios

1. Launch Excel if it is not currently running, or create a new worksheet by selecting New from the File menu.
2. Enter the text labels shown in Figure 6.31.
3. Select the range B5:D5 and type **1000**.
4. Type **9%** in cell B6, **11%** in cell C6, and **15%** in cell D6.

> **TIP**   You can enter percentages in a cell by either typing the decimal equivalent or typing the percent value followed by the percent (%) symbol.

5. Select the range B7:D7 and type **100** as the monthly contribution.
6. Select the range B8:D8 and type **10** as term of the investment.
7. Select cell B9, type **=FV(B6/12,B8*12,-B7,-B5)**, and press **(ENTER)**. Cash you pay out (deposits to savings or other payments) is represented by a negative number.
8. Use the fill handle to copy this formula through cell D9.
9. Create a folder on your disk named *Investments*.
10. Save your workbook to the Investments folder with *FV—Three Scenarios.xls* as the file name.

### 4. Using the Date Function

Excel stores dates as sequential serial numbers so that it can perform calculations on them. Excel stores January 1, 1900, as serial number 1. The Date function in Excel is used to return the serial number corresponding to a given date. In this exercise, you will create a simple clock that counts the number of days remaining until the new century. The workbook you will create is shown in Figure 6.32.

**FIGURE 6.32**

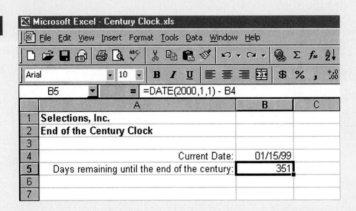

1. Launch Excel if it is not currently running, or create a new worksheet by selecting New from the File menu.

2. Enter the text labels shown in Figure 6.32. Format the text as shown.

3. Type **1/15/99** in cell B4, and change the format to a date format if necessary.

4. Type **=DATE(2000,1,1) – B4** as the formula in cell B5. This formula uses the Date function to return the serial number for January 1, 2000, and subtracts from this number the date listed in cell B4.

5. Format cell B5 as a number with zero decimal places, if necessary.

6. Save the workbook as *Century Clock.xls*.

7. Close the workbook.

# On Your Own Exercises

## 1. Creating Macros to Enable and Disable Protection for a Worksheet

Open the *Protected Loan Analysis.xls* workbook. Create two macros: one that sets the protection for the worksheet, and one that removes the worksheet protection. Save the workbook as *Protected Loan Y-N.xls*.

## 2. Repaying a Loan Early

Visit Microsoft's New Spreadsheet Solutions site, which contains spreadsheet solutions created by Village Software, to download a file called *Loan Manager*.

## Web Tip

You can download the *Loan Manager* file from the Web at
http://officeupdate.microsoft.com/downloadDetails/loan.htm
If you cannot access this site, ask your instructor for a copy of the file.

Download the Loan Manager self-extracting file (*Loan.exe*), and install the *Loan.xlt* template to your disk. Open the *Loan.xlt* file, and enter the loan data from this project. Make three additional payments of $100.00 each. Save the workbook as *Prepaid.xls*.

### 3. Modifying a Workbook

Open the *Prepaid.xls* workbook and make the following changes:

1. Create a macro to set the workbook to a predictable state.
2. Protect the cells containing critical formulas so they cannot be modified.

Save the updated workbook as *Prepaid Updates.xls*.

### 4. Comparing Multiple Amortizations

Create an Excel workbook containing two amortization schedule worksheets with two separate loan scenarios. Save the workbook as *Loan Comparisons.xls*.

### 5. Adding a Lump Sum Feature to the Loan Comparisons Workbook

When repaying a loan, it is common to make lump sum payments against the principal at periodic intervals. Modify the two worksheets in the *Loan Comparisons.xls* workbook to accept lump sum payments. Save the updated workbook as *Updated Loan Comparisons.xls*.

### 6. Summarizing Loan Comparison Data

Open the *Updated Loan Comparisons.xls* workbook and create a summary worksheet that summarizes the loan scenarios on one sheet. Use linking formulas and name the updated workbook as *Summarized Loan Comparisons.xls*.

# Excel 2000 Function Reference Guide

| Function | Mouse Action or Button | Menu | Keyboard Shortcut |
|---|---|---|---|
| AutoFormat | | Select the cells and choose Format, AutoFormat | Press (ALT) + O, A |
| Border, add | Select the cell(s), click the down arrow on ⊞▾, and click on the desired border | Select the cell(s) and choose Format, Cells, Border | |
| Cell, align | Select the cell(s) and click ≡, ≡, or ≡ | Select the cell(s) and choose Format, Cells, Alignment | |
| Cell, copy | Select the cell(s) and click 📋 | Select the cell(s) and choose Edit, Copy | Select the cell(s) and press (CTRL) + C |
| Cell, cut | Select the cell(s) and click ✂ | Select the cell(s) and choose Edit, Cut | Select the cell(s) and press (CTRL) + X |
| Cell, delete | | Select the cell(s) and choose Edit, Delete | |
| Cell, delete data in | | Select the cell(s) and choose Edit, Clear | Select the cell(s) and press (DEL) |
| Cell, format | Select the cell(s) and click the appropriate formatting button ( **B**, *I*, and so on) | Select the cell(s), choose Format, Cells, and click the desired tab | Press (CTRL) + 1 (one) |
| Cell, insert | | Select the cell(s) and choose Insert, Cells | |
| Cell, paste | Select the cell(s) and click 📋 | Select the cell(s) and choose Edit, Paste | Select the cell(s) and press (CTRL) + V |
| Cell, select | Drag the mouse pointer through the desired cells | | Press (SHIFT) + any navigation key |
| Chart, create | Click 📊 | Choose Chart from the Insert menu | Press (ALT) + I, H |

| Function | Mouse Action or Button | Menu | Keyboard Shortcut |
|---|---|---|---|
| Chart, move | Select the chart and drag | | |
| Chart, size | Select a handle and drag | | |
| Column, change the width | Drag the vertical border of the column in the column indicator row | Select the column and choose Format, Column, Width | Press ALT + O, C |
| Column, delete | | Select the column(s) and choose Edit, Delete | Press ALT + E, D |
| Column, insert | | Select the column(s) and choose Insert, Columns | Press ALT + I, C |
| Comments, add | | Select the cell and choose Insert, Comment | Press ALT + I, M |
| Data, edit | Select the cell, click in the formula bar, and edit as desired; double-click the cell | | Select the cell, press F2, and edit as desired |
| Data, enter | | | Select the cell, type the data, and press ENTER or any navigation key |
| Data, find | | Choose Edit, Find | Press CTRL + F |
| Data, sort | Select the cell(s) and click ⊉ or ⊋ | Select the cell(s) and choose Data, Sort | Press ALT + D, F |
| Exit Excel 2000 | Click ✖ in the application window | Choose File, Exit | Press ALT + F4 |
| Fill, add | Select the cell(s), click the down arrow on the ◆, and select a color | Select the cell(s) and choose Format, Cells, Patterns | Press ALT + O, C |
| Font, color | Click A▾ | Select the cell(s) and choose Format, Cells, Font | Press ALT + O, C |
| Footer, create | | Choose View, Header and Footer | Press ALT + V, H |

| Function | Mouse Action or Button | Menu | Keyboard Shortcut |
|---|---|---|---|
| Format dates | | Select the cell(s) and choose Format, Cells, Number | Press ALT + O, C |
| Format numbers | Select the cell(s) and click $ , % , , , .00 , or .0 | Select the cell(s) and choose Format, Cells, Number | Press ALT + O, C |
| Function, create | Click $f_x$ | Select Function from the Insert menu | Press ALT + I, F |
| Go to a cell | | Edit, Goto | Press CTRL + G or F5 |
| Header, create | | Choose View, Header and Footer | Press ALT + V, H |
| Help | Click ? | Choose Help, Microsoft Excel Help | Press F1 |
| Page break, change | | Choose View, Page Break Preview, and drag the page break line | Press ALT + V, P and drag the page break line |
| Page break, view | | Choose View, Page Break Preview | Press ALT + V, P |
| Preview | Click [preview icon] | Choose File, Print Preview | Press ALT + F, V |
| Print | Click [print icon] | Choose File, Print | Press CTRL + P |
| Row, change the height | Drag the horizontal border of the row indicator | Select the row(s) and choose Format, Row, Height | Press ALT + O, R, E |
| Row, delete | | Select the row(s) and choose Edit, Delete | Press ALT + E, D |
| Row, insert | | Select the number of rows you want to insert and choose Insert, Rows | Press ALT + I, R |
| Spell check | Click [spell check icon] | Choose Tools, Spelling | Press F7 |
| Start Excel 2000 | | Choose Start, Programs, Microsoft Excel 2000 | |

| Function | Mouse Action or Button | Menu | Keyboard Shortcut |
|---|---|---|---|
| Workbook, close | Click ☒ in the workbook window | Choose File, Close | Press (CTRL) + (F4) or (CTRL) + W |
| Workbook, create | Click ▯ | Choose File, New | Press (CTRL) + N |
| Workbook, open | Click ☞ | Choose File, Open | Press (CTRL) + O |
| Workbook, save | Click ▤ | Choose, File, Save | Press (CTRL) + S |
| Worksheet, delete | | Click the worksheet tab and choose Edit, Delete Sheet | Press (ALT) + E, L |
| Worksheet, insert | | Click the worksheet tab that should follow the new worksheet and choose Insert, Worksheet | Press (ALT) + I, W |
| Worksheet, move | Drag the worksheet tab to a new location | Select the worksheet tab and choose Edit, Move or Copy Sheet | Press (ALT) + E, M |
| Worksheet, name | Double-click the worksheet name and type new name | Right-click the worksheet tab and choose Rename | |

# Glossary

**3-D workbook** A workbook comprising of one or more worksheets that contain linking formulas for sharing information among worksheets.

**Absolute cell reference** A reference to a cell in a formula where both the column and the row reference are preceded by a dollar sign ($). The reference to the cell will never change, regardless of where the formula is copied.

**Active cell** The specific cell in a worksheet that has the focus. In a selection, the active cell is the cell from which the selection originated.

**Active sheet** The specific worksheet in a workbook that has the focus. In a selection, the active worksheet is the sheet from which the selection originated.

**Address** The row and column designation identifying a specific cell, such as A1 (column A, row 1).

**Adjacent cells** A selection of cells that compose a continuous range.

**Amortization** The process of spreading loan or other obligations (payments) over time.

**Amortization schedule** A listing of the payments required for paying back a loan or other obligation. A loan amortization schedule often specifies the portion of a loan payment that applies to the principal.

**Annuity functions** Excel functions calculating a series of constant cash payments made over a continuous period. In annuity functions, cash you pay out, such as a deposit to savings, is represented by a negative number; cash you receive, such as a dividend check, is represented by a positive number.

**Application title bar** The title bar for Microsoft Excel that appears above the workbook window for each open workbook, and contains the controls to minimize, maximize, restore, and close Excel.

**Argument** The values a function uses to perform operations or calculations. The type of argument a function uses is specific to the function. Common arguments used within functions include numeric values, text values, cell references, ranges of cells, names, labels, and nested functions.

**AutoSum** In Microsoft Excel, adds numbers automatically with the SUM function. Microsoft Excel suggests the range of cells to be added. If the suggested range is incorrect, drag through the range you want, and then press ENTER.

**Bar chart** A chart type that represents a data series as horizontal bars.

**Borders button** The button on the formatting toolbar for applying the specified border to a cell or range of cells.

**Cell** The intersection of a row and column in a worksheet. All worksheet data is contained in cells.

**Cell alignment** A setting for cell data that specifies whether data in the cell appears left, center, or right aligned.

**Cell border** A format applied to one or more cells specifying the format of a line surrounding a cell or range of cells.

**Cell reference** The reference to a specific cell using its address. Cell references are used in most formulas.

**Cell shading** A format applied to one or more cells specifying the format of a color or pattern in a cell or range of cells.

**Cell tip** A descriptive label that appears when you hover over a button on a toolbar or complete a procedure in Excel.

**Chart options** Options you can set for a chart to change one or more of its features.

**Chart sub-type** A specific chart type within a category, such as a 3-D exploded pie chart versus a simple two-dimensional pie chart.

**Chart type** The type of chart you use to communicate numeric data graphically. The type you select depends upon the structure of the data series. Common chart types include bar, column, line, pie, and X-Y scatter.

**Chart Wizard** An Excel wizard that walks you through the process of creating a chart.

**Column** The vertical areas of a worksheet, which are identified with a letter (A, B, C, and so on).

**Column chart** A chart representing data series as one or more vertical columns.

**Columns** A selection of more than one column in a worksheet.

**Currency style** A number format applied to one or more cells that displays a currency symbol, thousands separator, and two decimal places.

**Data integrity** A theoretical construct emphasizing the accuracy of data in a worksheet by minimizing redundant instances of data in multiple worksheets. You can use 3-D linking and consolidation formulas to minimize data redundancy, and thereby improve data integrity.

**Enter Formula button** A button on the formula bar for accepting a formula you have entered or edited. The button appears as a green checkmark.

**Fill handle** The black square in the lower-right corner of the active cell or selection. When the pointer is on the fill handle, the pointer changes from an arrow to a crosshair. Drag the fill handle down or to the right to fill cells with data based on the current selection.

**Font box** The box on the Formatting toolbar that lists the available fonts that you can apply to a cell or selection.

**Font Size box** The box on the Formatting toolbar that you can use to specify the size of a font in a cell or selection.

**Footer** Text appearing at the bottom of each page of a printed worksheet.

**Format Painter button** A button on the Formatting toolbar that copies the format from a selected object or text and applying it to the object or text you click.

**Formatting toolbar** The toolbar appearing at the top of the application window that contains buttons and boxes for formatting one or more cells.

**Formula** Cell data beginning with an equal sign (=) that performs a calculation or returns data.

**Formula bar** A bar near the top of the window that displays the constant value or formula used in the active cell. To enter or edit values or formulas, select a cell, type the data, and then press (ENTER). You can also double-click a cell to edit data directly in the cell.

**Formula palette** When you create a formula that contains a function, the formula palette helps you enter worksheet functions. As you enter a function into the formula, the formula palette displays the name of the function, each of its arguments, a description of the function and each argument, the current result of the function, and the current result of the entire formula.

**Function** A predefined formula that performs calculations by using specific values, called arguments, in a particular order, or structure.

**Header** Text appearing at the top of each page of a printed worksheet.

**Home cell** The uppermost left cell in a worksheet—cell A1.

**IF function** A function that returns one value if a condition you specify evaluates to TRUE and another value if it evaluates to FALSE.

**Label** Text in Excel that defines the structure of a worksheet.

**Landscape orientation** The page orientation for a worksheet in which the height of the page is smaller than its width.

**Line chart** A chart in which the data series are represented by one or more lines.

**Linking formulas** A formula containing a 3-D reference that displays data from a specific cell in a worksheet or workbook. 3-D references are updated automatically whenever the source data changes.

**Loan scenario** The principal, interest rate, and term of a loan, which determine the monthly payment.

**Logical function** A category of worksheet functions that make logical comparisons, conduct logical tests, and usually return a value based upon a logical condition.

**Macro** A program you write or record that stores a series of Microsoft Excel commands that you can later use as a single command. Macros can automate complex tasks and reduce the number of steps required to complete tasks that you perform frequently. Macros are recorded in the Visual Basic for Applications programming language.

**Mixed cell reference** A reference to a cell in a formula where either the column or the row reference is preceded by a dollar sign ($). The reference to the cell or column designated as absolute will never change when the formula is copied.

**Name** A stored name for a range of cells in a worksheet. Named ranges are viewed and selected using the Name box on the Formatting toolbar.

**Non-adjacent cells** A selection of worksheet cells that are not adjacent to one another.

**Number** An integer or decimal value entered into a cell. Numbers compose the worksheet data for performing calculations.

**Number formats** Cell formats that change the appearance of numbers, including dates and times, without changing the number behind the appearance (the actual cell value).

**Numeric constants** Numbers in an electronic spreadsheet upon which calculations are performed.

**Object** An image, chart, or other data added to an Excel worksheet.

**Office Clipboard** A clipboard shared among the Office applications that holds up to 12 entries that can be embedded or linked in Office documents and files.

**Operands** Specific operators that specify the type of calculation that you want to perform on the elements of a formula. Microsoft Excel includes four different types of calculation operators: arithmetic, comparison, text, and reference.

**Operator precedence** The specific order in which Excel performs calculations when you combine several operators in a single formula.

**Orientation** The direction in which text appears in a cell.

**Page Break Preview** A view of a worksheet that displays the current page breaks.

**Pie chart** An Excel chart type that is used to represent a single data series identifying the parts of a whole.

**Portrait orientation** The page orientation for a worksheet in which the height of the page is larger than its width.

**Principal** The amount of money borrowed for a loan, or the present value of an annuity.

**Print areas** A specified selection of cells that will print when a worksheet is printed.

**Print Preview** An Excel view of a worksheet or sheet in a workbook as they will appear when printed.

**Properties** Specification for a workbook file, such as the author and title of the workbook. Individual controls in Excel such as text boxes, images, and command buttons also have properties that can be set or changed.

**Range** A selection of cells referenced in a formula or selected when applying formats.

**Rate** The interest rate for a loan. This is a required element for the PMT function.

**Relative cell reference** A reference to a cell in a formula where neither the column nor the row reference is preceded by a dollar sign ($). The cell reference will change accordingly when the formula is copied.

**Row** A horizontal storage area in Excel.

**Rows** A selection of more than one row in a worksheet.

**Run** The action of applying the steps stored in an Excel macro.

**Scroll bars** The shaded bars along the right side and bottom of a window. To scroll to another part of the file, drag the box or click the arrows in the scroll bar.

**Select** The action of using the mouse or a keyboard shortcut to select one or more cells in a worksheet.

**Select All button** A button in the upper-left corner of a worksheet that selects all cells in the sheet.

**Selection** A cell or range of cells that have been highlighted.

**Sheet tabs** The tabs appearing in the lower portion of the workbook window that represent the worksheets in a workbook.

**Standard toolbar** A toolbar displayed in the application window containing buttons to accomplish common tasks such as saving files, opening files, printing, and so on.

**Status bar** The bar near the bottom of the screen that displays information about a selected command or an operation in progress. The right side of the status bar shows whether keys such as (CAPS LOCK), (SCROLL LOCK), or (NUM LOCK) are turned on. Choose Status Bar on the View menu to display or hide the status bar.

**Style** A collection of formats such as font size, patterns, and alignment, that you can define and save as a group.

**Syntax** Formula syntax is the structure or order of the elements in a formula. Formulas in Microsoft Excel follow a specific syntax that includes an equal sign (=) followed by the elements to be calculated (the operands) and the calculation operators. Each operand can be a value that does not change (a constant value), a cell or range reference, a label, a name, or a worksheet function.

**Template** A workbook you create and then use as the basis for other similar workbooks. You can create templates for workbooks and worksheets.

**Term** The length of time over which you make a loan or annuity payment. This is a required argument in some financial functions.

**Text** Letters and numbers added to worksheet cells.

**Text constants** Text data entered into a cell as a descriptive label, title, or heading.

**Universal Document Viewing** In Excel 2000, you can save a workbook in HTML file format and retain the fidelity of your native workbook format. By saving as HTML, you ensure that anyone with a Web browser can view your documents. Editing those documents is not a problem either because Excel 2000 allows you to "round-trip" them back into the original Office program without losing any of the functionality of the workbook file.

**"What if?"**   A "what if" analysis is the process of changing certain worksheet values to see the impact these changes have on other values.

**Workbook**   An Excel file containing one or more worksheets.

**Worksheet**   A two-dimensional grid of data in a row-and-column format in an Excel workbook.

**Worksheet area**   The specific portion of a worksheet in which you enter data, format cells, or enter formulas.

**X-Y scatter chart**   A chart type used to compare data series for pairs of values.

# Index

## Common Elements in Office 2000

## Excel 2000